Subject Cataloging:
Critiques and Innovations

1 0866727

Subject Cataloging: Critiques and Innovations

Sanford Berman
Editor

The Haworth Press
New York

Subject Cataloging: Critiques and Innovations has also been published as *Technical Services Quarterly*, Volume 2, Numbers 1/2, Fall/Winter 1984.

The Haworth Press,· Inc., 28 East 22 Street, New York, NY 10010

Library of Congress Cataloging in Publication Data
Main entry under title:

Subject cataloging.

    Published also as v. 2, no. 1/2, fall/winter 1984 of Technical services quarterly.
    Includes bibliographical references and index.
    1. Subject cataloging—Addresses, essays, lectures. 2. Subject headings—Addresses, essays, lectures. I. Berman, Sanford, 1933-
    Z695.S888 1984   025.4'7   84-10554
    ISBN 0-86656-265-6

Subject Cataloging:
Critiques and Innovations

Technical Services Quarterly
Volume 2, Numbers 1/2

CONTENTS

Subject Cataloging:
Critiques and Innovations

Introduction

This is our premise: That the subject approach potentially represents the most powerful and fruitful means to access library materials, but at present remains woefully undeveloped and underutilized.

This is our purpose: To pinpoint what's wrong with current subject cataloging, demonstrating why it often doesn't "work" and sometimes transmits undesirable messages, and then to either suggest constructive reforms or report on actual innovations that illustrate how subject cataloging *can* be at once responsive, sensitive, useful, and exciting.

To begin, John R. Likins amusingly identifies a primary source of "pain" in current Library of Congress nomenclature and practice. Ellen Koger then addresses the problem of subject headings for children's fiction, while Diane Choquette relates how the New Religious Movements Research Collection in Berkeley created its own thesaurus to effectively handle material on deprogramming, Eastern religions, and "New Age" phenomena.

In West Virginia, the State Library Commission pioneered in making information and referral (I & R) data accessible through library catalogs, Shirley A. Smith supplies details on that ongoing, soon-to-be-automated project.

Although both health information and public demand for it have mushroomed, Lionelle Elsesser argues that methods of arrangement and subject retrieval have not similarly evolved to make that information easier to find. She not only summarizes a terminology study among users, but also suggests practical ways to enhance findability—and incidentally makes some telling points about the ethics of information retrieval.

Audrey Taylor brilliantly critiques standard subject cataloging from both a school library and new technology perspective, afterwards propounding a remedy for the access malaise: PRECIS, the PREserved Context Index System, which has been successfully implemented in Ontario school resource centers and elsewhere.

1

People speaking Asian languages—especially Hmong, Lao, Korean, Vietnamese, Chinese, Thai, and Japanese—represent a fast-growing lingual minority. Paul R. Murdock describes a bold, imaginative project at the Jefferson County (Colorado) Public Library to provide multilingual access to Asian-language materials.

The SAC Ad-Hoc Subcommittee on Concepts Denoted by the Term "Primitive," charged with recommending how to eliminate "primitive" forms from the Library of Congress subject heading scheme, accomplished its mission with thoroughness, commitment, ingenuity, and sound judgment. That group produced careful, precise recommendations that LC can easily enact to end the catalog-transmission of one longstanding type of "undesirable" message and in so doing proved the efficacy of a targeted, task force approach to specific subject access problems.

"Two Changed Headings," documents why and how Hennepin County Library altered the conventional headings, LEPROSY and SHELTERED WORKSHOPS. In particular, these exchanges show that subject catalogers can profitably interact with interested and knowledgeable "outsiders," in effect positing a model for such cooperation.

Despite all the agitation to improve subject access to women's materials, much remains to be done. "Out of the Kitchen—But Not Into the Catalog" inventories LC delinquencies and proposes solutions.

"Beyond the Pale" probes the continuing bias in LC's Judaica-related vocabulary and praxis, as well as exemplifying user-"outreach," an attempt to inform and activate affected constituencies, for earlier versions of the paper had been directed solely to Jewish audiences.

"Teen Subject Headings" is at once an example of authority file construction and the development of exact, contemporary terminology that denotes real topics in language familiar to real-life library users, in this case teenagers.

Subject Headings, Silly, American—20th Century— Complications and Sequelae—Addresses, Essays, Lectures

John R. Likins

Nearly every day for the last twelve or thirteen years it seems I've encountered absolutely hilarious, outrageously offensive, or just plain mysterious subject headings. I have a real concern that these sorts of headings will be permanently embedded in the growing machine-readable databases of bibliographic information unless we catalogers *STOP AND THINK* about what we're putting into our catalogs!

Do we need, for example, to establish subject headings for churches, corporations, etc., in foreign languages? Or do we just do it because "the rules say so" or because it's cheaper ("cost-effective") or maybe to impress our patrons and colleagues with our vast learning? ("Oh wow, this library knows that the real name for Moon's Unification Church is SEGYE KIDOKKYO TONGIL SILLYONG HYPOPHOL. Silly me, I tried looking under 'Unification Church!' That'll teach me.")

MUST we be relentlessly stuffy and scholarly at all times? Why use AFRO—AMERICAN AGRICULTURAL LABORERS? What's wrong with BLACK FARM WORKERS?

And does it make sense to indiscriminately mix topical and form subdivisions? What do you suppose ordinary mortals think when they encounter catalog listings such as:

ANXIETY—ANECDOTES, FACETIAE, SATIRE, ETC.
BANKRUPTCY—POPULAR WORKS
SNEAKERS—ADDRESSES, ESSAYS, LECTURES

3

I'd like to suggest a brand new buzz-word: "service-effective." Is it service-effective to put garbage into library catalogs or bibliographic databases? Or are we simply trying to amuse and/or offend our patrons? Is it always more important to save bucks in this intrinsically labor-intensive service profession? Or shall we take advantage of the marvelous possibilities of the computer to produce usable, better access to library materials?

The list below is selected from a booklet, *From ADZES to ZUTPHEN*, a compilation of twenty of my regular columns in *PLAFSEP*. Most are subject headings from the MARC database, or *Library of Congress Subject Headings*, with a few series added, and a topical subdivision or two.

Some headings, I must say in fairness, are from Cataloging in Publication (CIP) information, and therefore based on very sketchy data furnished by publishers. Many CIP headings were later changed when the Library of Congress received the completed publications, or had its attention drawn to silly things by librarians and other CIP "consumers."

In some cases, headings do not reflect *current* Library of Congress cataloging practice. For example, the numerous headings in the pattern [topic] IN RELIGION, FOLK-LORE, ETC. are being replaced by LC with various subdivisions. The winner in the PLAFSEP Silly Subject Heading Contest a few years ago was BUTTOCKS (IN RELIGION, FOLK-LORE, ETC.). Under current LC policy, however, this important concept would be assigned:

1. BUTTOCKS—FOLKLORE
2. BUTTOCKS—MYTHOLOGY
3. BUTTOCKS—RELIGIOUS ASPECTS

Finally, I'd very much like to thank Sandy Berman, Carla Biermaier, Jan DeSirey, Chris Dodge, and other staff members at the Hennepin County Library [Minnetonka, Minn.] for the wonderful list of "Irresistibles" at the end of this article.

And here are my favorites:

AFRO-AMERICAN AGRICULTURAL LABORERS
AGED—UNITED STATES—AUDIO-VISUAL AIDS—CATA-
    LOGS
AGED, WRITINGS OF THE, AMERICAN
AMERICAN GIANT CHECKERED RABBIT

AMERICAN REVOLUTION BICENTENNIAL TWO DOLLAR BILL POSTAGE-STAMP CANCELLATIONS
ANUS (PSYCHOLOGY)
ANXIETY—ANECDOTES, FACETIAE, SATIRE, ETC.
APPLE GROWERS—UNITED STATES—BIOGRAPHY—JUVENILE LITERATURE [kid's book about Johnny Appleseed!]
ARCHITECTS—HOMES AND HAUNTS
ASPECTS OF GREEK AND ROMAN LIFE (ITHACA, N.Y.) [series]
ATOMIC WARFARE—POPULAR WORKS
AUSTRALIAN ABORIGINES—AUSTRALIA
  sa ART, BRITISH—GREAT BRITAIN
  sa GARDENS, JAPANESE—JAPAN
  sa SCULPTURE, AFRICAN—AFRICA, SUB—SAHARAN
AZTECS—URBAN RESIDENCE

BALLS (PARTIES)
BALLS (SPORTING GOODS)
BANANA RESEARCH
BANKRUPTCY—POPULAR WORKS
BEAST MARRIAGE
  x MARRIAGE OF PERSON TO ANIMAL
xx ANIMAL LORE
BOYS ANTI-TANK RIFLE
BUTTOCKS (IN RELIGION, FOLK-LORE, ETC.)

CATASTROPHICAL, THE
  sa COMIC, THE
  sa STATE, THE
  sa TRAGIC, THE
CATHOLIC CHURCH—DOCTRINAL AND CONTROVERSIAL WORKS, POPULAR
CATS—HOUSING
CHAIRS—ADDRESSES, ESSAYS, LECTURES
CHEMICAL WARFARE—HYGIENIC ASPECTS
CHILD ABUSE—STUDY AND TEACHING
CONCERTOS (HURDY-GURDY WITH CHAMBER ORCHESTRA), ARRANGED
CONTANGO AND BACKWARDATION
COUNTRY MUSICIANS—UNITED STATES—ICONOGRAPHY

CRABBING
CREATIVE ACTIVITIES AND SEATWORK
CRIME AND CRIMINALS—NEVADA—LAS VEGAS—FAM-
ILY RELATIONSHIPS—CASE STUDIES

DANDIES—ENGLAND—BIOGRAPHY
DEATH—SOCIAL ASPECTS
DENTISTS IN ART
DESSERTS—EARLY WORKS TO 1800
DIVING, SUBMARINE
DOG MASS
DRINKING IN ART
DUBLIN (DUBLIN) IN LITERATURE

FACE—SURGERY—PATIENTS—UNITED STATES—BIOG-
RAPHY
FAILURE (PSYCHOLOGY)—ANECDOTES, FACETIAE,
SATIRE, ETC.
FANTASTIC TELEVISION PROGRAMS
FECES, FOSSIL
FISHES, DRESSING OF
FOOD, JUNK
FRIENDLY SOCIETIES—CANADA
FROGS—ADDRESSES, ESSAYS, LECTURES
FROGS—LITERARY COLLECTIONS
FUELWOOD CUTTING—FOLKLORE

GASTROENTEROLOGY—POPULAR WORKS
GHOSTS—PICTORIAL WORKS
GOD—ADDRESSES, ESSAYS, LECTURES
GREAT TIT
   sa BLUE TIT—BEHAVIOR
GUERRILLAS—FRANCE—RIVIERA—BIOGRAPHY

HARVARD UNIVERSITY—SANITARY AFFAIRS
HEADS OF STATE—GERMANY—ICONOGRAPHY
HEART—INFARCTION—PENNSYLVANIA—ROSETO—MOR-
TALITY
HEMORRHOIDS—POPULAR WORKS
HOOPOES (IN RELIGION, FOLK-LORE, ETC.)
HORNER, JOYCE MARY, 1903- —BIOGRAPHY—LAST
   YEARS AND DEATH
HOT PEPPER SAUCE INDUSTRY—LOUISIANA

INEFFICIENCY, INTELLECTUAL—DICTIONARIES—POLY-
GLOT
INFANTS—ENGLAND—BIOGRAPHY
INSANE, CRIMINAL AND DANGEROUS

JESUS CHRIST—PERSON AND OFFICES

LABORATORY ANIMALS—CONGRESSES
LAWYERS—COSTUME
LOVE-NESTS—DIRECTORIES

MACADAMIA NUT INDUSTRY
MANURE HANDLING
MARINE INVERTEBRATES AS PETS
MARRIAGE—DRAMA
    sa ANTENUPTIAL CONTRACTS—UNITED STATES—POP-
    ULAR WORKS
    sa CHASTITY, VOW OF
    sa IMPEDIMENTS TO MARRIAGE
    sa MATRIMONIAL ACTIONS—NEW YORK (CITY)
    sa MARRIAGE WITH DECEASED WIFE'S SISTER
    sa SHIP'S HUSBANDS
MATERIA MEDICA, VEGETABLE
MIDDLE AGE—CARE AND HYGIENE
MORAL DEVELOPMENT—LONGITUDINAL STUDIES
MORAR, LOCH, SCOT.
MOTHERS—PRAYER-BOOKS AND DEVOTIONS—ENGLISH
    sa CHILDREN—CALIFORNIA—OAKLAND—TIME MAN-
    AGEMENT—CASE STUDIES
    sa CHILDREN—MANAGEMENT
    sa CHILDREN'S PARAPHERNALIA—COLLECTORS AND
    COLLECTING
    sa FOUL BROOD, AMERICAN
    sa FOUL BROOD, EUROPEAN
MOVING-PICTURE ACTORS AND ACTRESSES—HOMES
    AND HAUNTS—CALIFORNIA—HOLLYWOOD
MUD LUMPS

NAKED SINGULARITIES (COSMOLOGY)
NATURAL DISASTERS—POPULAR WORKS
NEUROTICS—ANECDOTES, FACETIAE, SATIRE, ETC.
NSZZ "SOLIDARNOSC" (LABOR ORGANIZATION)

ODORS IN THE BIBLE

OLD AGE—AUDIO-VISUAL AIDS—CATALOGS
ONE-LEGGED RESTING POSITION
OSTOMATES—CARE AND HYGIENE
OWLS—QUOTATIONS, MAXIMS, ETC.

PAINTING, MODERN—17TH-18TH CENTURIES
PENNY DREADFULS
   xx DIME NOVELS
PHONY PEACH DISEASE
PLANTS, EFFECT OF PRAYER ON
PLAY-PARTY
PRAYERS FOR ANIMALS
PROMPT NEUTRONS
PROSTITUTES—PENNSYLVANIA—PHILADELPHIA—COR-
RESPONDENCE, REMINISCENCES, ETC.

QUACKS AND QUACKERY

RAPE—JUVENILE LITERATURE
RAILROADS—MODELS—BIOGRAPHY
RULE OF THE ROAD AT SEA
REFUSE COLLECTION VEHICLES

SCRIPT OF A MOTION PICTURE OF THE SAME TITLE
SEGYE KIDOKKYO TONGIL SILLYONG HYPOPHOL—AD-
DRESSES, ESSAYS, LECTURES
SEGYE KIDOKKYO TONGIL SILLYONG HYPOPHOL—
BIOGRAPHY
SEGYE KIDOKKYO TONGIL SILLYONG HYPOPHOL—CON-
TROVERSIAL LITERATURE
SEPULCHRAL MONUMENTS
SEWAGE—COLLECTED WORKS
SEX INSTRUCTION FOR CHILDREN—JUVENILE LITER-
ATURE
SICK—FAMILY RELATIONSHIPS
SIERRA NEVADA MOUNTAINS—ADDRESSES, ESSAYS,
LECTURES
SKJEMSTAD, LORNS O. LANGRENNSBOKA FOR TUR-
GAERE OG KONKURRANSEL-OPERE. ENGLISH.
SNEAKERS—ADDRESSES, ESSAYS, LECTURES
SOCIAL WORK WITH THE SOCIALLY HANDICAPPED
SOUND—RECORDING AND REPRODUCING—EQUIPMENT
AND SUPPLIES—MAINTENANCE AND REPAIR

SOVIET UNION—COURT AND COURTIERS—BIOGRAPHY
SPECIAL LIBRARIANS
SPIRIT PHONE CALLS
SPIRITUAL LIFE—FRIEND AUTHORS
SPRANG
SQUASH PLAYERS
STORAGE BATTERIES—POPULAR WORKS
STRIKES AND LOCKOUTS—SOY SAUCE INDUSTRY
STRUCTURED PROGRAMMING—PROGRAMMED IN-
STRUCTION
SWIMMING—PHILOSOPHY
SWINE INFLUENZA—PREVENTIVE INOCULATION—PO-
LITICAL ASPECTS
TETRACHLORODIBENZODIOXIN—TOXICOLOGY—ITA-
LY—SEVESO
TONGUING (WIND INSTRUMENT PLAYING)
TRANSPORTATION OF ORGANS, TISSUES, ETC.
—TSUNAMI [subdivision, formerly—TIDAL WAVES]

URINARY DIVERSION
   sa URINE DANCE
   sa URINE (IN RELIGION, FOLK-LORE, ETC.)

VIDEO TAPES IN HISTORIOGRAPHY

WASPS (PERSONS)
WATERGATE AFFAIR, 1972- —STUDY AND TEACHING
(SECONDARY)—SIMULATION METHODS
THE WEST
   sa THE OLD WEST (ALEXANDRIA, VA.) [series, formerly
      THE OLD WEST (NEW YORK)]
   sa WEST (N.Y.) IN ART—CATALOGS
WHALEMEN'S WRITINGS, AMERICAN
WOMEN AND THE SEA
WOMEN—PSYCHOLOGY—PHILOSOPHY

*IRRESISTIBLES: COMMENTARY ON BEST-LOVED SUBJECT
HEADINGS FROM THE FIRST 20 ISSUES OF PLAFSEP*, com-
piled by Sandy Berman, Carla Biermaier, Jan DeSirey, Chris
Dodge, and other staff members, Hennepin County Library.

AMERICAN GIANT CHECKERED RABBIT
   sa PLAID FUR COATS

CATASTROPHICAL, THE
  sa HORRENDOUS, THE
CATS—HOUSING
  x CAT HOUSES (PET CARE)
CRABBING
  sa GROUCHING
  sa COMPLAINING
  sa WHINING
DOG MASS
  sa CAT MASS
  sa DOGMAS
FISHES, DRESSING OF
  sa GILL STRAPS
  sa GROOMING
  sa SCALE MODELS
FOUL BROOD, AMERICAN
  x SMELLY KIDS
FROGS—ADDRESSES, ESSAYS, LECTURES note: Assigned to
  The Miracle of One Kiss, by Prince Bertrand of Belgium.
GOD—ADDRESSES, ESSAYS, LECTURES note: Assign to the
  Ten Commandments.
ITALIAN LANGUAGE—AUDIO-VISUAL INSTRUCTION
  (FOR CAGE-BIRDS) [HCL heading]
NAKED SINGULARITIES (COSMOLOGY)
  x NUDE SINGULARITIES (COSMOLOGY)
ODORS IN THE BIBLE
xx RARE BOOKS, CLEANING OF
ONE-LEGGED RESTING POSITION
  sa ONE-EYED, ONE-HORNED FLYING PURPLE PEOPLE
    EATER
PHONY PEACH DISEASE
  sa HYPOCHONDRIA IN FRUITS
  sa HYPOCHONDRIA IN VEGETABLES
SCRIPT OF A MOTION PICTURE OF THE SAME TITLE
  sa WORDS OF A SONG FROM THE MOTION PICTURE OF
    THE SAME TITLE
  sa TEXT OF A POEM BASED ON THE WORDS OF A SONG
    FROM THE MOTION PICTURE OF THE SAME TITLE
  sa THEME OF A LECTURE ADAPTED FROM THE TEXT
    OF A POEM BASED ON THE WORDS OF A SONG FROM
    THE MOTION PICTURE OF THE SAME TITLE.

sa TELEPHONE DIRECTORY ENTRIES SIMILAR TO THE
THEME OF A LECTURE ADAPTED FROM THE TEXT
OF A POEM BASED ON THE WORDS OF A SONG FROM
THE MOTION PICTURE OF THE SAME TITLE.
sa THOUGHTS AND OTHER RAMBLINGS DERIVED
FROM CHITCHAT WITH MY NEXT DOOR NEIGHBOR
THAT DEVELOPED WHILE MOWING THE LAWN
PRIOR TO GOING TO THE GROCERY STORE
SEX AIDS (FOR CANARIES) [HCL heading]
SQUASH PLAYERS
  sa RUTABAGA PLAYERS
  sa EGGPLANT PLAYERS
  sa OKRA PLAYERS
  x WINTER SQUASH PLAYERS
  x SUMMER SQUASH PLAYERS
TESTES
  x BALLS (ANATOMY)

NOTE

From *ADZES to ZUTPHEN* is $5 (prepaid) from me at 332 Railroad Ave., Norwood, Mass. 02062. *PLAFSEP* is the newsletter of the Massachusetts Library Association, edited by me until last year. It's $6 yearly from Mass. Library Association, Box 7, Nahant, Mass. 01908.

Subject Headings for Children's Fiction

Ellen Koger

SEX. DRUGS. DEATH. DIVORCE and ADOPTION. Not to mention MONKEYS, SCHOOL, PARENTS, BROTHERS AND SISTERS, BASEBALL and LIFE ON OTHER PLANETS. What do you do when a child wants a fiction book on these or any other subjects? Only if adequate subject cataloging of all juvenile fiction has been done will a child, parent or librarian find books which satisfy such wants. As Meg McNelly has said, "Parents, teachers and kids who never heard of the term [bibliotherapy] want fiction on thumb-sucking, fear of the dark, responsibility, sharing."[1]

As one means of dealing with this need at Nampa Public Library, we established a rule: Every children's fiction book must have at least one subject heading. We applied the rule to E's (picture books), R's (beginning readers), general J fiction for 4th to 8th graders, and YA's (J fiction with a problem-oriented theme.)

Nampa Public Library is a small (50,000 volumes) public library in a rural Idaho community of 26,000. The children's collection includes 3,913 E's, 1,547 R's, and 8,056 J's (of which about 230 are YA's.) Annual circulation of children's fiction is over 50,000.

To test how well the collection satisfied the rule, I chose 113 cards at random from the shelflist—about 28 each in E, R, J and YA. This random method gave me 30 books that were issued before 1969, when the Library of Congress's Annotated Card Program was adopted as the national standard for cataloging children's materials. (I'll return to these pre-1969 titles later.)

In order to have a standard for judging subject access for this project, I compiled these principles from LC's introduction to the ACP headings list, the introduction to Sears, and the writings of Sanford Berman, Joan K. Marshall and others (in the past, Nampa's catalogers have used a more subjective and intuitive approach; i.e., no formal written statement exists):

13

1. Choose a single uniform term or phrase and apply it consistently to all the works on that subject in the library's collection.
2. Enter a work under the most specific term which adequately reflects its subject.
3. Assign sufficient subject entries to fully and fairly reflect the content of the work.[2]
4. Avoid sex, ethnic, age and other bias; prefer self-declared group names.[3]
5. Use English-language, popular terms in common American usage. Anglicize names of persons to concur with American usage. Follow natural word order and avoid inversions.
6. Establish new terms for new topics and concepts.
7. Indicate content of works with form and genre headings.
8. Indicate the geographic or historical setting of works of fiction.
9. Create headings to identify popular fictional characters, groups or places.[4]
10. Apply headings for major literary and media awards to the laureate works themselves.[5]
11. Indicate possible uses or curricular relationships of the material.[6]

Out of the 83 titles cataloged after the adoption of the 1969 standard, 30 had satisfactory subject headings. Nine were E, 9 were R, 5 were J and 7 were YA. In two cases NPL had added another heading: SCIENCE FICTION to *Beloved Benjamin is waiting* and FAMILY LIFE—FICTION to *Find a Stranger, Say Goodbye.*

For 41 of the 83 titles, however, the subject entries assigned by the Library of Congress were not adequate. This number included 13 E's, 6 R's, 10 J's and 13 YA's. Eleven more titles had no headings at all: 2 E's, 3 R's, 3 J's and 3 YA's. Generally I judged the headings to be inadequate or unsuitable because there were too few or those assigned were not specific enough to reflect the content of the work.

As Sanford Berman has demonstrated elsewhere,[7] it is easy to criticize LC's ACP subject cataloging by pulling a few horrendous examples out of the thousands of books handled in the program. I wasn't looking for all the awful things I could find, but this random search did turn up some good examples of bad subject cataloging. *Temporary Times, Temporary Places* (the joy and pain of first love form a bond between a teenager and her aunt when they discover they share the same feelings about their individual love affairs) was assigned only AUNTS—FICTION, totally missing the theme of the book. LOVE STORIES or TEENAGE ROMANCE—FICTION, a heading established by Hennepin County Library, would provide a more satisfactory entry. In *Weakfoot*, a boy living near the Okefenokee Swamp befriends a fugitive, slays a panther, and experiences his first romance, but the only subject access is OKEFENOKEE SWAMP—FICTION. Boys who would enjoy this coming-of-age story might find it under FUGITIVES FROM JUSTICE—FICTION, CRIME AND CRIMINALS—FICTION, or HUNTING STORIES. And *Garden of Broken Glass* (unable to work out a satisfactory relationship with his siblings and cope with their alcoholic mother, a young boy finds solace with neighborhood friends and in his relationship with a stray dog) got only FAMILY PROBLEMS—FICTION. Further access could be provided by assigning BROTHERS AND SISTERS—FICTION or CHILDREN OF ALCOHOLIC PARENTS—FICTION (with appropriate references from ALCOHOLICS of course) or even PETS—FICTION. These three YA titles illustrate the difficulty of providing adequate subject access to problem-oriented fiction for 6th to 9th graders.

But the 4- to 6-year-old who has suddenly become fascinated by imaginary playmates, frightened of the dark, or who wants to read (or be read to) about bathtubs, foxes or baby sitters is also sometimes poorly served. For example, *Reasons and Raisins* tells how Little Fox's box of raisins filched from the kitchen brings him adventures and causes him problems, but was assigned no subject entries. ADVENTURE STORIES and PARENT AND CHILD—FICTION (his mother forgives him and makes raisin pudding), as well as FOXES—FICTION, would provide suitable access. A mother might be pleased to find *A Bone for Breakfast* under BREAKFASTS—FICTION and IMAGINATION—FICTION if her child, like Henry, balks at breakfast by pretending to be a dog, seal, horse, monkey and mouse as his mother patiently fixes the appropriate food for each animal.

Girls seeking books with strong adventurous heroines won't find *Z for Zachariah, The Blue Sword, The Night Rider, Dragonsinger, The Darkangel, The Watch House* or *The Queen of Spells* through any subject headings assigned by LC. Hennepin County Library's GIRL ADVENTURERS could be added, but still doesn't really meet the criterion of specificity. (These titles are all identified with

YA spine labels at Nampa Public Library, and have such headings as FANTASY, SUPERNATURAL—FICTION, and GHOST STORIES, but lack an indication of the central character's sex or strengths. I'm strongly in favor of spine labels to identify every genre for which a label is available.)

In the best of all possible worlds, my 30 pre-1969 titles would be part of an ongoing, retrospective project to update and improve subject access and assign headings to titles which lack them. As a result, we would have subject access to such titles as *The Bears on Hemlock Mountain, Little Raccoon and the Thing in the Pool,* and *Tiny's Big Umbrella,* as well as to *The Legend of Sleepy Hollow, Homer Price* and *All the Mowgli Stories.* Failing such a project, what can be done is this: whenever a book comes to hand for any reason other than circulation or simple mending, evaluate its subject entries (if any) and make additional access points if they are needed.

If such an ongoing evaluation were undertaken, I suspect it would confirm some of the suspicions I now have about the state of the children's fiction subject entries at Nampa Public Library. Without a written statement, NPL catalogers have not consistently chosen a single term (in this small sample I found FANTASY, FANTASTIC FICTION and SCIENCE FICTION used apparently interchangeably.)

The rule has been "at least one" rather than "sufficient" headings; as a result, when LC assigned FOLKLORE—CHINA to *Liang and the Magic Paintbrush,* no additional headings were assigned to reflect the actual content of the book: A poor boy who longs to paint is given a magic brush that brings to life whatever he pictures.

Nampa had not officially adopted Principle 4, so in this small sample I found SPANISH-AMERICANS and MEXICAN-AMERICANS instead of LATINO TEENAGERS (an HCL form) or HISPANIC-AMERICANS (ACP-assigned) and CHICANOS (HCL form).

The sample entries also perpetuated the biases inherent in LCSH such as AGED and its sometimes less-than-current forms such as HOSIERY—FICTION. Can you imagine a 6-year-old or her mother asking, "Do you have any books about hosiery?"

On the plus side, NPL has consistently provided genre headings for SCIENCE FICTION, MYSTERY AND DETECTIVE STORIES, THE WEST—FICTION and the form heading SHORT STORIES. But other genres, such as ROMANCE or SPORTS STORIES, have fared less well.

Because it seemed too radical, NPL catalogers have hesitated to create headings for fictional characters or places—although PERN (PLANET) would do a lot to improve access to Ann McCaffrey's "Dragonriders of Pern" series. And we have relied on bookmarks and printed lists for access to Newbery and Caldecott winners without creating subject entries, although each year's children's literature students expect to find such entries.

For all titles, resources such as *The Bookfinder, The Elementary School Library Collection* and Wilson Company indexes can provide valuable access for reference librarians and readers' advisors if the catalog does not do the job.

When new titles are received, their subject cataloging should be evaluated against the principles outlined above (as well as your library's policy statements). Don't accept limited access blindly. Some jobbers do better than others at supplying the ACP headings; find one who will give you what you want.

And the ACP itself is doing better than it did at first. *Cataloging Service Bulletin 19* announces a new regular feature which will list "new subject headings that represent popular trends or concepts."[8] Included in the initial list are TRUCKING, CHILD MOLESTERS, JOINT CUSTODY OF CHILDREN, LATCHKEY CHILDREN, FOSTER GRANDPARENTS and HUGGING, all of which are of interest in the context of this article.

In addition, consider creating reading lists and bibliographies for types of books, such as the strong heroine titles listed above, in which the best available subject access still may not satisfy the needs of a particular audience.

The ultimate goal of subject cataloging, stated by everyone from Cutter and Haykin to Berman and Marshall is to serve the user. Paying attention to subject cataloging of children's fiction will move us closer to reaching that goal.

REFERENCES

1. Meg McNelly, "Faulty Subject Heads [letter]," *School Library Journal*, XXIII (October, 1976), 59.

2. Sanford Berman, "Proposed: A Subject Cataloging Code for Public, School, and Community College Libraries," in *The Joy of Cataloging* (Phoenix: Oryx Press, 1981), 151.

3. *Ibid.*

4. *Ibid.*, p. 150.

5. *Ibid.*

6. Theodore C. Hines and Lois Winkel, "A New Information Access Tool for

Children's Media," *Library Resources & Technical Services*, XXVII (January/March, 1983), 95.
7. Sanford Berman, "Follies and Deficiencies: LC's Cataloging of Children's Materials," *School Library Journal*, XXII (April, 1976), 50.
8. "Subject Headings of Current Interest," *Cataloging Service Bulletin*, No. 19, (Winter, 1982), 3-5.

SELECTED BIBLIOGRAPHY

Annotations for titles referred to in this article are taken from the summaries provided by the Library of Congress Annotated Card Program.

Berman, Sanford. "Follies and Deficiencies: LC's Cataloging of Children's Materials." *School Library Journal*, XXII (April, 1976), 50.
Berman, Sanford. *The Joy of Cataloging*. Phoenix: Oryx Press, 1981.
Berman, Sanford. "Kids' Stuff: a Grabbag of Hennepin County (MN) Library Subject Headings for (Mostly) Children's Media." *The Unabashed Librarian*, No. 25 (1977), 6-7.
Cataloging Service Bulletin, Nos. 15 (Winter, 1982), 19 (also called Winter, 1982), and 20 (Spring, 1983).
Chan, Lois Mai. *Library of Congress Subject Headings: Principles and Applications*. Littleton, Colo.: Libraries Unlimited, 1978.
Hines, Theodore C. and Winkel, Lois. "A New Information Access Tool for Children's Media." *Library Resources and Technical Services*, XXVII (January/March, 1983), 94-104.
Levitt, Jent G. "Cataloging for Children." *The Unabashed Librarian*, No. 19 (Spring, 1976), 15-16.
McNelly, Meg. "Faulty Subject Heads [letter]." *School Library Journal*, XXIII (October, 1976), 59.
Marshall, Joan K., comp. *On Equal Terms: a Thesaurus for Nonsexist Indexing and Cataloging*. New York: Neal Schuman Publishers, 1977.
Rose, Lois Doman and Duncan, Winifred E. "LC's National Standard for Cataloging Children's Materials." *School Library Journal*, XXII (January, 1976), 20-23.
United States. Library of Congress. Subject Cataloging Division. *Library of Congress Subject Headings*. Washington, D. C.: Library of Congress, 1980.
Westby, Barbara M., ed. *Sears List of Subject Headings*. 11th ed. New York: H. W. Wilson Co., 1977.

The New Religious Movements Research Collection: A History and Description of Alternative Subject Cataloging

Diane Choquette

The development and refinement of subject access to the ephemeral files of the New Religious Movements Research Collection (NRM Collection) at the Graduate Theological Union Library (GTU Library) in Berkeley, California, provides an interesting and perhaps instructive example of the pitfalls and creative possibilities of alternative subject cataloging. In 1977, concurrently with the start of the Center for the Study of New Religious Movements in America (CSNRM), directed by Dr. Jacob Needleman, Betty Roszak began the formidable task of acquiring and organizing materials for the NRM Collection. As decisions were made in the GTU Library concerning types of material collected and their housing, the need for special subject access became readily apparent. First, let us consider both the varied subject areas included in the NRM collection, followed by a description of the physical arrangement of materials within the library. These two elements clearly set the stage for departure from traditional Library of Congress subject headings.

The definition of the NRM Collection's scope evolved slowly over a period of a few years in response to perceived needs of a broad audience, staff time, and library resources. Those who use the collection include scholars, the general public, the media, teachers, clergy from mainstream churches, and members of new religious groups. Among the general public are family and friends of people who have joined cults (here used non-pejoratively to designate small religious groups, often centered around a charismatic leader whose teachings differ significantly from the estab-

lished religions of the larger culture). These people generally want
all the information they can get about the group in question, often
with information on the appeal of the cults. Rarely, however, are
they interested in primary sources from the cults. Teachers and
scholars, along with students, represent the academic community.
They are primarily interested in the history and teachings of various
groups, especially American forms of Eastern religions, and issues
of social concern related to cults. The needs and interests of the
scholars connected with the CSNRM (which incidentally closed at
the end of June 1983) helped to shape the scope of the collection
considerably. People in the communications field, especially
writers, often want what amounts to a broad survey of the current
scene. Members of the religious groups themselves sometimes use
the collection to prepare for court cases; at other times they appear
in the role of seekers looking for another group to join.

From the outset, the collection focused on religious and quasi-
religious movements that are not part of the mainstream Judeo-
Christian tradition, in particular groups new to the U.S. since the
mid-1960s. Of concern also are older alternative religions that
flourished during the 1960s and 1970s. Many researchers have observed significant growth in occultism, witchcraft, magic, Buddhism (especially Zen and Tibetan forms), and other Eastern religions. It is now apparent that specifically American forms of
Sufism, Sikhism, Hinduism and Buddhism are attaining some
moderate stability. Diverse communal organizations have flourished, many of short duration. Some have or had a New Age experi-
mental orientation; others are or were Christian fundamentalist
tending towards traditional roles for men and women. Some
scholars consider quasi-religious human potential movements such
as *est*, Arica and Lifespring to be part of the same spiritual ferment.
The presence of the Unification Church and the Peoples Temple
tragedy have stimulated considerable research and public interest.

Several aspects of this religious ferment have become matters of
social concern and litigation. The most widely debated of these has
to do with complex questions of civil liberties and religious freedom
surrounding indoctrination practices commonly called brainwashing
and the equally controversial practice of deprogramming. Organizations devoted to defending religious liberty have come into existence in opposition to deprogramming. The Peoples Temple
tragedy prompted anti-cult groups to seek legislation to regulate
questionable practices.

Public policy issues have come to the forefront when communal organizations, such as the Rajneesh Foundation, have sought, and in this case, secured, incorporation as towns. Taken together, the various spiritual orientations and concomitant cultural responses comprise a new interdisciplinary area of study. The NRM collection includes social scientific, theological and religious, historical, legal, and popular secondary materials in addition to primary materials from religious, human potential, counseling, religious liberty, and anti-cult organizations.

The initial work of the NRM collection staff centered around intensive acquisitions of materials and decisions concerning housing and organization. The GTU library staff decided to integrate books, periodicals, audiocassettes and phonodiscs with the main collection. The library's card catalogs provide traditional author/title and subject access, modified by the addition of a few local subject terms. This decision followed groundwork laid by J. Stillson Judah, Professor and Librarian Emeritus, who had researched and added significantly to the library's collection of materials on the metaphysical movements, including New Thought, Christian Science, and Spiritualism. His interest in Scientology, the Unification Church, and the International Society for Krishna Consciousness led him to make valuable depository agreements between each organization and the GTU library. These organizations have continued to send their publications to the library for several years now.

In addition, however, Betty Roszak and the CSNRM wanted to document the contemporary religious revival as fully as possible. In order to do this, the NRM collection staff solicited brochures, newsletters, broadsides and other types of ephemera from the religious groups of interest. Posters and flyers were retrieved from public places in the San Francisco Bay Area. Researchers donated unpublished papers and ephemera they had collected. It was an exciting and challenging beginning. New materials arrived every day, leading to sometimes intense discussions concerning what to keep and how to treat it.

Betty Roszak decided to arrange the fugitive materials in folders, within vertical file cabinets, alphabetically by names of the group from which materials originated, or to which they referred (Group Files). Research papers constitute a separate file arranged alphabetically by author. A third file contains items not appropriate to the other two, such as notices of conferences, subject bibliographies, and general materials on religions. These items are housed in folders assigned broad subject headings. The Group Files make up the bulk of the ephemeral collection, and their arrangement aids us in answering almost half of our reference questions.

In order to deal with the remainder of the reference questions, however, subject access is necessary. When I joined the NRM collection staff in January 1979 as an assistant to Betty Roszak, a perhaps unique form of subject access was in use. It was, and still is, deemed adequate and possible to provide subject access only to each Group File as a whole, not to the individual items within the files. Research papers receive individual cataloging and, as mentioned earlier, are filed separately.

In what I would call Phase One of subject cataloging, no subject authority governed the choice of terms used as access points. For each Group File a main entry was determined directly from the literature. A term to indicate type of religion was sometimes, but not always, assigned, i.e., Sufism, Hinduism. The spiritual leader's name and alternate group names or names of divisions of the group were assigned as access points, too. In addition, an unspecified number of terms for rituals or beliefs were assigned as access points. The main entry cards, which still have the same format, looked like this:

```
                 ARICA INSTITUTE

              x  Ichazo, Oscar
              x  Kensho
              x  Psychocalisthenics
              x  Trialectics
              x  Hypergnostic Analysis
              x  Zhikr
              x  Consciousness
             xx  ONE UNITED SYSTEM
              x  Radiant Light
              x  Pyramid West
```

The above card is filed in the Main Entry portion of the NRM catalog. Cards constructed for each term under the main entry refer the user to that Group File or back to the main entry card and are filed in the Subject section of the catalog. For example:

```
Ichazo, Oscar
   see ARICA INSTITUTE
```

The format is very simple, and on the surface the choice of access points appears to be justifiable. Oscar Ichazo created the Arica Institute, and we can expect to receive questions concerning him, particularly in cases where Arica is not known. KENSHO, PSY-CHOCALISTHENICS, TRIALECTICS, HYPERGNOSTIC ANALYSIS, ZHIKR, and RADIANT LIGHT are all exercises or practices described in Arica's literature. Most are unique; however, I doubt that RADIANT LIGHT is, and I know that ZHIKR is a spiritual practice borrowed from Sufism. CONSCIOUSNESS was used because the teachings and practices of Arica are aimed at changing one's consciousness, leading ultimately to a form of enlightenment. PYRAMID WEST is the name of a division of Arica and ONE UNITED SYSTEM is another organization, either a successor or offshoot. Its name has been capitalized to indicate that a Group File exists for it, and one will find a "see also" card from its name to Arica Institute in the subject section of the catalog.

The treatment of Arica Institute illustrates two important aspects of Phase One subject cataloging: 1) subject headings were usually taken directly from primary literature, and 2) there was no guideline concerning how special terms used by a particular group were chosen as subject access points. When all terms are taken from the literature it is difficult to link together similar organizations by using a common descriptive term. In this case, among the terms assigned, CONSCIOUSNESS most closely approximates a term designating the type of organization we are dealing with, but is not usefully applied here since all spiritual groups are in some way concerned with changing consciousness. In secondary literature, Arica has been referred to as a "Human Potential Movement." Not everybody wants to call Arica a Human Potential Movement, but enough people have so that it is a useful term to use as an access point that connects Arica to other similar groups.

In Phase Two of subject cataloging, when subject authority was established, HUMAN POTENTIAL MOVEMENT was applied to organizations that had been called that in secondary literature. This has proven helpful in dealing with questions such as "What human potential groups do you have information on?" or "I want to study practices of different human potential movements."

Subject headings covering practices and doctrines of groups were used extensively in Phase One in anticipation of questions regarding who taught or practiced them. In each case, the librarian chose terms from primary literature, often relying only upon a feeling for what might be appropriate. It is difficult to adequately describe here the proliferation of terms referring to spiritual practices, rituals, and beliefs which has occurred as a result of the greater popularity of Buddhism (Tibetan Buddhism alone has four major traditions), Hinduism, Sufism, and Sikhism, not to mention renewed interest in the occult. The librarian was faced with much to choose from.

Also, during the first year of the collection, reference questions were not recorded and, of course, the collection was so new that there was little to go on. There certainly was no other such library collection to refer to. And, too, the primary religious literature with its emphasis on newness calls forth the desire to break away from traditional ways of dealing with materials in libraries. In the beginning, there was room to experiment without encountering much frustration in finding materials. Also, the simple, flexible arrangement of materials and format of the NRM card catalog allowed for easy change.

In order to provide the broadest access to materials possible, no "see" or "see also" references were used, so when ZEN BUDDHISM was used, so was BUDDHISM, ZEN. Direct forms of types of yoga, such as SIDDHA YOGA or KUNDALINI YOGA were used in addition to the inverted form, but sometimes only one form was used, and then, of course, everyone had to remember to search under both forms.

In the summer of 1979 when I replaced Betty Roszak as librarian for the collection, we had 580 Group Files and about 200 research papers. The lack of control in the NRM catalog was causing frustration, and I feared I was not always finding information I wanted. Every time I established a new Group File or cataloged a research paper I wondered how useful unique terms for teachings and practices really were or could be conceived to be in the future. Which should I choose and how many? With a growing backlog of unprocessed materials and too little staff time available, I seized upon the opportunity to become involved in a grant proposal the CSNRM was preparing for the National Endowment for the Humanities. The main aim of the proposal was to process the backlog and I saw this as an appropriate time to create subject authority for processing new materials and to gain better control over processed materials.

NEH awarded the Graduate Theological Union a modest one-year grant, most of which paid for more staff time to process the backlog, update our current files, create subject authority and clean up the NRM catalog. So, at the end of 1980 we began Phase Two of subject cataloging, changing the course of action. I turned to reference questions and secondary literature in determining subject access, depending less on, but still using, primary materials.

The collection staff had begun to record reference questions early in 1978 and by mid-1980 we had dealt with 300. A study of those questions demonstrated that the alphabetical arrangement of the Group Files took care of forty-seven percent of the queries. Fifteen percent were general questions, usually from students writing term papers on cults. These people were given bibliographies covering general works on new religious movements, prepared by the collection staff. Thirty-eight percent of the questions, however, involved issues, spiritual leaders, and types of groups. Key terms which have been used include: religious liberties, feminist spirituality, brainwashing, anti-cult movement, Zen groups, Neo-Pagan groups, deprogramming, Christian and Jewish responses to cults, authoritarianism, and communal groups.

In addition, the study revealed that terms for unique spiritual practices and beliefs, such as those mentioned earlier in connection with the Arica Institute, did not appear in queries. With some feeling of discomfort, I decided to avoid using such special terms in future cataloging. Now I breathe more easily, since that type of subject access is still not needed.

Other changes in cataloging practices were made, all with consistency, control, and utility in mind. In the proposal to the National Endowment for the Humanities, the following criteria for subject cataloging were suggested:

1. Assign no more than two subject headings plus the name of the spiritual leader or director as access points for each Group File. Two subject headings are usually adequate for research papers, but use more if needed.
2. Select an appropriate heading to indicate the religious or non-religious orientation of the group, i.e., TIBETAN BUD-DHISM, NEO-PAGANISM, CHRISTIAN COMMUNITIES, and ANTI-CULT MOVEMENT. If the group cannot be readily typed from its literature, consult secondary sources. J. Gordon Melton's *Encyclopedia of American Religions* is a particularly comprehensive source.
3. If a group has an alternate name, use as an entry point if the name appears frequently on literature.
4. When establishing terms as subject authorities use Library of Congress headings only when truly useful. LC headings for religions are often quite applicable, but the new religious movements literature has developed a language of its own. Be responsive to these developments in choosing new terms.

The above criteria are in use now, not as hard and fast rules, but as guidelines based on experience. Flexibility is an important quality in dealing with the NRM collection.

While applying the criteria in cataloging new materials, I delved into the NRM catalog, making changes to bring the catalog in line with the new guidelines as much as possible. This work is still not finished, and, of course, since the subject headings are always changing, the catalog is always in a state of flux. In the following changes, however, I have attempted to use terms accurately and to create consistent usage which brings together materials in a way that is meaningful to the user:

1. In situations where two or more very similar headings have been used, one has been established as an authority. For example:

Former	Current
ESOTERIC SYSTEMS ESOTERIC TEACHINGS ESOTERIC STUDIES	ESOTERIC STUDIES AND TEACHINGS
NEW RELIGIONS NEW RELIGIOUS MOVE- MENTS	NEW RELIGIOUS MOVE- MENTS
COMMUNAL LIFE COMMUNITY COMMUNITIES ALTERNATIVE COM- MUNITIES	COMMUNITIES

2. "See also" references have been used frequently to connect closely related terms which had each been used several times during the first two years of the collection. These subject headings, although very close in meaning, derive utility from widespread acceptance in the literature and among users. For example:

SPIRITUALISM
  sa CHANNELED MESSAGES
    ASCENDED MASTERS

OCCULT CENTERS, GROUPS, ETC.
  sa ESOTERIC STUDIES AND TEACHINGS
    ESOTERIC CHRISTIANITY

GROWTH CENTERS
  sa HUMAN POTENTIAL MOVEMENT

3. In other cases, "see also" references were needed to bring together overlapping areas. For example:

LEGAL ASPECTS OF NEW RELIGIOUS MOVEMENTS

  x CONSERVATORSHIP
  sa DEPROGRAMMING
  sa CHURCH AND STATE IN THE U.S.
  xx RELIGIOUS LIBERTY
  xx TAXATION, EXEMPTION FROM

4. Forms of headings have been changed to create consistency.

For example:

YOGA, ANTHAR	YOGA, ASHTANGA
x ANTHAR YOGA	x ASHTANGA YOGA
ZEN BUDDHISM,	ZEN BUDDHISM,
SOTO	RINZAI
x SOTO ZEN	x RINZAI ZEN
BUDDHISM	BUDDHISM

The Subject Heading List gives further examples.

Finally, let me discuss one more heading here as an example of the difficulty in choosing accurate headings in a field fraught with emotion. The reader will note that EXTRAORDINARY SOCIAL INFLUENCE is used as a heading in place of BRAINWASHING. Although BRAINWASHING is used extensively by media and researchers to denote the result of strong influence exercised by some authoritarian cults in recruiting members, it is a term that most researchers find to be more suitably applied to processes forced on prisoners of war, as has occurred in China and Korea. As I listened to top scholars on both sides of the issue discuss the topic at the New Religious Movements conference in 1981, I saw that BRAIN-WASHING was a term they all struggled against using, while still doing so. EXTRAORDINARY SOCIAL INFLUENCE was brought up, along with a few other terms. I chose it because it does not carry the pejorative dimension of BRAINWASHING and appears to be more apropos, even though awkward.

In reviewing the history of subject cataloging of the NRM collection, one can see continued movement away from disparate terms available mostly in primary literature to terms applied by outsiders seeking to classify, compare, and understand. In some cases, members of groups represented in the collection have questioned the way in which their spiritual inclinations have been labeled. I am reminded of discussions among the collection staff a few years ago in which we agreed on the importance of adhering to self-definitions and not imposing labels on new doctrines. More recently an *est* graduate questioned the existence of materials about *est* in the collection. When I told him that I did not define *est* in any way myself, but that it was seen as a cult by some and by others to be a human potential movement bearing an impression of Zen Buddhism, he replied, in effect, that it wasn't anything like that at all; people just want to put things in categories.

His remark made me think back on the years when the collection had no subject authority. The lack of order and the unusual terms used reflected something exciting and curious about the materials collected. As a young child, the NRM collection was certainly unruly. Now we have placed most items in neat categories, tied down and located only by choosing the right entry, by appealing to the proper authorities, so to speak.

Perhaps I am naive to regret the compromises that subject cataloging entails. Surely the benefits have been worth the loss of a counter-culture rebellion against intellectual categories. But it is important to remember that subject cataloging is a responsive activity. The librarian must always be willing to change, seeking to most accurately represent sometimes complex works with the few words used for subject access. Then, too, the people in quest of information must be listened to, for they help us to organize information by keeping us aware of their needs. Subject cataloging exists between the information and the seeker as a subtle territory of categorized thought, which presents the librarian with a lively challenge.

SUBJECT HEADING LIST

NEW RELIGIOUS MOVEMENTS RESEARCH COLLECTION

AFRO-AMERICAN GROUPS
  x BLACK CHURCHES
ALTERED STATES OF CON-
  SCIOUSNESS
  xx CONSCIOUSNESS
AMERICAN INDIAN RELIGIONS
  see NATIVE AMERICAN
  RELIGIONS
ANIMALS, TREATMENT OF
ANTHAR YOGA
  see YOGA, ANTHAR
ANTI-CULT MOVEMENT
  sa DEPROGRAMMING
  sa LEGAL ASPECTS OF NEW
    RELIGIOUS MOVEMENTS
APOSTASY
  x CULTS-DEFECTORS
  x DEFECTORS

ASCENDED MASTERS
  xx CHANNELED MESSAGES
  xx SPIRITUALISM
ASHTANGA YOGA
  see YOGA, ASHTANGA
AUTHORITARIANISM
  sa PSYCHOLOGY OF NEW
    RELIGIOUS MOVEMENTS
  sa CHARISMA
BHAKTI, YOGA
  see YOGA, BHAKTI
BLACK CHURCHES
  see AFRO-AMERICAN GROUPS
BRAIN RESEARCH
  see also CONSCIOUSNESS
BRAINWASHING
  see EXTRAORDINARY SOCIAL
    INFLUENCE

BUDDHISM
BUDDHISM, HINAYANA
  see HINAYANA BUDDHISM
BUDDHISM, JAPANESE
  xx JAPANESE RELIGIONS
BUDDHISM, TIBETAN
  see TIBETAN BUDDHISM
BUDDHISM, ZEN
  see ZEN BUDDHISM
BUDDHISM AND CHRISTIANITY
CABALA
  sa HASIDISM
  x KABBALAH
CAMPS AND RETREATS
  x RETREATS
CELEBRATIONS
  see FESTIVALS, FAIRS, EXPO-
    SITIONS, CELEBRATIONS,
    ETC.
CEREMONIAL MAGICK
  see MAGICK, CEREMONIAL
  def. Occult magic; witchcraft
    (New Age Dict.)
CHANNELED MESSAGES
  xx ASCENDED MASTERS
  xx SPIRITUALISM
CHARISMA
  sa PSYCHOLOGY OF NEW
    RELIGIOUS MOVEMENTS
  sa AUTHORITARIANISM
CHARISMATICS
  sa PENTECOSTALISM
CHILDREN IN COMMUNITIES
  xx COMMUNITIES
CHINESE BUDDHISM
  x BUDDHISM, CHINESE
CHRISTIAN COMMUNITIES
  xx COMMUNITIES
CHRISTIAN GROWTH GROUPS
  x GROWTH GROUPS,
    CHRISTIAN
  x SPIRITUAL GROWTH,
    CHRISTIAN
CHRISTIAN MYSTICISM
  see MYSTICISM-CHRISTIAN-
    ITY
"CHRISTIAN NEW RIGHT"
  xx MORAL MAJORITY

CHRISTIAN PSYCHICAL RE-
  SEARCH
  see PARAPSYCHOLOGY AND
    CHRISTIANITY
CHRISTIAN RESPONSE TO
  NRMs
CHRISTIANITY AND HINDUISM
  see HINDUISM AND CHRIS-
    TIANITY
CHURCH AND STATE IN THE
  U.S.
  xx LEGAL ASPECTS OF NEW
    RELIGIOUS MOVEMENTS
  x RELIGION IN THE PUBLIC
    SCHOOLS
COERCIVE PERSUASION
  see EXTRAORDINARY SOCIAL
    INFLUENCE
COMMUNITIES
  sa CHRISTIAN COMMUNITIES
  x MONASTERIES
  also see various religions, such
    as Zen Buddhism, Hinduism,
    etc.
  sa CHILDREN IN COMMUNI-
    TIES
CONSCIOUS EVOLUTION
CONFERENCES, WORKSHOPS,
  SEMINARS
  x WORKSHOPS
  x SEMINARS
CONSCIOUSNESS
  xx ALTERED STATES OF
    CONSCIOUSNESS
  xx BRAIN RESEARCH
CONSERVATORSHIP
  see LEGAL ASPECTS OF NEW
    RELIGIOUS MOVEMENTS
CONVERSION
  sa PSYCHOLOGY OF NEW RE-
    LIGIOUS MOVEMENTS
    RECRUITMENT
COUNSELING
CULTS
  sa NEW RELIGIOUS MOVE-
    MENTS
CULTS-DEFECTORS
  see APOSTASY

DANCE

DEATH AND DYING

DEFECTORS
see APOSTASY

DEPROGRAMMING
xx ANTI-CULT MOVEMENT
xx LEGAL ASPECTS OF NEW
RELIGIOUS MOVEMENTS

DIET
see NUTRITION AND DIET

DREAMS AND DREAMING

DRUGS
xx MARIHUANA

DRUIDS

EDUCATION
sa EDUCATION, HUMANISTIC

EDUCATION, HUMANISTIC
xx EDUCATION
xx HUMANISTIC EDUCATION

ESOTERIC CHRISTIANITY
xx ESOTERIC STUDIES AND
TEACHINGS
xx OCCULT CENTERS,
GROUPS, ETC.

ESOTERIC STUDIES AND
TEACHINGS
see also OCCULT CENTERS,
GROUPS, ETC.
ESOTERIC CHRISTIANITY

EVANGELICALISM
see also TELEVANGELISM

EXPOSITIONS
see FESTIVALS, FAIRS, EXPO-
SITIONS, CELEBRATIONS,
ETC.

EXTRAORDINARY SOCIAL
INFLUENCE
x BRAINWASHING
x COERCIVE PERSUASION
x MIND CONTROL
sa PSYCHOLOGY OF NEW RE-
LIGIOUS MOVEMENTS

FAIRS
see FESTIVALS, FAIRS, EXPO-
SITIONS, CELEBRATIONS,
ETC.

FAITH HEALING
see SPIRITUAL HEALING

FEMINIST SPIRITUALITY
xx GODDESSES
xx WOMEN IN RELIGION

FESTIVALS, FAIRS, EXPOSI-
TIONS, CELEBRATIONS, ETC.
x FAIRS
x CELEBRATIONS
x EXPOSITIONS

FOOD
see NUTRITION AND DIET

FLYING SAUCERS
see UFOs

GAY SPIRITUALITY
x HOMOSEXUALITY AND
RELIGION

GLOSSOLALIA
sa PENTECOSTALISM
x TONGUES, GIFT OF

GODDESSES
xx FEMINIST SPIRITUALITY
xx WOMEN IN RELIGION

GROWTH CENTERS
sa HUMAN POTENTIAL
MOVEMENT

GROWTH GROUPS, CHRISTIAN
see CHRISTIAN GROWTH
GROUPS

GURDJIEFF WORK

HASIDISM
xx JUDAISM
sa CABALA
MYSTICISM-JUDAISM

HINAYANA BUDDHISM
x BUDDHISM, HINAYANA
x THERAVADA BUDDHISM

HINDUISM
x CHRISTIANITY AND HIN-
DUISM

HOLISTIC HEALTH

HOMOSEXUALITY AND RE-
LIGION
see GAY SPIRITUALITY

HUMAN POTENTIAL MOVE-
MENT
xx GROWTH CENTERS

HUMANISTIC EDUCATION
see EDUCATION, HUMAN-
ISTIC

HUMANISTIC PSYCHOLOGY
x PSYCHOLOGY, HUMAN-
    ISTIC
ISLAM
sa SUFISM
JAPANESE RELIGIONS
sa BUDDHISM, JAPANESE
JESUS PEOPLE
x JESUS MOVEMENT
JESUS MOVEMENT
see JESUS PEOPLE
JUDAISM
sa HASIDISM
sa CABALA
    MESSIANIC JUDAISM
    MYSTICISM-JUDAISM
KABALLAH
see CABALA
KUNDALINI
x YOGA, KUNDALINI
LEGAL ASPECTS OF NEW RE-
    LIGIOUS MOVEMENTS
x CONSERVATORSHIP
sa DEPROGRAMMING
sa CHURCH AND STATE IN
    THE U.S.
xx RELIGIOUS LIBERTY
xx TAXATION, EXEMPTION
    FROM
MAGIC
sa WITCHCRAFT
MAGICK, CEREMONIAL
x CEREMONIAL MAGICK
MAIL-ORDER CHURCHES
x ORDINATION BY MAIL
MARIHUANA
xx DRUGS
x MARIJUANA
MARIJUANA
see MARIHUANA
MEDIA RESPONSES TO NEW
    RELIGIOUS MOVEMENTS
x NEW RELIGIOUS MOVE-
    MENTS-MEDIA RESPONSES
x TELEVISION PROGRAMS
x RADIO BROADCASTS
MEDITATION
xx VIPASSANA MEDITATION

MEDITATION (BUDDHIST)
xx VIPASSANA MEDITATION
MESSIANIC JUDAISM
xx JUDAISM
METAPHYSICAL MOVEMENTS
see also NEW THOUGHT
MIND CONTROL
see EXTRAORDINARY
    SOCIAL INFLUENCE
MONASTERIES
see COMMUNITIES
also see various religions,
    such as Zen Buddhism,
    Hinduism, etc.
MORAL MAJORITY
sa "CHRISTIAN NEW RIGHT"
MUSIC
MYSTICISM
MYSTICISM-CHRISTIANITY
x CHRISTIAN MYSTICISM
MYSTICISM-JUDAISM
sa HASIDISM
NATIVE AMERICAN RELIGIONS
x AMERICAN INDIAN
    RELIGIONS
NEO-PAGANISM
xx WITCHCRAFT
NETWORKS
NEW RELIGIOUS MOVEMENTS
xx CULTS
NEW RELIGIOUS MOVEMENTS-
    MEDIA RESPONSES
see MEDIA RESPONSES TO
    NEW RELIGIOUS MOVE-
    MENTS
NEW THOUGHT
xx METAPHYSICAL MOVE-
    MENTS
NUTRITION AND DIET
x DIET
x FOOD
OCCULT CENTERS, GROUPS,
    ETC.
see also ESOTERIC STUDIES
    AND TEACHINGS
ESOTERIC CHRISTIANITY
ORDINATION BY MAIL
see MAIL-ORDER CHURCHES

PARAPSYCHOLOGY
  x PSYCHICAL RESEARCH
PARAPSYCHOLOGY AND
  CHRISTIANITY
  x CHRISTIAN PSYCHICAL
    RESEARCH
PENTECOSTALISM
  sa CHARISMATICS
  xx GLOSSOLALIA
PLANETARY CONSCIOUSNESS
PSYCHIC AWARENESS
PSYCHIC HEALING
  sa SPIRITUAL HEALING
PSYCHIC SURGERY
PSYCHICAL RESEARCH
  see PARAPSYCHOLOGY
PSYCHICS
PSYCHOLOGY, HUMANISTIC
  see HUMANISTIC PSYCHOL-
    OGY
PSYCHOLOGY OF NEW RE-
  LIGIOUS MOVEMENTS
  xx CONVERSION
  xx EXTRAORDINARY SOCIAL
    INFLUENCE
  xx AUTHORITARIANISM
  sa CHARISMA
RADIO BROADCASTS
  see MEDIA RESPONSES TO
    NEW RELIGIOUS MOVE-
    MENTS
RAS TAFARI MOVEMENT
  x RASTAFARIAN MOVEMENT
RASTAFARIAN MOVEMENT
  see RAS TAFARI MOVEMENT
RECRUITMENT
  sa CONVERSION
REINCARNATION THERAPY
RELIGION IN THE PUBLIC
  SCHOOLS
  see CHURCH AND STATE IN
    THE U.S.
RELIGIOUS LIBERTY
  see also LEGAL ASPECTS OF
    NEW RELIGIOUS MOVE-
    MENTS
RETREATS
  see CAMPS AND RETREATS

RINZAI ZEN BUDDHISM
  see ZEN BUDDHISM, RINZAI
SEXUALITY
SIDDHA YOGA
  see YOGA, SIDDHA
SOCIOLOGY OF NEW RE-
  LIGIOUS MOVEMENTS
SOTO ZEN BUDDHISM
  see ZEN BUDDHISM, SOTO
SPIRITUAL GROWTH, CHRIS-
  TIAN
  see CHRISTIAN GROWTH
    GROUPS
SPIRITUAL HEALING
  sa PSYCHIC HEALING
  x FAITH HEALING
SPIRITUALISM
  xx ASCENDED MASTERS
  xx CHANNELED MESSAGES
SUFISM
  xx ISLAM
TANTRISM
TAOISM
TAXATION, EXEMPTION FROM
  sa LEGAL ASPECTS OF NEW
    RELIGIOUS MOVEMENTS
TELEVANGELISM
  xx EVANGELICALISM
TELEVISION PROGRAMS
  see MEDIA RESPONSES TO
    NEW RELIGIOUS MOVE-
    MENTS
THERAVADA BUDDHISM
  see HINAYANA BUDDHISM
TIBETAN BUDDHISM
  x BUDDHISM, TIBETAN
TONGUES, GIFT OF
  see GLOSSOLALIA
UFO CONTACTEE CULTS
UFOs
  x FLYING SAUCERS
  x UNIDENTIFIED FLYING
    OBJECTS
UNIDENTIFIED FLYING
  OBJECTS
  see UFOs
WITCHCRAFT
  xx MAGIC

sa NEO-PAGANISM
  x WICCA
  xx WOMEN IN RELIGION
WOMEN IN RELIGION
  sa FEMINIST SPIRITUALITY
  sa WITCHCRAFT
  sa GODDESSES
YOGA, ANTHAR
  x ANTHAR YOGA
YOGA, ASHTANGA
  x ASHTANGA YOGA

YOGA, BHAKTI
  x BHAKTI YOGA
YOGA, SIDDHA
  x SIDDHA YOGA
ZEN BUDDHISM, RINZAI
  x RINZAI ZEN BUDDHISM
ZEN BUDDHISM, SOTO
  x SOTO ZEN BUDDHISM
ZEN BUDDHISM
  x BUDDHISM, ZEN

Problems in I & R Taxonomy, with a Grassroots Solution

Shirley A. Smith

Although the literature for information and referral services spans less than twenty years, the sheer quantity of material tends to put off all but the most determined researcher. This proliferation obviously results from the initial infusion of Federal funds in I & R and the inevitable reports required by that funding. But it offers few practical, how-to-do-it-good examples or instructions for persons starting an I & R program: for instance, how to devise subject headings for the resource file.

The 1978 report, "Evaluation of Human Services Taxonomy Project, Volume I: The State of the Art," identifies 372 domestic human services taxonomies and/or common languages and 5 international taxonomies. Of the 299 surveyed for that report, 72% were found to be either direct applications or modifications of the "granddaddy" of them all (and still the most comprehensive), the United Way of America Services Identification System (UWASIS). All the taxonomies focused on social welfare, social welfare/health, social welfare/education, health, health/education, education, and other human services fields. These taxonomies usually address such target groups as seniors, children and youth, disabled and low income persons, minorities, offenders, veterans, women, and workers.

The UWASIS scheme (Exhibit 1) is organized by life goals, service subsystems, service, and programs and is conceptually, but not literally, all-inclusive, which explains the "Add-if-Needed" (AIN) category in each section. Although it is beautifully adaptable to computer use due to intricate coding (Exhibit 2), its everyday use requires training and experience. To be used in libraries, it needs expanding far beyond the human services areas it covers.

A library contemplating a manual file would be better served by

EXHIBIT 1

UNITED WAY OF AMERICA SERVICES IDENTIFICATION SYSTEM (UWASIS)

Identification and Classification of Human Service Programs within the

Framework of Broad Human Goals, Services Systems, Services and Programs

GOAL I. ADEQUATE INCOME AND
ECONOMIC OPPORTUNITY

EMPLOYMENT SERVICES SYSTEM

Manpower Development &
Training Services

PROGRAMS
Job Finding
Pre-Job Guidance
Job Training
Job Placement &
Referral

Special Employment Services
for the Socially, Economically, & Politically
Disadvantaged

PROGRAMS
Employment Assistance to the
Socially & Economically
Disadvantaged
Bonding of Ex-Offenders
Exemplary Rehabilitation
Certification Assistance
Certification for Employment
of Non-Citizens
Special Employment Services
for the Aging and the
Physically & Mentally
Handicapped

PROGRAMS
Sheltered Remunerative
Employment
Homebound Employment

INCOME MAINTENANCE SERVICES
SYSTEM

Social Insurance Services

PROGRAMS
Health Insurance for the
Aged-Hospital Insurance
(Medicare)
Health Insurance for the
Aged-Supplementary
Medical Insurance
(Medicare)
Unemployment Insurance
Workmen's Compensation
Social Insurance for
Railroad Workers
Special Benefits for
Disabled Coal Miners
("Black Lung" Benefits)
Disability Insurance
Retirement Insurance
Survivors Insurance

Financial Aid Services

PROGRAMS
Aid to the Blind
Aid to the Permanently
and Totally Disabled
Aid to Families with
Dependent Children
Old Age Assistance

EXHIBIT 1 (continued)

GOAL I. ADEQUATE INCOME AND
ECONOMIC OPPORTUNITY

EMPLOYMENT SERVICES SYSTEM

PROGRAMS
Emergency Welfare
  Assistance
General Assistance
Special Benefits for
  Persons Aged 72 and
  Over

CONSUMER PROTECTION &
SAFETY SERVICES
SYSTEM

Consumer Education
  Services

PROGRAMS
Direct Consumer Advice
  and Guidance
Mass Consumer Education

Services for the Quality
  Control of Consumer
  Goods & Products

PROGRAMS
Calibration & Testing
Agricultural Product Grading
Meat, Poultry, & Egg Products
  Inspection & Supervision
Fishing Products Inspection
  & Certification

PROGRAMS
Protection Against Unfair
  Trade Practices Services

PROGRAMS
Commodity Exchange Regulation
Trade Practices Regulation

PROGRAMS
Commodity Exchange Regulation
Trade Practices Regulation

Consumer Safety Standards
  Services

PROGRAMS
Food Safety Standards
Drug Safety Standards
Product Safety Standards

Consumer Recourse Services

PROGRAMS
Consumer Complaints
  Processing &
  Investigation
Consumer Redress

EXHIBIT 1 (continued)

GOAL II. OPTIMAL ENVIRONMENTAL
CONDITIONS AND PROVISION OF BASIC

FOOD & NUTRITION SERVICES SYSTEM

Governmental Food Subvention
  & Assistance Services

PROGRAMS
Commodity Distribution
Food Stamps
Special Non-School Food
  Assistance for Children
School Breakfasts
National School Lunch Program
Special Milk Program for
  Children

Voluntary Food Services

PROGRAMS
General Food Service
Home Meals or Mobile Meals

CLOTHING & APPAREL SERVICES
  SYSTEM

Subsidized or Free Apparel
  Services

PROGRAMS
Collection & Pickup of
  Donated Apparel
Apparel Distribution Centers

HOUSING SERVICES SYSTEM
Urban Renewal and Redevelopment
  Services

PROGRAMS
Real Estate Acquisition,
  Renewal & Redevelopment
Relocation & Allocation Under
  Renewal

PROGRAMS
Housing Subvention Services

PROGRAMS
Low to Moderate Income Housing
  Loans
Mortgage & Loan Insurance
Rent Supplements
Interest Subsidy
Public Housing
Housing Assistance for Special
  Groups

General Housing Search &
  Location Services

PROGRAMS
General Assistance for Housing
Residence Service

TRANSPORTATION SERVICES SYSTEM

Earth, Water, & Air Transportation Development & Maintenance
  Services

PROGRAMS
Development & Maintenance of
  Earth Surface Transportation
Development & Maintenance of
  Water Surface Transportation
Development & Maintenance of
  Air Transportation
Special Transportation Needs
  of Selected Groups

Transportation (Traffic) Control
  & Safety Services

EXHIBIT 1 (continued)

GOAL II. OPTIMAL ENVIRONMENTAL
CONDITIONS AND PROVISION OF BASIC

FOOD & NUTRITION SERVICES SYSTEM

PROGRAMS
Earth Surface Traffic Control
  & Safety
Waterways Traffic Control &
  Safety
Air Traffic Control & Safety

PUBLIC PROTECTION, JUSTICE, &
SAFETY SERVICES SYSTEM

Administration of Justice
  Services

PROGRAMS
Law Enforcement
Dispensation of Justice &
  Resolution of Disputes
Legal Aid & Defense
Detention of Law Violators &
  Alleged Law Violators
Corrections

Crime & Delinquency Prevention
Services

GOAL III. OPTIMAL HEALTH

HEALTH (PHYSICAL) MAINTENANCE &
CARE SERVICES SYSTEMS

Community Health Maintenance
  Services

PROGRAMS
Prevention & Control of
  Communicable Diseases
Public Health Nursing
Environmental Sanitation
Occupational Health Concerns
Community Health Education
Blood Bank
Community Clinics
Home Health Care
Medical Supplies & Equipment
  Provision

Medical Care Services

PROGRAMS
Inpatient Medical Care
Outpatient Medical Care
Emergency Medical Care

MENTAL HEALTH MAINTENANCE
  & CARE SERVICES SYSTEM

Psychiatric Treatment Services

PROGRAMS
Inpatient Psychiatric Care
Outpatient Psychiatric Care
Emergency Psychiatric Care
Residential Treatment of the
  Emotionally Disturbed
Transitional Care

Mental Health Preservation
  & Maintenance Services

PROGRAMS
Alcoholism Prevention &
  Treatment
Drug Abuse & Narcotics Addiction
  Prevention & Treatment

EXHIBIT 1 (continued)

GOAL III. OPTIMAL HEALTH

HEALTH (PHYSICAL) MAINTENANCE &
CARE SERVICES SYSTEMS

MENTAL RETARDATION SERVICES
SYSTEM

Services for the Habilitation
of the Mentally Retarded

PROGRAMS
Special Day Care of the
Mentally Retarded

Residential Care Services for
the Mentally Retarded

PROGRAMS
Short-Term Residential Care
of the Mentally Retarded

PROGRAMS
Long-Term Custodial Care of
the Mentally Retarded

REHABILITATION SERVICES SYSTEM

Therapeutic Services for the
Handicapped

PROGRAMS
Inpatient Rehabilitation
Outpatient Rehabilitation

GOAL IV. ADEQUATE KNOWLEDGE
AND SKILLS

FORMAL EDUCATIONAL SERVICES
SYSTEM

Preschool Services

PROGRAMS
Early School Admissions

Elementary & Secondary School
Services

PROGRAMS
Kindergarten
Primary or Elementary School
Education
Secondary or High School
Education

Higher Educational Services

PROGRAMS
Community Colleges or Junior
Colleges Education
Undergraduate College Education
Universities, Professional
Schools, and
Technological Institutes

INFORMAL & SUPPLEMENTARY
EDUCATIONAL SERVICES SYSTEM

Informal Educational Services
for Self-Instruction

PROGRAMS
Libraries

EXHIBIT 1 (continued)

GOAL IV. ADEQUATE KNOWLEDGE
AND SKILLS

FORMAL EDUCATIONAL SERVICES
SYSTEM

PROGRAMS
Occupationally or Professionally
   Oriented Groups or Specific
   Goal-Oriented Groups &
   Associations

Supplementary Educational
   Services

PROGRAMS
Adult Education

PROGRAMS
Special Educational Services
   for the Gifted & the
   Disadvantaged
Special Educational
   Opportunities for Gifted
   Children
Special Educational
   Opportunities for the
   Disadvantaged

GOAL V. OPTIMAL PERSONAL AND
SOCIAL ADJUSTMENT AND

INDIVIDUAL & FAMILY LIFE
SERVICES SYSTEM

Family Preservation &
   Strengthening Services

PROGRAMS
Counseling
Homemaker
Family Growth Control &
   Planning

Family Substitute Services

PROGRAMS
Adoption
Day Care
Foster Home Care
Group Home
Institutional Care

Crisis Intervention &
   Protective Services

PROGRAMS
Suicide Prevention & Protection
   Against Physical Self-Harm
Protection from Neglect, Abuse
   & Exploitation

Supportive Services to
   Individuals & Families

PROGRAMS
Retirement Preparation
Friendly Visiting
Assistance to Travelers,
   Newcomers, Migrants,
   Immigrants and Mobile Families
Emergency Assistance

SOCIAL ADJUSTMENT, SOCIAL
   DEVELOPMENT & SOCIAL
   USEFULNESS SERVICES SYSTEM

EXHIBIT 1 (continued)

GOAL V. OPTIMAL PERSONAL AND
SOCIAL ADJUSTMENT AND

INDIVIDUAL & FAMILY LIFE
SERVICES SYSTEM

Recreational Services

PROGRAMS
Participatory Recreation
Spectator or Non-Participatory
  Recreation

Social Group Services

PROGRAMS
Social Adjustment
Social Development
Troop Type

Intergroup Relations Services

PROGRAMS
Special or Single Interest
  Group Promotion
Multi-Interest Community
  Relations

CULTURAL & SPIRITUAL ENRICHMENT
& DEVELOPMENT SERVICES SYSTEM

Arts & Humanities Development
  & Subvention Services

PROGRAMS
Community Facilities for Arts
  & Humanities
Arts & Humanities Subsidization

Artistic & Cultural
  Opportunities Services

PROGRAMS
Personal Involvement & Active
  Participation in Artistic
  Pursuits
Arts Appreciation & Enjoyment

Religious or Spiritual Services

PROGRAMS
Group Worship
Independent Spiritual Pursuits

GOAL VI. ADEQUATELY ORGANIZED
SOCIAL INSTRUMENTALITIES

MOBILIZATION OF PEOPLE
SERVICES SYSTEM

Community or Organization
  Services

PROGRAMS
Neighborhood Developoment
Community Planning &
  Development

Political Organizations
  Services

PROGRAMS
Political Parties
Elections & Election
  Campaigns

EXHIBIT 1 (continued)

GOAL VI. ADEQUATELY ORGANIZED
SOCIAL INSTRUMENTALITIES

MOBILIZATION OF PEOPLE
SERVICES SYSTEM

Volunteer Services

PROGRAMS
Volunteer Recruitment &
  Training
Volunteer Placement &
  Supervision

RESOURCE DEVELOPMENT
SERVICES SYSTEM

Human Service Programs
  Funding Services

PROGRAMS
Governmental Fund Raising
  or Public Sector Program
  Funding
Voluntary Fund Raising
Acquisition of Charitable
  Foundations Support
Acquisition of Governmental
  Grants and Contracts

Economic Development
  Services

PROGRAMS
Promotion of Tourism, Busi-
  nesses & Industries
Small Business Development

ADMINISTRATION & MANAGEMENT
CAPABILITY SERVICES SYSTEM

Administrative Services

PROGRAMS
Personnel Recruitment &
  Training
Budgeting, Allocations &
  Agency Relations
Purchasing
Plant & Facilities
  Operation & Maintenance
Planning & Evaluation

Communications & Public
  Information Services

PROGRAMS
Public Relations

Research Services

PROGRAMS
Demonstration or Pilot
  Projects
Causational Research
Social Simulations
Social Forecasting

EQUAL OPPORTUNITY
SERVICES SYSTEM

Equal Opportunity Promo-
  tion Services

PROGRAMS
Civil Rights Promotion
  (Legally Mandated)
Equal Employment
  Opportunity Promotion
Promotion of Fair Housing
  Policies & Practices

EXHIBIT 1 (continued)

GOAL VI. ADEQUATELY ORGANIZED
SOCIAL INSTRUMENTALITIES

MOBILIZATION OF PEOPLE
SERVICES SYSTEM

Equal Opportunity Recourse
Services

PROGRAMS
Equal Opportunity-Mediation
of Disputes (Non-
enforcement)

PROGRAMS
Equal Opportunity Recourse
Through Legal Enforcement

SOURCE: People and Programs Need Uniform and
Comparable Definitions...UWASIS-
United Way of America Services
Identification System,
θ United Way of America, Alexandria,
Virginia, 1972. Appendix D.

EXHIBIT 2

OUTLINE OF UWASIS II

1.0.00.00

GOAL I: OPTIMAL INCOME SECURITY AND
ECONOMIC OPPORTUNITY

1.1.00.00	EMPLOYMENT SER-VICES SYSTEM	1.1.02.00	Employment Training Service
1.1.01.00	Employment Procure-ment Service		Programs
	Programs	1.1.02.01	Job Training (Un-specified)
1.1.01.01	Employment Assess-ment and Guidance	1.1.02.02	Apprenticeship
1.1.01.02	Pre-Job Guidance	1.1.02.03	Internship
1.1.01.03	Job Search Assistance and Placement (Unspecified)	1.1.02.04	On-the-Job Training
		1.1.02.05	AIN—Employment
		to	Training Service
1.1.01.04	Add If Necessary	1.1.02.99	Programs
to	(AIN)—Employment		
1.1.01.99	Procurement Service Programs		

EXHIBIT 2 (continued)

1.1.03.00	**Special Employment Assistance Service for Exceptional Individuals and Groups (Aged, Handicapped, and other Disadvantaged)**	**1.1.04.00 to 1.1.99.99**	**AIN—Employment Services System, Services and Programs**
	Programs	*1.2.00.00*	*INCOME SECURITY SERVICES SYSTEM*
1.1.03.01	Employment Assistance to the Socially and Economically Disadvantaged (Unspecified)	**1.2.01.00**	**Social Insurance Service**
			Programs
		1.2.01.01	Unemployment Insurance
1.1.03.02	Public Service Employment	1.2.01.02	Social Insurance for Railroad Workers
1.1.03.03	Emergency Employment	1.2.01.03	Disability Insurance
1.1.03.04	Bonding of Ex-Offenders	1.2.01.04	Retirement Insurance
		1.2.01.05	Survivors Insurance
1.1.03.05	Exemplary Rehabilitation Certification	1.2.01.06	Life Insurance for Veterans
1.1.03.06	Sheltered Remunerative Employment	1.2.01.07	Workmen's Compensation (Unspecified)
1.1.03.07	Work Activity Centers	1.2.01.08	Longshoremen's and Harbor Workers' Compensation
1.1.03.08	Homebound Employment	1.2.01.09	Disabled Coal Mine Workers' Compensation ("Black Lung" Benefits)
1.1.03.09	Vocational Rehabilitation		
1.1.03.10	Federal Employment for the Handicapped	1.2.01.10 to 1.2.01.99	AIN—Social Insurance Service Programs
1.1.03.11 to 1.1.03.99	AIN—Special Employment Assistance Service for Exceptional Individuals and Groups Programs		

employing various indices to the major taxonomies, such as the alphabetical subject index to ICSIS, the Information Center Services Identification System (Exhibit 3), and modifying them for local resources.

Although there is a universal call for common language and a definitive taxonomy, the sheer number of existing lists, as well as the AIN principle in UWASIS, indicates that local or regional peculiarities dictate the subject headings used by individual I&R operations, standardized lists being most useful for computer applications and consistent reporting.

EXHIBIT 3

ICSIS

ALPHABETICAL SUBJECT INDEX

SUBJECT DESCRIPTION	GOAL	BEGINS AT ICSIS NUMBER
CRIME PREVENTION	2	5777
CRISIS INTERVENTION COUNSELING	5	42307
CRISIS INTERVENTION SAFETY CHECK BY TELEPHONE	5	42348
CRISIS INTERVENTION SUICIDE PREVENTION/PROTECTION AGAINST PHYSICAL SELF-HARM	5	42225
D		
DAY CARE	5	40818
DELINQUENCY PREVENTION	2	5818
DEMONSTRATION/PILOT PROJECTS	6	51140
DENTAL CARE INPATIENT	3	23598
DENTAL CARE OUTPATIENT	3	23747
DETENTION OF LAW VIOLATORS AND ALLEGED LAW VIOLATORS	2	5680
DIABETES CONTROL	3	9047
DISABLED SUPPLEMENT SECURITY INCOME	1	1650
DISASTER RELIEF	2	6112
DISCUSSION GROUPS	5	42859
DISEASE CONTROL COMMUNICABLE	3	7865
DISEASE CONTROL NONCOMMUNICABLE	3	8828
DISEASES PREVENTION AND CONTROL OF COMMUNICABLE	3	7152
DISTRIBUTION CENTERS CLOTHING/ACCESSORIES/HOUSEHOLD GOODS	2	4237
DRUG ABUSE/NARCOTICS ADDICTION—PREVENTION AND TREATMENT	3	29423
DRUG SAFETY STANDARDS	1	3321
DRUG THERAPY FOR LPN COURSE	4	35344
E		
EARTHQUAKE HAZARDS REDUCTION	2	6030
ECONOMIC DEVELOPMENT PROMOTION OF TOURISM, BUSINESS, AND INDUSTRY	6	50452
ECONOMIC DEVELOPMENT SMALL BUSINESS DEVELOPMENT	6	50575

The professional organization in the field, Alliance of Information and Referral Services (AIRS), in their "National Standards for Information and Referral Services" (AIRS, 1978)[1] calls for using a classification system to standardize definitions, enhance information retrieval, increase data reliability, make comparisons and evaluations consistent and reliable, and facilitate networking. The standards suggest adoption of a national classification system such as IRMA, UWASIS I or II, SEARCH, etc. Throughout, the standards reflect a human services orientation.

In the taxonomies cited by the AIRS standards (UWASIS, IRMA, etc.), the file arrangement is topical rather than alphabetical, usually covering at least these areas:

1. Human Development
2. Welfare services
3. Physical health services
4. Mental health services
5. Educational services
6. Protective services
7. Environmental services
8. Public safety and Justice services
9. Consumer services
10. Housing services
11. Employment services
12. Transportation services
13. Recreation
14. Entertainment
15. Religion
16. Animals
17. Miscellaneous

These are minutely subdivided (Exhibit 2).

When seeking library-generated I&R, the subject heading authority file takes quite a different approach, usually being alphabetical and much simpler in format. The TIP project at Detroit Public Library, although developed at about the same time as UWASIS (1971-2), definitely reflects the library approach to subject indexing (Exhibit 4).[2] Helen Marshall, formerly with the

---

[1] Revision due Fall 1983.
[2] See complete listing in Jones' *Public Library Information and Referral Service.*

EXHIBIT 4

TIP SUBJECT HEADINGS

This is a combined list of subject headings used both in the TIP card file and in the TIP pamphlet file. (Because some subject headings apply only to pamphlet material, there will not be a card in the file for every entry on the list.)

ABORTION REFERRAL

   see also
PREGNANCY COUNSELING
RIGHT TO LIFE

Abused wives
   see
WOMEN-ABUSED

ACCOUNTING

Actors & acting
   see
PERFORMING ARTS EDUCATION
THEATRE
THEATRE, SUMMER

ADOPTION

ADOPTION-FOREIGN BORN

ADULT EDUCATION

   see also
Names of subjects, e.g.,
   FOREIGN LANGUAGE LESSONS,
   PHOTOGRAPHY
ENGLISH AS A SECOND
   LANGUAGE
G.E.D. PREPARATION
G.E.D. TESTING

ADVERTISING

Afro-Americans
   see
BLACKS

AGED

   see also
AGED-INFORMATION &
   REFERRAL
CAMPS-AGED
CONSUMER DISCOUNTS-AGED
DAY CARE-ADULTS
EMPLOYMENT-AGED
FOSTER HOME CARE
HANDICAPPED-AGED
HEALTH CARE-AGED
HOME VISITING
HOMES FOR THE AGED

HOUSING-AGED
NURSING HOMES
PROTECTIVE SERVICES-AGED
RECREATION-AGED
SOCIAL SECURITY
TEACHERS-RETIRED
TELEPHONE REASSURANCE
TRANSPORTATION-AGED
VETERANS
VOLUNTEERS-AGED
WIDOWS/WIDOWERS

Aged-Day care
   see
DAY CARE-ADULTS

Aged-Foster home care
   see
FOSTER HOME CARE

AGED-INFORMATION & REFERRAL

Agriculture
   see
FARMS
GARDENS & GARDENING

AIR POLLUTION

   see also
CONSERVATION

ALCOHOLISM

Aliens
   see
IMMIGRATION & NATURALIZA-
TION

ALUMNI

AMPUTEE

Animal pick-up
   see
ANIMALS-NUISANCE & STRAY
DEAD ANIMAL PICK-UP

ANIMALS

   see also
Names of animals, e.g.,
   BIRDS, DOGS.

EXHIBIT 4 (continued)

DEAD ANIMAL PICK-UP
LEADER DOGS
ZOOS

ANIMALS-NUISANCE & STRAY

ANIMALS-STERILIZATION

ANTIQUES

Appliances-Second hand
   see
FURNITURE/APPLIANCES-
SECOND HAND

APPRENTICESHIP INFORMATION

ARAB

ARBITRATION

ARCHITECTS

ART
   see also
   ARTS & CRAFTS
   FOLK ART
   MUSEUMS

ART EDUCATION

ART GALLERIES

ARTHRITIS & RHEUMATISM

ARTS & CRAFTS
   see also
   Names of arts & crafts,
    e.g., BALLET, PHOTOGRAPHY,
   WEAVING

ART
ART EDUCATION
FOLK ART

ASTHMA

ASTRONOMY
   see also
   PLANETARIUMS

Athletics
   see
   RECREATION

AUCTIONS

AUTISM

AUTO RECOVERY

AUTOMOBILE DRIVER
EDUCATION

AUTOMOBILE DRIVER EDUCA-
TION-HANDICAPPED

AUTOMOBILE RACING

AUTOMOBILES
   see also
   CAR POOLS

Automobiles, Abandoned
   see
   AUTO RECOVERY

Automobiles, Insurance
   see
   INSURANCE, AUTOMOBILE

Langston Hughes Community Information Center of the Queens Borough Public Library, maintains that—based on her experience with both computer and manual systems—computerized databases are not always the answer because computers are so numerically-oriented that much of the information just doesn't fit a program that is so people-oriented. Comparing TIP to UWASIS clearly shows this.

The key to access of any body of information or file is the ability of the person accessing it to use the "proper" term. Human services professionals (or even their trained volunteers) are familiar with the terminology used in UWASIS, IRMA, etc.; librarians, on the other hand, have had an entirely different type of training, exemplified by

Sears List of Subject Headings, Library of Congress Subject Headings, the Wilson indexes, and the *New York Times Index*. In developing library-based I&R, the problem then becomes whether librarians shall learn a whole new way of indexing in order to conform to widely-used national thesauri or adapt their old familiar lists to the resource file, despite repeated warnings in the literature not to "reinvent the wheel."

The answer lies somewhere in-between, depending on the situation, for when it comes right down to it, accessing the file is a one-to-one proposition, whether it is the person seeking help or an I & R worker dealing with an inquiry. It is also important to know from the start that the development of the list will be an ongoing operation subject to constant change; yesterday's "wife abuse" is today's "woman battering."

When the *S*tatewide *I*nformation *R*eferral (SIR) file was set up in West Virginia in 1979, the philosophy behind it was basically:

1. Inclusion of a comprehensive listing of all government agencies, their services and programs and private agencies.
2. Inclusion of regional or national sources for topics not covered by states and private sources.
3. Provision for local emergency and non-emergency resources.
4. Provision for miscellaneous data not readily available in small, isolated libraries.
5. Employment of "user friendly" terms.

Working in the Capitol Complex, we knew the vast variety of services and programs available to West Virginia citizens, and were determined to advertise this as widely as possible. Since West Virginia's sources are relatively limited compared to other states, we included national sources where we lacked a state source, e.g., for anorexia nervosa.

The explanatory information sent out with the file included specific instructions for adding local information, e.g., an all-night drugstore, local recreation facilities, 24-hour dental and medical care, etc.

Since most of the state's libraries are small, located in isolated rural communities, and have very limited funds, it was decided to include miscellaneous information that they often didn't have access to like state statistics, census data, presidential greetings, Privacy Act details, translators, Grand Ole Opry facts, etc. Working with representative librarians from around the state at our annual training institute made this type of input feasible.

The last criterion, that of "user-friendly" terminology, was the easiest—and hardest—to achieve. It meant going against what we had been taught and what was traditional. Librarians know that people ask for information about *cars*, but the term "automobiles" persists. Very few persons look under "Motor-trucks" when searching for a truck repair manual. Knowing this, it was decided when developing the resource file to use the most specific term a person might ask for, adding cross-references—"see also" or "see" references—only when absolutely necessary.

There were, of course, problems with this. For example, resources for the elderly were scattered under "Housing for the Elderly," "Daycare, Elderly," etc., with "see also" references from "Elderly." The rationale for this was that few people would ask for everything available on the elderly, they usually had a specific problem.

In setting up the file, several existing library subject heading lists were used to consolidate data describing community resources into a comprehensive format that could be used by the general public. The two basic lists used were the TIP list from Detroit Public Library (Exhibit 4) and the one from Cabell County Public Library's Information and Referral Service in Huntington, West Virginia (Exhibit 5). These two were compared to the subject headings indexed in *Information For Everyday Survival: What You Need to Know and Where to Get It* in order to increase the scope of the headings.

The brief examples in Exhibits 4, 5, and 6 reveal that the headings denote services rather than things, and as such would have to vary from standard library lists. Many of the headings used (because they

EXHIBIT 5

Cabell County I & R

COUNTY HISTORY
CRAFTS
   SEE ARTS & CRAFTS
CREDIT COUNSELING
CREDIT DENIAL
CREDIT RATING
CREMATION
   SEE DEATH RELATED SERVICES
CRIB DEATH
CRIME PREVENTION—CITY/
   COUNTY

CRIME PREVENTION PROGRAMS
   FOR GROUPS
CRIPPLED CHILDREN—SEE CHIL-
   DREN-HANDICAPPED
CRISIS INTERVENTION
   —CHILDREN
   —OHIO
   —YOUTH
CRISIS INTERVENTION CENTERS
CRUTCHES SEE MEDICAL
   APPLIANCES/SUPPLIES

EXHIBIT 5 (continued)

CULTURE—SEE ARTS & CULTURE
CYSTIC FIBROSIS

DALE CARNEGIE ASSOCIATES
DAY CARE CENTERS
 —OHIO
DAY CARE SERVICES
 —WAYNE COUNTY
DEAFNESS
DEAFNESS SEE ALSO HEARING
 CLINICS
DEAFNESS—SIGN LANGUAGE
 INSTRUCTION
DEATH AND DYING
DEATH RELATED SERVICES
 —CREMATION
DEBT COLLECTION
DENTAL ASSOCIATIONS
DENTAL CARE—REFERRAL
DENTAL CLINICS
DENTURES
DIABETES
DIABETES CLINICS
DIAL-A-PRAYER
DIAL-A-STORY
DIETING SEE WEIGHT CONTROL
DISABLED SEE HANDICAPPED
DISABLED VETERANS
 SEE VETERANS
DISASTER RECOVERY INFORMA-
 TION
DISASTER RELIEF SEE EMER-
 GENCY ASSISTANCE
DISCRIMINATION SEE CIVIL
 RIGHTS

DIVORCE
DOGS
 —SEEING EYE
DOGS, GUARD
DOLLS
DRIVER EDUCATION
DRUG ABUSE
 —I & R
DRUG ABUSE—PREVENTION/
 TREATMENT/REFERRAL
DRUGS
DWARFS

EARLY CHILDHOOD EDUCATION
 SEE PRE-SCHOOL
EARLY PERIODIC SCREENING
ECONOMIC STATISTICS
EDUCATION SEE
 —INFORMATION
ELDERLY
ELDERLY SEE ALSO RETIREMENT
 —DAY CENTER
 —DISCOUNT
 —EXERCISE
 —HOMEMAKER SERVICES
 —PHYSICAL EXAMINATIONS
 —SCHOOL LUNCHES
 —TRANSPORTATION
 —WAYNE COUNTY
ELECTIONS
EMERGENCY ASSISTANCE
 —ALCOHOLISM
 —APPLIANCES

EXHIBIT 6

S I R SUBJECT HEADINGS
July, 1983

LOCAL EMERGENCY SOURCES
EMERGENCY
ABANDONED PROPERTY
ABC (ALL BY CALLING)
ABORTION
ABSENTEE VOTING—
 SEE VOTING
ACCOUNTANTS
ACTION
ADOPTION

ADULT EDUCATION
ADVOCACY—SEE
 INDIVIDUAL TOPICS
AERIAL SPRAYING
AGING—SEE ALSO HOME
 HEALTH CARE, NUTRITION
AGING—AREA AGENCIES
AGING—DAY CARE
AGING—EMOTIONAL, MENTAL
AGING—EMPLOYMENT

EXHIBIT 6 (continued)

AGING—HEALTH CARE
AGING—HOT LINE
AGING—RECREATION
AGRICULTURE
AID TO FAMILIES WITH
  DEPENDENT CHILDREN
AIR FREIGHT
AIRLINES
AIRPORTS
AIR POLLUTION—SEE
  POLLUTION—AIR
ALCOHOLISM
ALLERGIES
AMBULANCES
AMATEUR RADIO
AMTRAK
ANALYSIS
ANIMALS
ANOREXIA NERVOSA—
  SEE EATING DISORDERS
APPLIANCES
APPRAISALS
ARCHIVES/HISTORY
ARMY—SEE RECRUITING
ART GALLERIES
ARTHRITIS
ARTS/CRAFTS
ASSOCIATED PRESS
ASSOCIATIONS
ASTHMA
ATTORNEYS
AUDIO VISUAL EQUIPMENT
AUTISM
AUTOMOBILES—SEE CARS
BABIES—SEE ALSO CHILDREN
BACKPACKING
BAIL BONDS
BANKRUPTCY
BANKS/BANKING
BARTER
BASIC EDUCATION GRANTS
  & LOANS
BASEMENTS, FLOODED
BATTERED WOMEN
BEEKEEPING
BEER
BEHAVIOR PROBLEMS
BETTER BUSINESS BUREAU
BIG BROTHERS/BIG SISTERS
BIRTH/DEATH RECORDS
BIRTH CONTROL
BIRTH DEFECTS
BLACK LUNG

BLIND—SEE VISUALLY
  HANDICAPPED
BLOOD
BOOKS—APPRAISAL
BOOKS ON TAPE
BOY SCOUTS
BRAILLE
BREASTFEEDING
BRIDGES—SEE ALSO
  COVERED BRIDGES
BUDGET COUNSELING—
  SEE CREDIT
BUILDING INSPECTION
BUILDING PERMITS—SEE
  PERMITS
BURIAL SOCIETIES
BUS SERVICE—SEE
  TRANSPORTATION
BUSINESS ADVICE—SEE SMALL
  BUSINESS
BUSINESS/INDUSTRY—SEE
  COMPANIES
CABLE TELEVISION
CAEL
CAMPFIRE GIRLS/BOYS
CAMPGROUNDS
CAMPING—SEE ALSO
  CAMPGROUNDS
CANCER
CANOEING
CAR POOL
CAR REGISTRATION
CAR RENTAL
CAR SAFETY
CAREER PLANNING
CARS
CARS—USED
CB RADIOS
CENSUS
CEREBRAL PALSY—SEE ALSO
  DEVELOPMENTALLY DISABLED
CETA
CHAMBER OF COMMERCE
CHARITIES
CHARLESTON
CHARLESTON CIVIC CENTER
CHARLESTON DISTANCE RUN
CHEMICALS
CHILD ABUSE
CHILD CARE—SEE DAY CARE
CHILDBIRTH—SEE PREGNANCY/
  CHILDBIRTH
CHILDREN

EXHIBIT 6 (continued)

CHILDREN'S HOMES
CHRISTMAS BUREAU
CITIES
CITIZENSHIP—SEE NATURALIZA-
  TION
CIVIL DEFENSE
CIVIL RIGHTS—SEE DISCRIMINA-
  TION
CIVIL SERVICE
CLEP
CLINICS
CLIPPING SERVICE
CLOTHING RESOURCES
CLOWNS
CLUBS
COAL
COAL MINING—SEE JOBS
COLLEGE CREDIT
COLLEGE SELECTION
COLLEGES & UNIVERSITIES
COLOSTOMY
COMMERCE
COMMODITY FUTURES
COMMUNICABLE DISEASES
COMPANIES
CONGRESSMAN
  US HOUSE
  US SENATE
CONSERVATION
CONSUMER INFORMATION
CONTACT
CONTINUING EDUCATION
CONVALESCENT CENTERS
COPYRIGHT
CORPORATION
CORRESPONDENCE SCHOOLS
COUNSELING
COUNTY DATA
COUNTY GOVERNMENTS
COUPONS
COURTS
COVERED BRIDGES
CPR
CRAFTS—SEE ARTS & CRAFTS
CREDIT
CREDIT CARDS
CREDIT COUNSELING—SEE CREDIT
CREDIT RATING
CRIPPLED CHILDREN—SEE
  PHYSICALLY HANDICAPPED
CRISIS INTERVENTION
CULTURAL ADVISORY AGENCIES
CULTURAL EVENTS

CULTURAL RESOURCES
CYSTIC FIBROSIS
DAY CARE—CHILDREN—SEE
  ALSO HANDICAPPED
DAY CARE—SENIOR CITIZENS
DEAF
DEATH—SEE BIRTH/DEATH
  RECORDS
DEEDS
DENTAL SERVICES
DESERTION
DESIGNER CLOTHER
DEVELOPMENTALLY DISABLED—
  SEE ALSO SSI
DIABETES
DIAL-A-NUMBER
DIETING—SEE ALSO WEIGHT
  CONTROL
DISABLED ADULTS & CHILDREN
DISABILITY BENEFITS
DISASTER RELIEF
DISASTER UNEMPLOYMENT
  ASSISTANCE
DISCRIMINATION
DISCRIMINATION—FAIR HOUSING
DISCRIMINATION—JOBS
DISCRIMINATION—SEX
DIVORCE
DIVORCE—NO FAULT
DOCTORS
DOCTORS—REFERRAL
DOOR-TO-DOOR SALES
DRIVERS LICENSES/TESTS—
  SEE LICENSES
DRUG ABUSE
DRUGS/DRUG ABUSE
EAR CARE—SEE DEAF;
  HEARING
EATING DISORDERS
EDUCATION
EDUCATION-COLLEGE &
  UNIVERSITY. . .SEE *WV BLUE
  BOOK* FOR LISTS
EDUCATION—DISCRIMINATION
EDUCATION—FINANCIAL AID—
  SEE ALSO SCHOLARSHIPS
EDUCATION—JOB OPPORTUNITIES
EDUCATION—OLDER ADULTS
EDUCATIONAL TESTING SERVICE
ELDERLY—SEE AGING, DAY CARE,
  EDUCATION, NUTRITION
  PROGRAM
ELECTIONS

EXHIBIT 6 (continued)

ELECTROLYSIS—SEE HAIR
REMOVAL
ELECTRONIC FUND TRANSFER
EMERGENCY AID
EMOTIONAL PROBLEMS—SEE
MENTAL HEALTH
EMPLOYMENT—SEE JOBS
EMT TRAINING
ENERGY
ENERGY CONSERVATION
ENVIRONMENTAL SERVICES
EPILEPSY—SEE ALSO DEVELOP-
MENTALLY DISABLED
EROSION CONTROL
ETHNIC ORGANIZATIONS
EX-OFFENDERS
EXPECTANT MOTHERS—SEE
PREGNANCY/CHILDBIRTH
EYES
FACTORY OUTLETS
FAIR HOUSING—SEE DISCRIM-
INATION
FAIRS
FAMILY COUNSELING
FAMILY PLANNING
FARMER'S MARKETS
FARMING
FEDERAL GOVERNMENT
INFORMATION
FEDERAL JOB INFORMATION
CENTER
FESTIVALS
FILM SOCIETIES & SERIES
FILMS/FILMSTRIPS (FREE)
FILM/FILMSTRIP (RENTAL)
FINANCIAL AID
FIRST AID INSTRUCTION
FIREFIGHTING
FISHING
FISHING AREAS
FLOOD INSURANCE
FOOD
FOOD—SEE ALSO NUTRITION
PROGRAM FOR THE ELDERLY
FOOD COOPERATIVES
FOOD HANDLER PERMITS—SEE
PERMITS
FOOD LABELS
FOOD STAMPS
FOREIGN LANGUAGES—SEE
TRANSLATORS
FORESTS
FOSTER GRANDPARENTS

FOSTER GRANDPARENTS
PROJECT
FOSTER HOMES/CARE
FOSTER PARENTS
FOUNDATIONS—WV
FOUNDATIONS—SEE ALSO
FUNDRAISING
FOUR-H CLUBS
FRATERNAL ORGANIZATIONS
FREEDOM OF INFORMATION
ACT (1966)
FRIENDSHIP FORCE
FUNDRAISING
FUNERALS
FURNITURE—USED
GAMBLING
GARBAGE
GARDENING
GASOHOL
GASOLINE
GAY RIGHTS/LESBIANS
GED
GENEALOGY
GIFTED CHILDREN
GIRL SCOUTS
GLASS COMPANIES
GLASSES—SEE EYES
GOLDEN AGE PASSPORTS
GOLF COURSES
GONORRHEA—SEE VENEREAL
DISEASES
GOVERNMENT DOCUMENTS
GOVERNMENT OFFICIALS
GRANGE
GRIEF INTERVENTION
HAIR/HAIR COLORING
HAIR REMOVAL
HALFWAY HOUSES
HANDICAPPED
HAZARDOUS PRODUCTS
HEALTH
HEALTH CLINICS
HEALTH—FAMILY PLANNING
HEALTH MAINTENANCE
ORGANIZATIONS
HEARING
HEART
HEATING OIL
HIGH SCHOOL EQUIVALENCY
EXAM—SEE GED
HIGHWAY INFORMATION
HIKING
HISTORICAL SOCIETIES

EXHIBIT 6 (continued)

HOBBIES
HODGKINS DISEASE
HOME ECONOMICS
HOME HEALTH CARE (AGING)
HOMEBOUND INSTRUCTION
HOMEMAKER SERVICES
HOMESTEADING
HOSPITALS
HOTEL/MOTEL RESERVATIONS
HOTLINE—NEWSPAPERS
HOTLINE
HOUSEHOLD ORGANIZATION
HOUSEHOLD PESTS
HOUSING
HOUSING—TEMPORARY SHELTER
HUMANE SOCIETIES
HUNTING
HUNTINGTON CIVIC CENTER
HYPNOSIS
IDENTIFICATION CARDS
ILLITERACY
IMMIGRATION
IMMUNIZATION—SEE HEALTH
  CLINICS
INCEST
INCOME TAX—SEE TAXES
INCORPORATION
INDUSTRY—SEE COMPANIES
INFANT CARE—SEE CHILDREN
INFORMATION & REFERRAL
INSANE—SEE MENTAL HEALTH
INSPIRATIONAL MESSAGES
INSURANCE
INTERNAL REVENUE—SEE TAXES
JOB CORPS
JOBS—SEE ALSO FED. JOB.
  INFORMATION CENTERS
JOBS—CAREER PLANNING
JOBS—COAL MINING
JOBS—DISCRIMINATION—SEE
  DISCRIMINATION
JOBS—HOTLINE
JUDGES—SEE COURTS
JUNIOR ACHIEVEMENT
JURY DUTY
JUVENILES
JUVENILES—ASSISTANCE
KANAWHA VALLEY RAILROAD
  CLUB
KENTUCKY PARKS
KIDNEY
LABOR
LABOR ORGANIZATIONS
LABOR STATISTICS

LAND—SEE HOMESTEADING
LARYNX (ARTIFICIAL)
LAWN & GARDEN INFORMATION
LAWYERS—SEE ATTORNEYS
LEARNING DISABILITIES
LEATHER
LEFT HANDERS
LEGAL AGE
LEGAL AID—JUVENILES
LEGAL AID
LEGISLATION LESSONS
LEUKEMIA SOCIETY OF
  AMERICA, INC.
LIBRARY SERVICES
LICENSES
LIFE SAVING
LITERARY ORGANIZATIONS
"LIVING WILL"
LOANS
LOBBYING
LOW-INCOME CONSUMERS
LUPUS
MAGAZINES
MAIL ORDER
MAILGRAM/TELEGRAM
MANUFACTURER'S—ADDRESSES/
  PHONE NUMBERS
MAPS
MARINES—SEE RECRUITING
MARKET BASKET SURVEY
MARRIAGE COUNSELING—SEE
  FAMILY COUNSELING
MARRIAGE RECORDS
MATERNITY—SEE PREGNANCY/
  CHILDBIRTH
MEALS, FREE
MEAT
MEDICAID
MEDICAL SERVICES
MEDICARE
MENSA
MENTAL HEALTH
MENTAL RETARDATION
MENTAL RETARDATION—DAY
  CARE
MENTALLY HANDICAPPED
METRIC
MIDWIVES
MILITARY PERSONNEL
MILLS—SEE OLD MILLS
MIME
MINERAL RIGHTS
MINES
MINORITY BUSINESS

EXHIBIT 6 (continued)

MINORITY GROUPS
MISSING PERSONS
MONEY MARKET FUNDS
MORTGAGES
MOTELS
MOVING-HOUSEHOLD
MULTIPLE SCLEROSIS
MUSCULAR DYSTROPHY
MYASTHENIA GRAVIA
NADER, RALPH
NAME CHANGE
NATIONAL GUARD
NATURAL RESOURCES
NATURALIZATION
NAVY—SEE RECRUITING
NEWSPAPERS
NUISANCE CALLS
NURSERY SCHOOLS—SEE
    DAY CARE
NURSING
NURSING HOMES
NUTRITION—SEE ALSO FOOD
NUTRITION PROGRAMS FOR
    ELDERLY
OCCUPATIONS—SEE JOBS
OLD MILLS
OSTOMY
OUTPATIENT
OUTREACH
PARENTS ANONYMOUS
PARKS
PARKS-LOCAL
PAROLE
PAROLEES
PASSPORTS/VISAS
PATENTS
PEACE CORPS—SEE ACTION
PENSIONS
PERFORMING ARTS
PERIODICALS
PERMITS
PERSONAL CARE HOMES
PEST CONTROL
PETS
PHOTOS—PROCESSING
PHYSICALLY HANDICAPPED
PHYSICALLY HANDICAPPED—
    JOBS
PHYSICALLY HANDICAPPED—
    PARKING PERMITS
PHYSICALLY HANDICAPPED—
    SPORTS
PILOT WEATHER INFORMATION
PLANNING COMMISSIONS

POINTS OF INTEREST-WV
POISON
POLICE
POLITICAL PARTIES/ORGA-
    NIZATIONS
POLLUTION
POLLUTION—AIR
POLLUTION—ENVIRONMENT
POLLUTION—WATER
POST OFFICES
POW
PREGNANCY/CHILDBIRTH
PRESERVATION
PRESIDENTIAL GREETINGS
PREVENTICARE
PRISONERS—FAMILY COUNSELING
PRIVACY ACT
PROBATION
PRODUCT SAFETY
PROFESSIONAL ORGANIZATIONS
PRO-LIFE
PROPERTY RIGHTS—SEE
    MINERAL RIGHTS
PROTECTIVE SERVICES
PSYCHIATRIC SERVICES—SEE
    MENTAL HEALTH
PURCHASING
RABIES
RACING
RADIO EQUIPMENT
RADIO—PUBLIC
RADIO—STATE POLICE BANDS
RAFTING
RAILROAD CLUBS—SEE KANAWHA
    VALLEY RAILROAD CLUB
RAPE
REACH FOR RECOVERY PROGRAM
READING IS FUNDAMENTAL
    PROGRAM (RIF)
REAL ESTATE
RECREATION—SEE INDIVIDUAL
    SPORTS, CLUB: SEE ALSO
    TRAVEL—WV, CAMPING—WV,
    SKI AREAS, TENNIS COURTS
RECRUITING
RECYCLING—ALUMINUM
RECYCLING
RED CROSS
REFUGEES
RELOCATION
RETARDED—SEE MENTAL
    RETARDATION
RETIREMENT
ROADS

EXHIBIT 6 (continued)

RSVP PROGRAM—SEE ACTION
RUNAWAYS
RURAL ISSUES
SANITARIUMS—SEE HOSPITALS
SAVINGS ACCOUNTS
SCHOLARSHIPS
SCHOOLS
SCHOOLS & COLLEGES
SCORE PROGRAM—SEE ACTION
SECURITIES—SEE STOCKS &
  BONDS
SELF-HELP
SENIOR CITIZENS—SEE AGING
SHELTER, TEMPORARY-SEE
  HOUSING, TEMPORARY
SHOES
SIGN LANGUAGE
SINGLE PARENT
SKI AREAS
SKIN CARE
SMALL BUSINESS
SOCIAL SECURITY
SOCIAL SECURITY RETIREMENT
SOIL
SOLAR ENERGY
SPCA
SPEAKERS
SPEECH
SPINA BIFIDA
SPORTS—SEE INDIVIDUAL
  LISTINGS
SSI—SEE SOCIAL SECURITY
STARTING YOUR OWN BUSINESS—
  SEE SMALL BUSINESS
STATE FOREST
STATE GOVERNMENT
STATE PARKS
STERILIZATION—SEE BIRTH
  CONTROL
STOCKS & BONDS
SUDDEN INFANT DEATH SYN-
  DROME
SUICIDE—SEE CRISIS INTER-
  VENTION
SUPPLEMENTAL SECURITY
  INCOME
SURGERY
SURPLUS GOVERNMENT
  PROPERTY
SURVIVORS—SOCIAL SECURITY
  BENEFITS
SWAPPING HOMES

SYPHILIS—SEE VENEREAL
  DISEASE
TALKING BOOKS—SEE VISUALLY
  HANDICAPPED
TAX EXEMPTION/NON PROFIT
  ORGANIZATION
TAXES
TEETH—SEE DENTAL SERVICES
TELEGRAPH
TELEPHONE
TELEPHONE SERVICES DAILY
  CHECK-IN
TELEVISION
TENNIS COURTS
TICKETS
TITLE IX
TOBACCO
TOLL FREE INFORMATION
TOURIST INFORMATION
TOURS
TOXIC SHOCK SYNDROME
TRADEMARKS
TRANSLATORS
TRANSPORTATION
TRAVEL—SEE ALSO FAIRS,
  FESTIVALS, RAFTING
TRAVEL INFORMATION
TRAVELER'S AID
TRIP—TRANSPORTATION RE-
  MUNERATION INCENTIVE
  PROGRAM
TRUCK RENTING/LEASING
TRUCKERS
TUTORING
TV STATIONS
UFOs
UNEMPLOYMENT COMPENSATION
UNION MISSION, INC.
UNIONS
UNWED MOTHERS
UPI
URBAN HOMESTEADING
UTILITIES
UTILITIES—COMPLAINTS/
  INQUIRIES
VACCINATION
VENEREAL DISEASE
VETERANS ADMINISTRATION
VETERANS AFFAIRS—EDUCATION
  AID
VETERANS AFFAIRS
VIDEO TAPES

EXHIBIT 6 (continued)

VISAs—SEE PASSPORTS/VISAs
VISTA VOLUNTEERS—SEE
   ACTION
VISUALLY HANDICAPPED
VOCATIONAL REHABILITATION
VOLUNTEERS
VOTING
WASTE MANAGEMENT
WASTEWATER
WEATHER INFORMATION
WEATHERIZATION
WEIGHT CONTROL
WEIGHT WATCHERS
WEIGHTS & MEASURES
WELCOME WAGON

WELFARE
WEST VIRGINIA
WEST VIRGINIA—STATISTICS
WHITE WATER RAFTING—SEE
   RAFTING
WIDOWS/WIDOWERS
WIFE ABUSE—SEE BATTERED
   WOMEN
WILLS
WIN PROGRAM
WOMEN'S GROUPS
WORK PERMITS
WORKMEN'S COMPENSATION
YOUNG ADULTS
YOUNG SERVICES

were needed, not because they fit a grand scheme) do not appear at all in standard lists: "Organ Donations," "Cars," "Banner Permits," "Sitters," "Absentee Voting." Some headings appear in a more practical order, such as "Housing for the Elderly" rather than "Elderly-Housing."

In comparing the formal major taxonomies with the library lists, the latter clearly illustrate the pitfall of mixed classification, that is, they list services, problems and agencies in one sequence. Why this is a "problem" may not be immediately apparent except perhaps to purists; in the West Virginia experience with the SIR file, and elsewhere, it seems to work quite well.

In West Virginia this specificity is especially important since the intent was to have the I & R cards interfiled in smaller libraries' card catalogs, thus enabling patrons to "help themselves." This meant choosing terms from the user's point of view and keeping terms in their language.

"See" and "see also" references were kept to a minimum for several reasons: most people won't bother to look more than one place in the card catalog, and it cut down on the total number of cards (the original file contained 1100). To assist librarians and/or patrons in finding a topic, a subject heading list was provided that included more cross-references than the file itself. Cards in the file were checked on this list to facilitate updating and revising.

Librarians were encouraged to add local information to the state and national resources in the file and to expand the subject headings as necessary. Several libraries utilized volunteers to do this. At this point, the subject heading authority list is no longer uniform from site to site. It has been found that at this stage it simply doesn't matter; the question is academic.

West Virginia is currently in the process of a statewide automation project with the central node in the network being at the Library Commission. It is anticipated that the SIR file will be put on-line as soon as possible to facilitate updating. Eventually, even the most remote library will have access to this central file via toll-free telephone lines. Although the details are yet to be worked out, the file will probably be created and put on-line following MARC format requirements. Local additions will be made to the central data file, which will allow us to get a county printout when needed. Updating of statewide agencies, services, and miscellaneous information will continue to be done at the state agency every six months.

Since one-third of West Virginia's 160 libraries are essentially one-person operations (Instant and Outpost Libraries), the present method of interfiling I & R cards in the card catalog has worked very well. It saves the librarian's time as well as providing the patron a certain amount of privacy in obtaining information. Despite unfamiliarity with the whole concept, a well-planned publicity campaign at the local level, coupled with in-service workshops for librarians, has made the SIR file very effective (Exhibit 7).

EXHIBIT 7: Sample catalog cards

CONSUMER AFFAIRS—WEST VIRGINIA   187

CONSUMER PROTECTION DIVISION
Attorney General's Office
3410 Staunton Ave., S.E.
Charleston, WV 25304
(304) 348-8986

. . .records of complaints about companies or consumer products; publications of general interest to consumers. Records of investigations or prosecution of companies most likely will not be available until the cases are closed.

CRISIS INTERVENTION   219

CONTACT OF KANAWHA VALLEY
c/o Christ Church Methodist
Quarrier & Morris Streets
Charleston, WV 25301
346-0826
24 hrs. a day/7 days a week

EXHIBIT 7 (continued)

FINANCIAL AID   341

HEATING BILLS: Apply thru local community service organizations, or senior citizens organizations for monies available under the Energy Crisis Assistance Program

(45 CFR Part 1061)

FOOD STAMPS   356

Food Stamp Regional Outreach Program
WV Dept of Welfare
Economic Services Division
1900 Washington Street, East
Building 6
Charleston, WV 25305

1-800-642-8670 (toll free)
348-8290 (Charleston)

10/81 Replacement

HOUSEHOLD PESTS   422

W. Va. Dept. of Agriculture
State Capitol
Charleston, WV 25305
348-2217

OR COUNTY EXTENSION AGENT

MENTAL HEALTH   496D

Kanawha, Boone, Clay, Putnam Counties

Mental Health Association
702½ Lee St., E.
Charleston, WV 25301
services   346-6005
referrals   M-F 9:00 to 4:00
speakers
self-help aftercare

SELECTED BIBLIOGRAPHY

Alliance of Information and Referral Services. *National Standards for Information and Referral*, 1978.
American Rehabilitation Foundation. *Information and Referral Services: The Resource File.* (working draft) Administration on Aging, USDHEW, 1971. ED 055 634.
Gotsick, Priscilla et al. *Information for Everyday Survival; What you Need To Know and Where To Get It.* Appalachian Adult Education Center, Morehead State University, Morehead, KY (ALA) 1976.

The Information Center of Hampton Roads. *Information and Referral-How To Do It.* Volume I, Part II, The First Step: Establishing the Resource Data Base. DHEW No. (OHDS) 77-20401, 1975.

_____. Volume I, Part III, ICSIS-Information Center Services Identification System. USDHEW No. (OHDS) 77-20402, 1975.

Jones, Clara Stanton. *Public Library Information and Referral Service.* Syracuse, NY, Gaylord Bros., 1978.

Long, Nicholas, Reiner, Steven and Zimmerman, Shirley. *Information and Referral Services: The Resource File.* USDHEW No. (OHD) 75-20111, nd.

National Assembly of National Voluntary Health and Welfare Organizations. *Evaluation of Human Services Taxonomy Project.* Volume I, *The State of the Art.* Prepared for Office of the Assistant Secretary for Planning and Evaluation (HEW), Washington, 1978. NTIS SHR-0002431.

Ohio Service Identification System (OSIS) Community Chest and Council of the Cincinnati Area, 2400 Reading Road, Cincinnati, Ohio, 45202. nd

United Way of America. *UWASIS II*; a taxonomy of social goals and human service programs. 2nd edition, Alexandria, VA, UWA, 1976.

A Case of "Cirosis":
The Subject Approach to Health Information

Lionelle Elsesser

The reasons for organizing a collection of any type of materials are generally the same for all libraries. Librarians want to establish control of content for the professional staff's economical information use as well as for promoting patron ease of access. Unfortunately, although most standard library cataloging systems and tools serve the informed librarian well enough, the client must often be a vigorous and undaunted sleuth. Many librarians have found that they have had to rethink the application of formal cataloging systems because they are so often out of sync with professional service ethics and goals.

Health information may be broadly defined as materials relating to physical and mental or emotional states that provide factual or theoretical guidance, explanation, or insight into those states. Health information may be transmitted by such "high tech" formats as interactive videodisc and computer printouts, or in more conventional media from ordinary print to the gamut of audiovisual options. The distinguishing features of health information are more perceived than real. Consequently, materials on child abuse, vegetarian cooking, homosexuality, stress in the workplace, body-building, assertive behavior, single-parent families, and hospices may or may not be considered by catalogers to fall under the rubric "health information." For purposes of this chapter, and generally for public library reference purposes, the position is taken that catalogers should err on the side of generosity in defining health-related materials and issues.

In accumulating health information for the lay public, one assumes that the intent is to make these materials readily available. If the collection is not a private one, it should be readily apparent to the prospective user that he or she will not encounter any censorship

63

in ferreting through the guide to that collection, that is, the catalog. Here I am not addressing the normal conscientious collection limitations inherent in selection, but rather the arrogant censorship imposed when we "codify" materials using jargon, obtuse logic, or judgement-laden terms.

The ethics of professional information services to diverse groups have been admirably addressed in library literature.[1,2,3] Frequently not addressed is the notion that the ethical standards applied to materials selection, rendering of services, and physical access to the library must be applied to cognitive access as well. This lack of discussion no doubt reflects the need to rely on "tried and true" tools, rather than any malevolence on the part of librarians. However, in practice, this omission can undermine the most conscientious collection-building and public service effort.

When we attempt to describe people, print or audiovisual materials, we are forced to do so using language that reflects our perceptions. Thus such terms as "clear," "easy to read," "useful" and "for the layperson" may well say more about the librarian reviewer than the intended, or optimal, reader. Unfortunately, much of the terminology we use in our initial designation of materials is both perception-based and inconsistent from user to user. Terms used to indicate audience may also reflect inappropriate age bias by labelling something as "adult," "youth," or "juvenile" that perhaps could be better described with phrases such as "elementary," "intermediate" or "advanced."

Why does any of this really matter? Why dredge up issues after libraries have settled into comfortable situations and practices? Although it is tempting to "go with the flow," the facts of publishing life in health-related subject areas indicate that flood alerts are more appropriate than basking in the warmth of past decisions. This growth in publishing plus the unrelenting barrage of the third-wave—the revolution of consumerism, self-care or self-sufficiency—would indicate only increasing demands for access to prohibitively expensive resources.

Library users seeking health information can be quite obscure in a reference interview, and, more often, quite reluctant to ask for help. The factors contributing to these problems are not atypical of dealings with the public in any area, but deserve special recapping in order to uphold later contentions. Frequently, library users are reluctant to disclose concerns of a personal nature. They may also be uncomfortable with the terminology used or embarrassed about their lack of sophistication. Some may perceive the staff as being unavailable to help them, while others may incorrectly assume the completeness of the catalog or of their search strategy. They suffer, as G. K. Chesterton suggests, because "it isn't that they can't see the solution. It is that they can't see the problem." Seeing the problem may be as elemental as finding the client's "key word" in the catalog or index. . . the way they *think* it is spelled.

As early as 1976,[4] librarians were concerned in their professional meetings with the cataloging and retrieval problems presented by health information resources. Sadly, the standard tools that were inadequate then remain less than satisfactory now.

The principal aspects of cataloging are materials organization and materials description. Organization may be the area of least concern here since good and generally adequate classification systems exist and since the ripple effects of the freewheeling manipulation of them in an established collection may be more *de*structive than *in*structive. Suffice it to say that the dangers of Dewey, NLM and LC are, to varying degrees: the emphasis on disease states; the presumption that the browsers know what ails or interests them and how (where) it fits into the classification system; and the tendency to isolate and separate interrelated areas. Most of the systems available are built upon the philosophy expressed in the preface to the *Manual on the Use of the Dewey Decimal Classification System*[5] that "a classification system is used most productively in those libraries where the larger segments of works are analyzed and a class number assigned to each. . ." This often imposes a mindset of generalization that becomes more problematic to access when the descriptive phase is entered.

In pre-coordinate indexing systems such as LC, Sears and Dewey, descriptive terms are set down at the time of indexing rather than when searching the material. With this pre-coordinate system, one must know the rules and principles of use in order to retrieve materials. These systems are usually predictable, have controlled vocabularies, limit the number of entries, and some would say, facilitate browsing. They are hampered by slow incorporation of new terms and subjects; a dependence upon knowledgeable users; and an inflexible ordering of elements.

Post-coordinate indexing systems allow elements to be entered at the time of application rather than at the time of indexing. Thus, by knowing the names by which a subject is called, one can readily use the system. Problems can arise with loose control of the vocabulary, but such systems are quick to accommodate new subjects, concepts and terminologies. Aspects of a work can be arranged in any order in post-coordinate indexing systems. The systems generally available and in use are pre-coordinate systems, and the general limits cited apply with particularly frustrating results when handling health care information.

It is possible that the ideal classification system (e.g., one geared to the needs of the browsing layperson) would be constructed along the lines of the "hambone" song. That is, works on the head bone would be connected to works on the neck bone, and works on the hipbone connected to those on the leg bone. The logic here is that, ailing or not, most of us can name the part of the body that concerns us. . .and a collection arranged anatomically quickly reveals itself. Within Dewey there is generally sufficient flexibility to utilize this logic. Well planned and positioned shelf guides may provide identification and liaison. To rely on users' exploration of the card or printed catalog is probably shortsighted in all but academic situations.

In selected settings, another arrangement (or highlighting system) suggests itself because of changing consumer emphasis in health care. Since reduction of health risk factors provides the greatest health care dollar cost-return, a system of arrangement or display by risk factors may be valid. This would group materials on smoking risk with materials on behavior modification, materials on obesity with special cookbooks, etc. Admittedly, such permanent physical arrangements are impractical for most, but as before, shelf guides can bridge some of the gaps. Such a system of display, like the other mentioned, is predicated on the assumption that the client does not knowledgeably exploit the catalog.

Finally, while such alternative arrangements may be impossible for existent monograph collections, there may be justification in applying them to pamphlet, audiovisual, and display materials particularly in patient libraries, schools, and rotating public library collections. Clearly, if an alternative classification system is used, a written guide to its logic is necessary. This may take the form of a decision file, public notes or catalogers' notes. Whatever the final choice of systems employed, it must be thought out in light of service objectives rather than familiarity.

If one chooses to serve the public with Dewey, a recitation of a few of the fractures should suffice to emphasize the need for thoughtful application:

TOPIC	CLASSIFICATION NUMBER
Occupational health & industrial hazards as social problems	362
Occupational health & industrial hazards as technical or scientific problem	613.62
Physiological aspects of diet	612.3
Therapeutic aspects of diet	615.854
Diseases aspects of diet	616.39
Home economics aspects of diet	641.1
Adverse actions of drugs	615.704
Allergic reactions to drugs	616.975
Comprehensive works on drugs	615.1
Diseases of the mouth and throat	616.31
Diseases of the teeth and gums	617.63
Addiction to food	616.39 (see above)
Addiction to other substances	616.86
Hospices as social institution	362.
Hospice care	616.
Wellness	613
Therapeutics and illness	615.8

There is considerable overlap between 613 and 615.8 (e.g., breathing, diet, exercise).

While the *Manual* on the use of DDC is an invaluable aid to the cataloger, it is not generally available to the library user—nor is the patron prepared to second-guess the decisions the manual represents.

While exploring alternative classification and arrangement schemes may be an interesting exercise in improving access, the issue of subject cataloging is the blood and sinew of rendering a collection fully usable. Anyone who has attempted to catalog health information for the layperson will be familiar with the general frustrations. Sensitive catalogers know intuitively the truth of Francis Bacon's acknowledgement that "the ill and unfit choice of words wonderfully obstructs understanding."

Accurate, intelligible (i.e., relevant), and adequate subject cataloging can be called the lynchpin of library service. Poorly done subject cataloging can frustrate and mislead the wisest reference librarian and the most patient, articulate client. While reliance upon standard tools such as the Library of Congress Subject Headings, Sears Subject Headings, or NLM's Medical Subject Headings may reflect traditional wisdom, a desire to provide service with economy of effort and a sort of logical rightness, it may in fact be as H. L. Mencken said "neat, plausible and wrong."

Subject headings and descriptors available in the traditional tools may be demonstrably archaic, inflexible, judgmental, or non-existent. As this problem relates to health information, it can have several causes. Health information is continually expanding and recombining as new information leads to new practices. The lack of clear boundaries for many subject areas (alluded to in the discussion of classification) makes provision of precise descriptive terminology challenging. The language and judgments of traditional medicine carry with them an authority and limiting logic that most librarians and library tools accept and incorporate into their cataloging—arguably to the detriment of service and objectivity. Knowing that these tools are pre-coordinated, one can understand their lack of flexibility.

It is critical that those providing subject access bear in mind the ethical need to avoid the pitfalls of perception-based service. Just as relevant as the reader-level terms employed are the terms by which we name conditions and populations. For years, the emotion-laden term "leprosy" has been used in catalogs to provide access to works on Hansen's Disease. While this is in fact the term most familiar to laypeople, it is a source of continuing anguish to the patients and families living with the disease because it allows the perpetuation of a false and painful stereotype. It will be argued here that the catalog must reflect the vernacular, but it is also argued that the catalog can (must?) instruct. "Leprosy" is no less offensive a term than "nigger," "wop," or "kike." While the common term for the disease probably cannot be eliminated from the catalog for some time, a *see* reference to Hansen's Disease can begin to sensitize library users.

Librarians have a responsibility to avoid employing labels which connote or imply a judgment of deviancy, aberration, abnormality, or unfitness just as we attempt to avoid sexist or racist terminology. As an ethical matter, this seems an unassailable position; as a practical matter, it can help avoid the inconsistencies and cataloging trauma inherent to a field as prone to revision as medicine.

The unfamiliar vocabulary of medical writing is perceived by some librarians as a barrier to extrapolative cataloging. The problems of translating medical terms and concepts are not significantly different from those encountered in describing works in other unfamiliar fields, whether engineering, agronomy, clothing design and construction, or cooking. The tools that facilitate interlocution between the work and the user are similar: internal guides to the cataloging tools; reference tools; and catalog ''public notes.'' Perhaps the most useful, and overlooked tool is the user.

In 1978, the library services of the Minneapolis Veterans Administration Medical Center undertook a project to ascertain the degree of variance between the two subject authorities in use there and the common terms used by patients and lay people seeking health information in the patient library.[6] A concurrent project at the V.A. Medical Center in San Francisco was an attempt to develop a lay taxonomy based on LC subject headings and the practiced intuitions of the librarians.[7] The Minneapolis project was influenced and encouraged by the on-going efforts at Consumer Health Information Programs and Services Projects (CHIPS) in Los Angeles County,[8] and the concern at Hennepin County Library (Minnesota) to provide lay-oriented catalog access.[9]

The Minneapolis study involved surveying patient and staff vocabulary choices using 20 open-ended questions. The questions were formatted to elicit the terminology used by laypeople to describe the 10 most common surgeries and diagnoses of the previous year's population. Typical questions included:

1. Recent books and films have been about people with ''split personalities.'' What terms would you use to find information about this?
2. A friend has liver disease from drinking too much. You want to learn more about this condition. Under what words would you look?
3. You want to know more about why people change [their] behavior when they get older. Under what words would you look for this information?

4. Your doctor has recommended surgery to remove your gall-bladder. What words would you look under to find more information about the gallbladder and this surgery?
5. You are scheduled to have surgery to remove the prostate. What terms would you use to find information about this?

Wording of the questionnaire was intended to keep it at approximately the sixth grade reading level and to supply only words the patient would likely be given by health care staff. Question format was highly repetitive to minimize the impact of distractions at the survey sites. The survey was distributed personally to clinic waiting areas, drug treatment program in-patients, and walk-in patients using the patient library. Non-medical hospital staff were also invited to participate. All were assured that the survey was voluntary and anonymous.

Patients and non-medical staff responses were summarized and ranked in order of occurrence. It should be noted that while sophisticated terminology was often used (e.g., cirrhosis, schizophrenia, neurology), terms were frequently misspelled, with rather consistent errors.

Responses to the questions were then compared to the terms available in the current Sears List of Subject Headings (11th ed.) and the 1976 Medical Subject Headings (MeSH) of NLM. The summary of responses below illustrates the gap between tools and clients.

QUESTION	PATIENT RESPONSES	SEARS	MeSH
#1	Split Personalities Schizophrenia Psychology	Personality Disorders Mental Health	Schizophrenia Schizoid Personality
#2	Liver Disease Cirrhosis Alcohol and effects	Alcohol— Physiological Effect	Liver Cirrhosis
#3	Senility Geriatrics Aging	Elderly—Habits and behaviors Human Behavior Aging	Psychoses, Senile Geriatric psychia- try Aged
#4	Gallbladder Gallbladder surgery Digestive system	Stomach Digestion	Gallbladder dis- eases Cholecystitis
#5	Prostate Glands Urology	Glands Men—Diseases	Prostatic diseases Exocrine glands

Clearly, neither Sears nor MeSH can "speak" directly to the lay-person. Even in combination, the two tools provide only second-choice access in many instances. Particularly striking, in light of its use by public libraries, was Sears' failure to provide specific access for materials dealing with diabetes, hernia, gallbladder disease, amputations, schizophrenia, and stroke.

While MeSH is certainly not intended to be used for lay collections, it was tempting to assume that its detailed specificity would be preferable to Sears' inconsistency. The limits of MeSH are apparent when one realizes that the terms for stroke, senility, high blood pressure, and cancer are respectively: cerebrovascular disorder; psychoses, senile; hypertension; and neoplasms, specific cancers, carcinoma or sarcoma. Merging the two tools might increase the accuracy of the catalog vocabulary, but would be unwieldy.

Although LC Subject headings were not included in the Minneapolis study, similar problems exist as the following terms illustrate. For some of the subjects queried, the terms of choice were: schizophrenia; alcoholics or alcoholism; senile psychosis, geriatric, geriatrics, geriatric nursing, aged; prostate gland—diseases. Looking for subject headings for other common health concerns we find such questionable terms as: herpevirus diseases, rather than herpes; bulimarexia or women—mental health, rather than bulimia; cerebrovascular disease, rather than stroke; coronary heart disease, rather than heart attack; terminal care or terminal care facilities, rather than hospice. As with Sears and MeSH, the system available is not consistent with the vernacular.

When the comparison of the Minneapolis patient vocabularies with Sears and MeSH was completed, a second stage of investigation began. The assumption was made that the indices to lay health encyclopedias were post-coordinate systems and therefore probably more flexible and responsive to popular language. Although each of the works examined was incomplete in terms of covering all the concerns of the questionnaire, there was almost a 70% correlation between index and lay vocabulary. Two factors affected the number and type of terms found in the indices. First, topic coverage was finite, and the purpose of the index was to provide maximal specific access. Second, because terms used in indexing are not standardized, an all-encompassing variety of terms and manner of subdivision was found. A final note: post-1978 index checks yield ever higher correlations between index terms and lay vocabularies.

In light of the experiential and studied evidence of a gap between tools and audience, several concerns seem evident. First, as Sanford Berman has noted, ". . .standard cataloging authorities or schemes. . .can no longer be regarded as sacrosanct or immutable. Rather, they should be considered as cataloging aids, to be tailored or transmuted as necessary to meet the requirements of the library's materials and clients."[10] Or, to paraphrase Andrew Lang, we should take care lest we use cataloging tools "as a drunken man uses lamp-posts—for support rather than illumination."

Significant in addressing the concerns of cataloging for the end user is the issue of the level at which subject cataloging is done. In most settings, the work is treated as a whole, in line with Needham's statement that:

> A fundamental theoretical rule of subject cataloging is that each heading, whether a notational symbol or a term in natural language, should be coextensive with the subject of the document.[11]

As the plethora of information continues to threaten us with live burial, as the cost of materials to be acquired increases, as the consumer appetite for information increases, and as the multidisciplinary treatment of many health topics becomes common, this "whole subject" approach seems less and less sensible. Tools which for years have adequately (if not admirably) served this wholistic approach to cataloging will be found wanting. Topics and subtopics of chapters and sections take on increased import.

Systems designed for laypeople must take some special considerations into account. One is that most of us have a lot of difficulty spelling unfamiliar medical terms. V.A. patients, presumably not unlike the population at large, made some consistent and significant spelling errors. Less than tenacious catalog users might decide nothing was available on the subject if they initially searched under the common misspellings: cirosis, prostrate, ofthalmology, or skizophrenia. So, too, a southerner accustomed to calling diabetes "sweet blood," or anyone using regional phrases or pronunciations, might find the technically correct public catalog unfulfilling. Libraries serving large foreign language-speaking populations may also need to examine the use of translating guide cards in the catalog.

Examples of sophisticated medical concerns coming into the

public conscious abound. . .one has only to look at the covers of popular magazines in any public library reading room. Yet catalogers, in relying on their trusted tools, persist in ignoring the popular terms used by every television doctor and talk show host. Standard tools continue to ignore such terms as hemorrhoids, home safety, family violence and hospice. Catalogers are faced with premenstrual syndrome instead of PMS, diethylstilbestrol instead of D.E.S., tobacco instead of smoking, phencyclines instead of PCP, in vitro fertilization instead of "test tube babies," deoxyribonucleic acid instead of DNA or recombinant DNA, and countless others.

While there is no argument that the library, and by extension its catalog, should uplift, illuminate, and foster clear and accurate thought, etc., it seems a bit arrogant to require the patron to come up to the artificial level of erudition imposed by our technically correct tools. Libraries should also attend to the ethical considerations of serving people at the level at which they present themselves. Then, too, such considerations might also serve the librarians at *their* level.

While the National Library of Medicine may seem the most likely institution to take a leadership role in devising a health information taxonomy for laypeople, the legal mandate to NLM is strictly related to meeting the needs of the medical professions. However, recent interest in exploring the needs of the lay public regarding access to health information has included recognition of the need for such a project.[12] Whether NLM can secure the necessary resources remains to be seen.

While LC subject headings are for many the national standard, it is important to note that LC is charged with serving Congress. . . not the public or the library profession. Tools developed by LC may be responsive to public need only incidentally, and it does not seem reasonable at this time to expect LC to take on the responsibility of meeting the library profession's needs.

The Medical Library Association and ALA are charged with the task of responding to the needs of the professionals they represent. One way to meet the needs of a profession is to coordinate the provision of necessary tools and the studies needed to validate them.

Schools providing graduate programs in Library Science are frequently faulted for their ivory tower aloofness from the workaday world. Projects responsive to the professional dilemmas that will be faced by the students they train would seem one way to encourage a reassessment of that perception.

There is a tradition in art and architecture that may be particularly relevant to this aspect of librarianship as well. "Charette" (little cart) comes from a French art students' practice of carting their paintings into Paris for sale. While en route, other travellers and farmers would suggest changes (more red, more flowers, etc.). Everyone got into the act, perhaps making it analogous to brainstorming or Type Z management. In education, the term denotes a design and implementation of innovation by involving a wide cross-section of the community. It would seem wise, timely and economical to begin involving the total library community (from the large agencies that serve it, to the school children beginning to use it) in the pursuit of accurate, appropriate library language. As Oliver Wendell Holmes might have said, cataloging "is a first-rate piece of furniture for a [person's] upper chamber, if [one] has common sense on the ground floor."

NOTES

1. American Library Association Code of Ethics Committee, "Code of Ethics for Librarians. . .adopted. . .Dec., 1938" *ALA Bulletin* 33:128-30 (Feb., 1939); ALA Special Committee on Code of Ethics, "Statement on Professional Ethics. . .1975," reprinted *ALA Yearbook, 1976* (Chicago, ALA, 1976).

2. D.J. Foskett, *The Creed of a Librarian—No Politics, No Religion, No Morals.* (Library Association, Reference Special and Information System. North Western Group. Occasional Papers no. 3) London, Library Assn., 1962.

3. Emmett Davis and C. Davis, *Mainstreaming Library Service for Disabled People.* Scarecrow, 1980.

4. Program note by Barbara Cox in, *Bulletin of the Medical Library Association,* 65 (1):142 Jan., 1977.

5. John Comaromi, ed. 19th ed. Albany, NY, Forest Press, 1982.

6. Unpublished student paper by Jacqueline Wulff, University of Minnesota Graduate Library School June, 1978. For information, contact Chief, Library Service, V.A.M.C. Minneapolis.

7. Private Communication, Sen Yee, Librarian, V.A.M.C. San Francisco.

8. Judith Furman, "CHIPS," *California Librarian* 39(1):23, Jan, 1978.

9. Sanford Berman "The Cataloging Shtik" *Library Journal* 102:1251-3, June 1, 1977, and issues of *Hennepin County Library Cataloging Bulletin.*

10. In "Automated Cataloging: More or Less Staff Needed?," *Library Journal* 103(4): 416. Feb 15, 1978.

11. In *Organizing Knowledge in Libraries; An Introduction to Information Retrieval,* p. 98. Gower Pub. Co., Lexington Books, 1971.

12. Private communication, Lois Ann Colaianni, Deputy Associate Director of Library Operations, NLM, May, 1983.

But I Have Promises to Keep—PRECIS, an Alternative for Subject Access

Audrey Taylor

Today's electronic culture has created user expectations for information systems that respond instantly and accurately to an enquiry. Library systems, even in the automated environment, continue to perpetuate precomputer principles developed over the last one hundred years, when information was thought to be linear and sequential rather than three-dimensional and dynamic.[1] Customary left-to-right, step-by-step methods of finding and dealing with information have been overtaken by instant information patterns released by electronic technology. Comparisons with sophisticated information systems used by business and by industry invite the conclusion that libraries and the library catalog may achieve immortality as fossilized relics of the Gutenburg revolution.

The proliferation of COM catalogs and current developments in online technology merely create the illusion that, at last, the "perfect" catalog has been achieved. It is no secret that the impoverished subject cataloging embedded in existing machine-readable bibliographic records used for catalog production provides, at best, limited access to information.[2] Any planning for the future must consider a dramatic change in the approach to subject access.

Until recently, scant attention has been paid to general user dissatisfaction with the library catalog as an information retrieval tool. "I can't find anything in this library ABOUT. . .!" is a painfully recurring exclamation. Exploration of the cause of the frustration has been largely neglected. There are exceptions that plead the rights of the user to fast, easy and precise access, exceptions that stress self-reliance, independence and confidence.[3]

In North America, librarians seem to be inextricably wedded to the century-old subject heading system, using either the *Library of Congress Subject Heading List* or the *Sears List*. Awareness that the method was designed to meet the needs of a vastly different technical and sociocultural era is beginning to surface in library literature.[4]

The Library of Congress Task Force (1977) acknowledged that the subject heading system was developed "in an environment of card and book catalogs," and that subject cataloging in the age of automation could provide a "more efficient and thorough access to the world's literature."[5] Blume looked to the changing nature of books as a cause for re-evaluation, pointing out that "monographs have become much more specific, there are more interdisciplinary works. . ."[6] Current sophisticated methods of storing information, e.g., computer discs, serve to increase the invisibility of and to decrease the accessibility to that information. Regrettably, promises of change meant only more of the same. The unveiling of the document, *Freezing the Library of Congress Catalog*, made a commitment only to the overhauling of terminology.

Changing user behaviour and the need for improved subject access were subjects of discussion at the University of Maryland's symposium, "Subject Access, Old Problems—New Solutions for the 1980's" (June 1982), and at the 1982 ALA Annual Conference. Still, most librarians continue to struggle with LCSH or Sears, some oblivious to the problems faced by the library user, others attempting to improve subject access by replacing or augmenting the subject cataloging used in standard cataloging copy. Tinkering with terminology while forcing information into an anachronistic straitjacket serves only to perpetuate the life of a retrieval tool that confounds the intelligence of the library user, threatens the credibility of the librarian, ignores current indexing theory, and misuses a powerful technology.

School libraries have not been spared the repercussions of the information revolution. Changes in educational philosophy, curriculum, and teaching methodology have impacted on school library service and the role of the teacher-librarian. Textbook and teacher-centred learning has given way to resource-based learning with greater emphasis on research skills (the retrieval and manipulation of information), and independent, individualized study programs. The teacher-librarian must use professional skills not only to assist students in the learning process but also to contribute as a member of the teaching team in the planning and implementation of the programs.[7] The library catalog, however, has remained unchanged, an impediment rather than an asset to learning.

User behaviour in school resource centres has altered significantly over the past ten years. School library clients, particularly students, have become consumers of high technology. They are trained in computer literacy and computer science. They are gaining familiarity with online search strategies required for accessing commercial databases. In their leisure, they play computer and video games passionately. Their teachers, meanwhile, are using microcomputer lessonware and courseware to enhance the learning environment.

Students and teachers are constantly hampered in their efforts to become confident and independent users of libraries. Unable to penetrate the mystique of subject cataloging, they are forced to rely upon the librarian who must function as an intermediary between the catalog and the enquirer. Lack of good subject access and inevitable lapses of memory can leave valuable materials to gather dust on the shelves.

Contrary to popular belief, broad general requests for information by students are no longer the norm, enquiries are specific and frequently specialized. The traditional school library catalog does not respond effectively to a search for information about, for example, "world food production related to the problems of overpopulation in the Third World." Nor can the catalog help the teacher locate specific microcomputer lessonware dealing with addition, subtraction and multiplication when confronted with a listing of more than 100 programs under the subject heading, MATHEMATICS. The titles, unfortunately, do not always reveal the contents.

Teacher-librarians have traditionally used Sears for the subject cataloging of curriculum support materials. An introductory sentence from Sears makes it clear that the objective of the application of the system is not to index information. "The purpose of subject cataloging is to list under one uniform word or phrase all the books on a given subject that a library has in its collection."[8]

There has been no clear professional consensus acknowledging the need for better subject access to curriculum resources. More often than not, the failure of subject headings to respond to curriculum-oriented enquiries has been rationalized by claims that the search for information, slow and frustrating though it may be, is a necessary part of the learning process. What nonsense!

Generally, research on library service to children and young adults has concentrated on every other aspect but the access question.[9] There have been some exceptions. In 1975, Moll concluded that the subject card catalog "does not provide effective access to information for children."[10] In 1976, Wehmeyer observed that "traditional subject cataloging is inadequate for curriculum needs. . . . What we seek is a retrieval system that will list materials in response to a student's specific needs. . . ."[11] Taylor's research using PRECIS to improve subject access to school library materials began in 1972.[12]

A student, required to write a research essay contrasting old and new lifestyles in China, is faced with a laborious search through materials listed under the broad heading, for example, CHINA—History. Not only will some of the titles be totally irrelevant, but pertinent information in geographical and sociological sources are likely to be overlooked. How much more useful the students would find the specificity of *PRECIS* subject entries such as:

CHINA
Families. Structure

CHINA
Social structure, to 1949

CHINA
People's Republic of China. Agricultural communes

CHINA
People's Republic of China. Daily life. Effects of communism

CHINA
People's Republic of China. Society. Role of peasants

Clearly, newer indexing systems such as PRECIS, the PREserved Context Index System, permit both the degree of specificity and the use of natural language in context that ensure intelligibility, predictability, and therefore, satisfaction for the school library user.

An interest in the relationship between linguistics and indexing languages materialized in the 1970s with the recognition that computer manipulation of words with no regard for syntax accomplished little to improve information retrieval.[13]

Both in speech and written composition, people decode the intended meaning of a term because they receive it generally in the context of another word or words; its meaning is, therefore, context-dependent on the words with which it is associated. The idea of context-dependency is an essential characteristic of all communication systems including natural language.

In Great Britain, the machine production of the British National Bibliography from MARC records called for a new indexing method designed for maximum efficiency in the computer production of the subject index. PRECIS was created and implemented by Derek Austin of the British Library. The system grew out of Austin's interest in linguistic theory and his work with the Classification Research Group (CRG) to develop a machine-readable faceted classification scheme (1969).[14]

PRECIS belongs to the family of documentation systems known as paralanguages. These systems share many characteristics in common with natural language, using some portion of both its vocabulary and structure. PRECIS is based on linguistic logic, possessing both semantic and syntactic features.

Unlike the traditional subject heading system with its prescribed lists of terms and phrases "based neither on principles nor on standards,"[15] PRECIS is a method, a set of working procedures.

The subject analysis and the indexing of a document (book, film, microcomputer software, videodisk, etc.,) result in the formulation of one or more subject statements or "strings" made up of natural language terms set in a predetermined context. The user enters the alphabetical subject index at any one of the terms which together make up that subject statements and realizes the full context in which the term has been used. Thus a complete statement or kind of "precis" is presented to the searcher under each term in the "string." For example, a book containing information about "the effects of acid rain on the fish in the lakes of northern Michigan," can be found by searching under MICHIGAN, NORTHERN MICHIGAN, LAKES, FISH, and ACID RAIN. The entries will appear alphabetically as follows:

ACID RAIN. Northern Michigan
  Effects on fish in lakes

FISH. Lakes. Northern Michigan
  Effects of acid rain

LAKES. Northern Michigan
  Fish. Effects of acid rain

MICHIGAN
    Northern Michigan. Lakes. Fish.
    Effects of acid rain

NORTHERN MICHIGAN
    Lakes. Fish. Effects of acid rain

Regardless of the starting point of the search, each *lead term* or point of entry generated by the "string" takes the user to the same information.

The five subject entries illustrated are produced by computer from the single input "string" of coded terms, i.e.,

$z01030$aMichigan$inorthern$zp1030$alakes$z11030$afish$win
    $zs0030$aeffectsvofwon$z31030$aacid rain

The codes embody a set of computer instructions that determine which terms become access points, the position of the terms in each entry, any intervening punctuation, and the typography.

As the entries from all the strings are produced, they are automatically placed in alphabetical order in the subject catalog. The user, having selected a search term—for example, FISH—will find other entries which could serve to narrow or broaden the enquiry:

FISH
    Adaptation to environment

FISH
    Species. Interspecific competition

FISH. Columbia River. Washington
    Effects of pollution—*Statistics*

FISH. Lakes. Northern Michigan
    Effects of acid rain

FISH. Rivers. United States
    Stocking—*Surveys*

Because PRECIS has the advantage of producing multiple entries from a single "string" of terms, the user approaching the index with a different subject in mind—for example, INTERSPECIFIC COMPETITION—will find the lead under *that* term equally valid for his or her search:

INTERSPECIFIC COMPETITION. Species of fish

In each case, the subject statement in the catalog is followed by the bibliographic citation(s), for example:

FISH. Food
Cooking—*Recipes*

> 641.5944 GOR The Dione Lucas book of natural French cooking. Gorman, Marion. c1977
>
> 641.5972 HAN Mexican cookery. Hansen, Barbara. 1981, c1980
>
> 641.692 FIS Fish. c1979

(Aurora High School Catalog)

The link between the PRECIS strings and the materials is made in the 691 field of the MARC records.

A search may be refined further by using the standardized reference network, an integral part of the PRECIS methodology generated from the machine-held thesaurus. The user, selecting the term, FISH, is reminded of specific kinds of fish:

FISH
See also
  PIKE
  SALMON
  TROUT

If the chosen term is not used in the index, the user is directed to the preferred term, for example:

PISCES
See FISH

Because the system is based on the concept of an open-ended vocabulary, any term encountered in the materials can be admitted to the file immediately, ensuring currency of terminology. The computer-held thesaurus determines that the same subject is consistently indexed under the same form of the word. When a new term is admitted to the files, the relationships with existing terms are handled in two different ways: the one establishes the context or syntactic relationships in the "string"; the other provides the semantic or hierarchical network in the thesaurus.

In Canada, The York Region Board of Education, Ontario, has, over the past decade, been responsible for a research and development project dedicated to the improvement of both the physical format of the library catalog and its function as an information retrieval tool. The school board's administrative staff had questioned the effectiveness of the card catalog in relation to its cost as early as 1969. Observational studies showed that the catalog was remarkably underused in the secondary school resource centres. Students were seen to browse the shelves rather than to consult the catalog when seeking subject information.

Taylor and McCordick corroborated the findings, suggesting that limited subject access was one of the major causes of user disenchantment with the library catalog. Experience in both elementary and secondary school libraries demonstrated that 85-90 percent of enquiries were subject-oriented. A large percentage of students were seen to abandon searches in the subject catalog because of lack of specificity in the subject headings, the unnatural order of inverted headings, and terminology out of touch with their needs and thoughts.[16]

In choosing an indexing system, it was decided that good subject access depended on a number of identifiable criteria: the information-seeking behaviour of the target audience; depth and specificity in subject analysis and indexing to prevent information loss; more subject access points per document than the subject heading system permitted; current and open-ended vocabulary drawn from the materials rather than a printed, outdated list such as Sears or LCSH; natural language structures to ensure intelligibility; and a potential for future online access by the user. A tall order, indeed! PRECIS more than met these requirements.

In 1971, the school board agreed to the implementation of PRECIS in the new Aurora High School, with the expectation that improved use of the library catalog could lead to the acceptance of PRECIS in other new schools. The experiment began with the manual application in a card catalog. From 1972-1975, observation by library staff and faculty provided evidence of a significant increase in student use of the subject catalog.[17]

In 1976, The Ontario Ministry of Education awarded The York Region Board a Grant-in-Aid of Educational Research to build an automated model for an Ontario-wide cataloging/information retrieval network for school libraries. The PRECIS project, based on the Aurora High School experience, became a user of a Canadian bibliographic utility, UTLAS (The University of Toronto Library Automation Systems). This service housed the only PRECIS computer program in existence in North America.

The research addressed five major areas:

i. the feasibility of networking and developing machine-readable files of bibliographic data (full MARC records) for school library materials;

ii. the building of PRECIS computer files of subject data for school library materials;

iii. the linking of the two files, (i) and (ii), for the creation of computer-produced catalogs, first in book form and later in COM (Computer Output Microform) as interim steps towards the development of an online catalog;

iv. the evaluation of the new subject catalog's capability to provide fast and easy access to information;

v. the development of a skilled central technical services staff, including PRECIS indexers, capable of serving a school library network.

Careful planning by the project team involved a number of activities: consultation with teaching staff about curriculum and the concepts being taught; the terminology used to express the concepts; examination of Ministry of Education and local curriculum guidelines; and consultation with library staff about the information-seeking behaviour of students and teachers. This planning was rewarded by an enthusiastic acceptance of the catalogs. Teachers and librarians were astounded to observe both the confidence and interest displayed by students in their use of the subject catalog. The successful retrieval of information was documented in the bibliographies of student research papers. As well, some teachers began to use the subject catalog as a tool for planning units of study based on available resources. They were able, as a result, to make informed recommendations for purchase of new support materials because the in-depth indexing made visible weaknesses in the collection.

Success in the secondary school experiment led to a grant of further research funds from the Ministry of Education in 1979 to investigate the feasibility of using PRECIS to index elementary school materials. Subject access using Sears has always presented insurmountable problems at this level. Not only are the language and structures of the subject headings inhibiting to young users, but information useful to teachers is frequently overlooked.[18]

Once again careful planning preceded implementation. McCordick prepared a field guide for the PRECIS indexers following an extensive investigation of needs based on her own experience and discussions with elementary teachers and librarians.

With the exception of literary works, no appreciable differences were found in curriculum-related terminology for identical subject content at elementary and secondary levels. The indexers were surprised by the level of difficulty of terms encountered in the primary materials. It was found, for example, that an author deliberately introduced complex scientific terms, accompanied by a definition. Complaints about the use of these terms by several teachers indicated that they were unaware of both current learning materials and curriculum guidelines. To exclude these terms from the subject catalog would be a disservice to the students.

Because the terminology derives from the library materials being indexed, the subject catalog reflects curriculum content and concepts. Experience has proved that students and teachers using a PRECIS subject index discover directions of enquiry that they had not considered when beginning their search. One elementary school teacher-librarian recently observed a grade 7 teacher and one of her students working together at the subject catalog looking up the topic, "pollution." They were able to work side-by-side, reading over the many subject strings and bibliographic citations made available in the COM catalog. They discussed which aspect of "pollution" might be appropriate for the student to pursue and which materials seemed most suitable. The librarian commented that this sort of learning partnership did not occur with traditional indexing and the card format.

Teacher-librarians also report that the subject catalog helps them enormously in retrieving materials, particularly on short notice. For example, a grade 1 teacher responding to a problem that had occurred during recess, requested a book called *The Fight*. The specific title was not immediately available. The librarian was able to respond quickly with an alternative, *I Was So Mad*, located by using the string,

CHILDREN
Anger—Stories

Surveys of student opinion of the catalogs by elementary school teacher-librarians showed that 75 percent of the student population, grades 4-8, preferred PRECIS to traditional subject cataloging. One grade 8 student commented that she likes the subject catalog because of the way the subjects are "organized and broken down." While students at the primary level use the subject catalog with confidence, they were omitted from the surveys because it was felt they might not fully understand the survey questions.

Over the years, seminars on the use of PRECIS in school libraries have produced a positive response to the claim that a PRECIS subject catalog not only responds well to the curriculum needs of students and teachers, but also has applications as a learning tool. Precise use of language, terms set in context, and the specificity of the subject entries are three of the powerful features that help the user in formulating an intelligent and comprehensive search. Success builds confidence!

It was noted in the early days of the project that one of the most grossly under-indexed of resources is fiction, including both children's and young adult literature. If it is a part of education to encourage reading that "stimulates the intellect, fires the imagination, develops language skills, enhances concept of self and promotes understanding,"[19] then these materials must be made visible, both in the school and the public library. There are encouraging signs of awareness that *all* fiction requires subject access based on known user needs.[20]

The standard subject cataloging of picture books, for example, is woefully wanting. Requests are made not only for specific topics but also for particular uses. Recurring themes such as "fear of the dark," "acceptance of a new baby," and "sibling rivalry," as well as abstract concepts related to the process of growing up, are seldom present.[21]

Contrast the two subject approaches to the title, *The Missing Piece Meets The Big O*, by Shel Silverstein. Only one subject heading has been assigned by the Library of Congress,

(i)   Circle—Fiction

PRECIS indexing generated two strings,

(i)   CHILDREN
        Self-image. Development—Stories

(ii) CHILDREN
        Self-reliance—Stories

Those familiar with this title will know that the book is not really about circles!

There are other criteria to be considered in the indexing of fiction. Pejtersen, familiar with the indexing capabilities of PRECIS, has developed a theory for determining "aboutness" based on user needs and interests from the public library point-of-view.[22] Criteria developed for the PRECIS project reflect student interests and curriculum. These criteria include setting (locale), main plot (action), major character(s), themes, and genre. For example, the title, *Dragonsinger*, by Anne McCaffrey, was assigned three strings:

(i)　TELEPORTATION—*Science fiction*

(ii)　SPACE COLONIES
　　　Defense by dragons—*Science fiction*

(iii)　TEENAGE MUSICIANS
　　　Ambition—*Novels*

The Aurora project's application of the PRECIS method differs from that of other institutions in that PRECIS is used for analytical indexing. There are no rules that stipulate "no more than 3 strings per document." Books, for example, can be indexed chapter by chapter, if such detail seems warranted.

The effectiveness of analytical indexing can best be illustrated through examples comparing LCSH entries taken from the MARC source record and PRECIS strings generated by the project staff. For the secondary school title, *A Foremost Nation: Canadian Foreign Policy and A Changing World*, two subject headings have been assigned in the CAN/MARC record:

(i)　Canada—Foreign relations—Addresses, essays, lectures

(ii)　Canada—Foreign economic relations—Addresses, essays, lectures

The following PRECIS strings were produced by the project indexers, based on their knowledge of curriculum needs:

(i)　CANADA
　　　Federal government. Foreign relations related to energy resources.

(ii) CANADA
     Federal government. Economic policies. Effects
     on multinational corporations.

(iii) CANADA
      Foreign trade. Policies of federal government.

(iv) CHINA
     People's Republic of China. Foreign relations
     with Canada.

(v) OCEANS
    Territorial rights. International law.

(vi) UNITED NATIONS
     Role of Canada.

One significant contribution made by this project to the use of PRECIS in library catalogs has been the development of the first computer-produced one-stage subject catalog, illustrated earlier in the paper. PRECIS was programmed originally to generate a back-of-the-book index to the classified catalogs of the British National Bibliography. Such a format was considered to be totally unsuitable for a student population. The one-stage format, linking the PRECIS string directly to the bibliographic citation rather than to a classification number, has since been implemented in slightly varying versions by the British Education Index[23] and the National Film Board of Canada.[24]

In the mid-seventies, other institutions and research projects in Canada recognized the need to improve subject access to specific kinds of documents. Each deliberately chose PRECIS.

In 1974, the Ontario Ministry of Education and the Metropolitan Toronto School Board jointly funded ONTERIS, the Ontario Education Resources Information System. At that time, there was a critical need to collect and provide access to educational research generated by school boards, the Ministries of Education and of Colleges and Universities, teachers' associations, and other educational organizations and authorities. Over the years, the database has expanded to include curriculum guidelines, reports, reviews, and other materials related to Ministry-funded activities. Subject access using PRECIS is made available both through a printed index and through online retrieval. In 1983, the ONTERIS database became available to the public through the facilities of Bibliographic Retrieval Services (BRS).[25]

Difficulty in capturing and making accessible information about Canadian-made films and other nonprint media led to a series of studies in the mid-1970s to assess the feasibility of establishing an automated Canadian nonprint information system.

The National Film Board of Canada, a major film producer and distributor, was aware that many of its current products remained invisible to its target audiences. A study commissioned to determine the cause of underuse concluded that poor subject access was the major problem. PRECIS was recommended as a superior method of indexing to improve information retrieval.[26]

Since then, NFB has established an online information/distribution system called FORMAT. The system is bilingual, capable of handling both bibliographic and subject information in French and English. The cataloging information is stored in the computer facilities of UTLAS and is later transferred to FORMAT in the form of magnetic tape. The UTLAS files are used for the computer-production of printed and COM catalogs; FORMAT handles the online enquiries of the NFB's regional offices.

In the last two years, other Canadian film production and collecting agencies have added their materials to the FORMAT system. In 1983, the National Library of Canada and the Public Archives agreed to collect and store bibliographic data in FORMAT for the purpose of producing *Film Canadiana*. In a radical departure from traditional LCSH subject cataloging, subject access to *Film Canadiana* will use PRECIS in French and English for both the printed catalogs and online subject enquiry.[27]

Despite the rejection of PRECIS by the Library of Congress in 1978, other American institutions have welcomed the method for its elegant use of computer technology and its pragmatic approach to user behaviour. The most familiar application is the Control Data Corporation's PLATO courseware for which PRECIS provides online subject access.

The need for improved subject indexing of curriculum support materials has been slow to gain acceptance in spite of growing evidence of user dissatisfaction, even rebellion. In Ontario, the creative energy of teacher-librarians and school library consultants is being expended on the automation of the traditional catalog and on the implementation of resource-based learning. The general laissez-faire attitude to information access has placed the PRECIS project's service to eight schools in a "sundown" position.

The promise of PRECIS lies in its growing international acceptance by institutions that recognize not only the immense importance of information retrieval in today's society but also their own responsibility in making information both visible and available.

REFERENCES

1. Deanna Marcum and Richard Boss. "Information Technology," *Wilson Library Bulletin*, Vol. 56, No. 10 (June 1982).

2. Bohdan S. Wynar. *Introduction to Cataloging and Classification*. 6th ed. Littleton, Colorado: Libraries Unlimited, 1980.

3. Nancy J. Williamson. "Is There a Catalog in Your Future? Access to Information in the Year 2006," *Library Resources and Technical Services*, Vol. 26, No. 2 (April/June 1982).

4. Michael Gorman. "Thinking the Thinkable: A Synergetic Profession: Online Catalogs Go Beyond Bibliographic Control," *American Libraries* (July/August 1982).

5. United States. Library of Congress. Task Force on Goals, Organization and Planning. *Report to the Librarian of Congress*. Washington: Library of Congress, 1977.

6. *The PRECIS Index System: Principles, Applications, and Prospects*. Edited by Hans H. Wellisch. New York: H.W. Wilson, 1977.

7. Ontario. Ministry of Education. *Partners In Action: the Library Resource Centre in the School Curriculum*. Toronto: Ministry of Education, 1982.

8. *Sears List of Subject Headings*. Edited by Barbara M. Westby. 10th ed. New York: H.W. Wilson, 1972.

9. Shirley Fitzgibbons. "Research on Library Services for Children and Young Adults: Implications for Practice," *Emergency Librarian*, Vol. 9, No. 5 (May/June 1982).

10. Joy Kaiser Moll. *Children's Access to Information in Print: An Analysis at the Vocabulary (Reading) Levels of Subject Headings and Their Application to Children's Books*. (PhD dissertation: Rutgers University, 1975).

11. Lillian Wehmeyer. "Cataloging the School Media Centre as a Specialized Collection," *Library Resources and Technical Services*, Vol. 20, No. 4 (Fall 1976).

12. Brian Burnham and Audrey Taylor. *PRECIS Indexing: The Development of a Working Model for a School Library Cataloging/Information Retrieval Network*. Toronto: Ontario Ministry of Education and Ministry of Colleges and Universities, 1982.

13. Constance Rinehart. "Subject Cataloging in 1982," *Library Resources and Technical Services*, Vol. 27, No. 3 (July/Sept. 1983).

14. Derek Austin. "The Development of PRECIS: A Theoretical and Technical History," *Journal of Documentation*, Vol. 30, No. 1 (March 1974).

15. Michael Gorman. "Fate, Time, Occasion, Chance and Change: Or How the Machine May Yet Save LCSH," *American Libraries*, Vol. 11 (Oct. 1980).

16. Audrey Taylor and Irene McCordick. "PRECIS: Indexing to Revolutionize Subject Access to Information in School Resource Centres," *Canadian Library Journal*, Vol. 33, No. 6 (Dec. 1976).

17. Brian Burnham, Irene McCordick and Audrey Taylor. *A Computer-Based Catalogue Linking the PRECIS Subject Indexing System to School Library Materials*. Aurora: York County Board of Education, 1978.

18. Op. cit. Brian Burnham (1982).

19. S.D. Neill. "Knowledge or Information—A Crisis of Purpose in Libraries," *Canadian Library Journal*, Vol. 39, No. 2 (April 1982).

20. Sanford Berman. "Reference, Readers and Fiction: New Approaches," *The Reference Librarian*, Nos. 1 & 2 (Fall/Winter 1981).

21. Theodore C. Hines, Lois Winkel and Rosann Collins. "The Children's Media Data Bank," *Top of the News*, Vol. 36, No. 2 (Winter 1980).

22. Annelise Mark Pejtersen. "The Meaning of 'About' in Fiction Indexing and Retrieval," *ASLIB Proceedings*, Vol. 31, No. 5 (May 1979).

23. Christine Shaw. *Analysis of Questionnaires on the Format of the British Education Index*. London: British Library Bibliographic Services Division, 1979.

24. Canada. National Film Board of Canada. *PRECIS Index to 16 mm Films*. Montreal: National Film Board of Canada, 1982.

25. Ontario. Ministry of Education. *ONTERIS: Access to Ontario Education Information*. Toronto: Ministry of Education. (pamphlet).

26. Mary Dykstra. "A Complete Delivery Service for Canadian Non-Print Media," *Canadian Journal of Information Science*, Vol. 3 (1978).

27. Canada. National Library of Canada. "Film Canadiana," *National Library News*, Vol. 15, No. 3 (March 1983).

BIBLIOGRAPHY

Alcock, Miranda. "The Learning Materials Recording Study: A Joint British Library/Inner London Education Authority Research Project," *The Audiovisual Librarian*, Vol. 5, No. 2 (Spring 1979).

Austin, Derek. "PRECIS in a Multilingual Context."
Part 1, "PRECIS: An Overview," *Libri*, Vol. 26 (March 1976)
Part 2, Sorensen, Jutta and Derek Austin. "A Linguistic and Logical Explanation of the Syntax," *Libri*, Vol. 26 (June 1976)
Part 3, Sorensen, Jutta and Derek Austin. "Multilingual Experiments, Proposed Codes, and Procedures for the Germanic Languages," *Libri*, Vol. 26 (September 1976)
Part 4, Lambert, G. "The Application of PRECIS in French," *Libri*, Vol. 26 (December 1976)

Austin, Derek. *PRECIS: A Manual of Concept Analysis and Subject Indexing*. London: The Council of the British National Bibliography, 1974.

Bell, Brian. "School Libraries and UTLAS: Building Now for the Future," *School Libraries in Canada*, Vol. 3, No. 2 (Winter 1983).

Dykstra, Mary. "The Lion That Squeaked," *Library Journal*, Vol. 103, No. 15 (September 1, 1978).

Gardhouse, Judy. "NFB Develops Delivery Service for Canadian Non-print Media," *Canadian Library Journal*, Vol. 37, No. 2 (April 1980).

Janke, Richard V. "Time for an Alternative," *Ontario Library Review*, Vol. 63, No. 3 (September 1979).

Ramsden, Michael J. *PRECIS: A Workbook for Students of Librarianship*. London: Bingley, 1981.

Robinson, C. Derek. "PRECIS Canada: Achievements and Prospects," *Canadian Journal of Information Science*, Vol. 4 (Spring 1979).

Schabas, A. H. "Post-coordinate Retrieval: A Comparison of Two Indexing Languages," *Journal of American Society for Information Science*, Vol. 33, No. 1 (January 1982).

Sive, Mary. "PRECIS—A Better Way To Index Films," *Sightlines*, Vol. 13 (Winter, 1979-80).

Wellisch, Hans H. "Year's Work in Subject Analysis: 1980," *Library Resources & Technical Services*, Vol. 25, No. 3 (July/Sept. 1981).

Younger, Jennifer A. "Year's Work in Subject Analysis: 1981," *Library Resources & Technical Services*, Vol. 26, No. 3 (July/Sept. 1982).

Multilingual Access:
The Jefferson County Public Library Experience

Paul R. Murdock

INTRODUCTION

Consider the following bibliographic records:

RECORD 1
NUC VOL. 26

'68-'72

Duyên-Anh.
 Ngày xu'a còn bé; truyên dài. [Saigon? Khai-Tri] 1971.
 161 p.
 I. Title.

RECORD 2
OCLC
7677311

OCLC: 7677311 Rec. stas: n Entrd: 810818 Used: 81228
Type: a Bib lvl: m Govt pub: Lang: Vie Source: d illus:
Repr: Enc lvl: I Conf pub: O Ctry: vs Dt tp: s
M/F/B: 11 Indx: O Mod rec: Festschr: O Cont:
Desc: a Int lvl: Dates: 1970.
1 010
2 040 CLE c CLE
3 092 b
4 049
5 100 00 Duy^en Anh, ḍ 1935- w 4n
6 245 10 Ng`ay x-a c^on bbe : b truy^en d`ai / c Duy^en Anh.
7 260 0 [s.1. : b s.n.] , c 1970.
8 300 161 p. ; c 21 cm.

  91

Each of these records contains cataloging data for the novel, *Ngày xu'a còn bé truyên dài*, by the popular Vietnamese author, Duyen-Anh. Roughly translated, the title might be rendered "When I Was Young." The story relates the romantic escapades and first loves of several Vietnamese students about high school age. Not exactly a ground-breaking contribution to the sociological literature concerning the etiological foundations of adolescent Vietnamese sexual mores, but that's beside the point. Except perhaps to note that if it were something other than a contemporary Vietnamese novel, the first two cataloging records *would* include a subject tracing or two.

If you happened to be a Vietnamese-American longing to read (and hear) your natural language, you might just muster a lot of courage and visit your local public library in search of *Ngày xu'a còn bé truyên dài*. If you discovered your local library does not buy ethno-cultural materials, you'd be disappointed. But if your library did, and your search landed you in front of the catalog, chances are good that you'd not only be disappointed, but confused, disoriented, horrified, terrified, in fact, utterly baffled by what you might find (Record 2). Or did not find (Record 1). About this time you perhaps would ask a librarian to help you decipher the "gestalt" of the very tool they designed for your assistance. Actually, this gets pretty ridiculous. But not at the Jefferson County (Colo.) Public Library's Villa Italia Branch.[1]

Consider Record 3.

RECORD 3
JEFFCAT
82001142

*NGAY XUA CON BE TRUYEN DAI ASIAN MODEL LIBRARY
   AUTHOR: $3.95 PUBLISHER: SONG MOI
     DUYEN ANH, 1935-1970S CLASSIFICATION: SP YA
     FICTION VIETNAMESE
   SUBJECTS:

     FICTION VIETNAMESE 20TH CENTURY
     HIGH SCHOOL STUDENTS FICTION
     LOVE STORIES VIETNAMESE
     TRUYEN TINH CAM TIENG VIET
     TRUYEN TUONG TUONG HOC SINH TRUNG HOC
     TRUYEN TUONG TUONG TIENG VIET
     TRUYEN TUONG TUONG TIENG VIET THE KY 20
     VIETNAMESE LANGUAGE MATERIALS FICTION
   HOLDINGS:
     VILLA

THE ASIAN MODEL LIBRARY

The Jefferson County Public Library received a $25,000 LSCA grant in September 1981. The purpose of this grant, awarded by the Colorado State Library, was to fund development of machine-readable cataloging data for a variety of Asian language library materials held chiefly in public libraries throughout Colorado. Perhaps the core of these dispersed holdings was the Asian Model Library at JCPL's Villa Italia Branch. This collection was developed during 1980-81 by Branch Librarian Natalia Greer with monies from an earlier LSCA grant.

Ms. Greer correctly perceived that a significant and growing population block in Jefferson County was comprised of recently arrived Asian language speaking emigrés.[2] Many in this emerging ethno-cultural minority had what literally could be termed an "emergency" need for basic survival skills information and resources. Others had urgent need for materials in their own non-English languages.

Prompted by these critical needs and mindful of librarianship's inherent relationship with ethnicity, the Asian Model Library was established. It was and remains squarely within the larger framework of the White House and Governor's Conferences' stated goals for libraries—those of enhancing lifestyles and preserving national heritages.[3]

From the original collection development grant and supplemented by donations from Colorado libraries, the collection has grown to more than 4,000 items incorporating East and Southeast Asian popular fiction, literary classics, periodicals, newspapers, pamphlets, reference materials, and audio-visual items including video tapes, cassette recordings, and kits.

Given the unique scope of the Asian Model Library, it was evident that the materials must be brought under bibliographic control. This was absolutely imperative not only in terms of ethnic collection development within the Villa Library, but also as the key step in making these materials available to Asian-Americans intrastate via the Colorado Union Catalog.

Consequently, the Asian Model Library Cataloging Project was conceived and funded from September 1981 through June 1982.

Inventory of the materials needing cataloging revealed a daunting list of items: 250+ Korean titles, 200+ Thai titles, 300+ Vietnamese titles, 250+ Japanese titles, and 200+ Chinese titles. Also, an interesting but seemingly endless assortment of vernacular, bilingual, and multilingual Hmong, Lao, Thai, Cambodian, Vietnamese, Japanese, Korean, Chinese, and English state, local, and federal documents. And assorted non-print items. All quietly begging for cataloging.

The goal of the Asian Cataloging Project was, then, the creation of machine-readable bibliographic data that were cost effective within the parameters of available funding. These catalog records, first and foremost, must be user-sensible and easily retrieved primarily in an online public catalog environment and secondarily off-line via microfiche catalogs.

Additionally, the following guidelines were presumed or established:

1. Cataloging data would be romanized according to nationally or internationally accepted standards. (More about this eternal controversy later.)
2. Translation personnel would be hired in order to achieve necessary romanizations.
3. All cataloging data would be created for natural interface with the online non-MARC formatted public catalog "JEFF-CAT."[4]
4. All cataloging data would be subject to the rigorous authority control routinely practiced at JCPL.

And most important,

5. All cataloging data, especially subject data, would be *findable, intelligible*, and *usable* not only by Asian language speakers, even though to this latter group the meaning of such data was linguistically unintelligible.

Mindful of the high percentage of subject searches a library catalog must support, it was apparent that subject access was of vital importance. It was also to be the thorniest problem.

CONTEMPORARY ACCESS METHODOLOGIES

In his 1980 report "Bibliographic Access to Multilingual Collections," Wellisch detailed findings of his survey ". . .On methods currently used by public libraries to provide bibliographic access to their foreign-language collections."[5] Among methodologies identified were: alphabetical author-title and subject catalogs but with subject headings in the dominant language (i.e., English in many cases); alphabetical author-title and classified subject catalogs with subject index in the dominant language; alphabetical author-title catalogs with separate subject catalogs by language or script; several variants of author-title-subject catalogs; and the infamous, justifiably impugned "separate shelving technique."[6]

Wellisch proposed several changes in or improvements upon current methodologies: the conventional author-title-subject catalog augmented with cross-references in non-English languages; separate subject catalogs in non-English languages; classified subject catalogs with multilingual indexes; and a combination alphabetical and classified catalog.[7]

Each of these methodologies and Wellisch's proposed improvements have merit. But with regard to the catalogs of the Asian Model Library, every one was rejected on an assortment of grounds ranging from technical to economic to philosophic. Not one of the catalog formats provides online integrated access irrespective of primary language orientation. By "integrated" is meant avoidance of split files, physically isolated or manual catalogs, and maximum avoidance of user-inhibiting language-related barriers for staff and patron alike.

PROBLEMS

There were two major problems implicit in this integrated language catalog access desideratum.

First, of course, how to handle the endless complexities of non-roman scripts.

The logographic characters used in Chinese, Japanese, and Korean are especially difficult. The traditional method, "romanization," is criticized on a variety of grounds. Since the library literature is bursting with passionately argued points of view on the topic, I need only reiterate several salient facts.[8]

Philosophically, there can be little doubt that input and retrieval of vernacular script bibliographic records is the ideal and one we will achieve with time and on a very grand scale. However, embracing the ideal reflects a too simplistic view of the scope of the complex problems that exist on a fundamental level (i.e., in JCPL.)

For example, American libraries involved in collection development in logographic (and other) script languages, rely primarily on card catalog or other hard copy formats to describe and access their collections. In the hard copy catalog environment, many good manual techniques suffice for vernacular input and retrieval. But the Jefferson County Public Library has not had a card catalog for nearly twenty years. Understandably, JCPL was not especially enthusiastic about championing its return.

Despite the impact of the MARC and UNIMARC formats, the National Program for Acquisitions and Cataloging, the automated vernacular Japanese records being developed by the National Diet Library (Tokyo),[9] or even such recent developments as the RLG/CJK computer terminal[10] and Telex Computer Products Multiple Language Keyboard with complete ALA/MARC character set,[11] despite these and numerous other developments underway, one very simple fact remains excruciatingly clear: We do not yet have *widely available and affordable* machines capable of manipulating most non-roman scripts. As a result, the complex problems associated with vernacular Asian script input and access in online public catalog environments are only now being addressed, not to mention solved.

For the time being, most libraries with collections in non-roman scripts accessed via online bibliographic records *must* use transliterated entries. (Optimizing the use of these data is entirely another matter.)

And for many libraries, operating as they must under severe budgetary, technical, and personnel constraints, this produces a painfully lucid either/or dilemma. Either accept romanized data as it is created or becomes available through cooperative or centralized services, or attempt no bibliographic control over such items. Unfortunately, the latter is truly a worst-case scenario, translating as it often seems to into the decision not to buy ethnic-related materials. It also guarantees that even if purchased and irrespective of the scope, size, or popularity of an ethnic collection, access to it and understanding of it will be severely, perhaps irreparably, damaged. No library mission statement anywhere condones this reckless attitudinal posture.

The second problem involved the meaning and use of these data, particularly but not exclusively subject data.

While vernacular script or language bibliographic data are unquestionably useful to non-English readers, these data may impart a needless layer of disadvantageousness to English-speaking staff trying to help patrons of specific ethnic orientations. When considering "user-oriented" subject cataloging data in the context of Asian languages, "user" must encompass the needs of staff members expected to cope with the unusual demands of unfamiliar languages or scripts. Because the Asian catalogs were to be distributed throughout Colorado for support of interlibrary loan activities, a methodology had to be developed that would allow staff to access Asian language records virtually "automatically."

Given the sufficiently documented fact that contemporary library catalogs produce "peine forte et dure" for seemingly everyone except their creators, a miserable situation can only be rendered hopeless by the addition of impenetrable linguistic barriers. Whether the obstacles manifest themselves in the form of vernacular scripts or romanized vernacular substitutes is beside the point. When staff are befuddled by the catalog (or its contents), the mind reels at what non-staff Asian language users might experience.

Briefly stated, the challenge was: how to optimize the use of "friendly," mixed-language, online catalog records while minimizing the practical and psychological effects of unfamiliar languages for the entire set of perceived and potential users.

SOLUTION

One solution to the problem of non-discriminatory, equitable language access, with emphasis on subject access in particular, is Mozartean in its elegance. If the catalog can accommodate this:

ENGLISH HEADING "A"

see/see also

ENGLISH HEADING "B"

then why not this:

WORLD WAR II 1939-1945 FICTION

see also

TI ERH TSU SHIH CHIEH TA CHAN 1939-1945
HSIAO SHO
DI ER CI SHIJIE DAZHAN 1939-1945 XIAOSHUO
NIYAI SONG KRAM LOK TRUNG TE 2 2482-2493

or this:

BIRTH CONTROL

see also

VASECTOMY
CONDOMS BIRTH CONTROL
CONTRACEPTIVE FOAMS AND JELLIES
BAO CAO SU NGUOI THUA
BOT NGUA THAI
SANJI SEIGEN
KAN KHOOM KAM NURD
KAN HEAD MAN KHONG PHOUSAI

or this:

SHOSETSU NIHON BUNGAKU 20 SEIKI

see also

FUKAKAI SHOSETSU NIHONGO
NIHON BUNGAKU RENAI SHOSETSU
SF SHOSETSU NIHON BUNGAKU
SHOJO SHOSETSU
SHOJO SHOSETSU NIHONGO

THE MULTILINGUAL ACCESS CONCEPT

Thus the multilingual access concept was formulated and applied to all bibliographic records representing titles in the Asian Model Library.

As a working technique, the concept dictated that English language subject headings be translated into vernacular equivalents and both the English and non-English headings be assigned to the bibliographic record. All such pairings of headings were linked in the subject catalog using conventional "see" and "see also" techniques. In fact, physical descriptions, bibliographic notes, referral notes, informational notes—all of these were formulated bilingually or multilingually as the situation required.

The result of this work is a linguistically multi-layered catalog where subject access points are accessed online irrespective of the user's primary language orientation.

GETTING STARTED

Early in the project, it became obvious that little precedent was available to assist in realizing the goals mentioned earlier. Nevertheless, each goal was achieved. But only through application of a finely tuned balance between the intelligent use of people and peoples' intelligent use of their machines. Among the more important people in this respect were the members of the translation staff.

As expected, it was frustratingly difficult and time-consuming to locate and hire translators capable of performing complex romanization work. Endless telephone calls to state, local, federal, civic, educational and religious institutions and agencies finally resulted in the hiring of ten translators: Vietnamese, Chinese, Lao, Hmong, Japanese, and Thai. Professionally, this staff was intriguing: 2 librarians, 1 systems analyst, 1 pharmacist, 1 university professor, 1 bilingual educator, 1 school bus mechanic, 1 restaurateur, 2 university students. An altogether fascinating mixture of ethnic heritage, attitude, language, and cultural sensitivity. They were, without exception, creative, resourceful, dedicated people demonstrably sensitive to the importance of the work they performed. Despite their own busy professional schedules, they made themselves available, frequently on weekends and during evenings.

Prior to assembling this group, there had been concern about the implications of placing people in a technical services environment quite mystifying to the great uninitiated. Of particular concern was the level of meaningful communication vital for their understanding of the "raison d'être" of unfamiliar bibliographic practices in a cataloging environment.

It seemed best to design a generic and unimposing worksheet for the collection of raw cataloging data prior to automated systems input (see Figure 1). This technique worked quite well. And to our delight, it was found that some of these folks really loved to write. And write. And write. At some point, then, the translator and supervisor would review the worksheet and discuss its content (this was always interesting), whereafter the supervisor would formulate the appropriate cataloging record. Later on, members of the translation staff provided indispensable assistance in data entry.

The staff was superlative in calling to attention matters related to nuances in meaning, modes of expression, semantic esoterica, cultural pluralities, difficulties inherent in romanized vocabulary, unfamiliar bibliographic practices, and countless other matters.

FIGURE 1. Worksheet for Asian Materials

WORKSHEET FOR ASIAN MATERIALS

| | FOR TS USE |

Is the item on hand (check one):

☐ Book or pamphlet   ☐ Other (map, tape, etc.)

Language(s) of item: _____

Dialect(s): __ _____

If the item is bilingual or in more than two languages
indicate languages: _____

_____

_____

FOR TS USE

Tag _____ Status _____ Quantity _____

Pub. date _____ Class _____

Vendor _____ P. O. _____ Pub. _____

Price _____ LCISBN _____

Title _____

_____

Location/accession _____

_____

A. TITLE INFORMATION

Please check if you've romanized the title ☐

Control Number _____

Title of item in language of title page: (if title is romanized, enter romanized title)

_____

_____

_____

Subtitle of item in language of title page:

_____

_____

English translation of title:

_____

_____

English translation of subtitle:

_____

_____

If you have not transcribed title from title
page, please check the appropriate box or boxes:

Is there additional title information which is
important? (volume numbers, added titles, series
or volume set titles, etc.)

☐ Title taken from cover
☐ Title taken from spine of book
☐ Title taken from label or container
☐ Other _____

_____

_____

_____

_____

ADDITIONAL TITLE INFORMATION

_____

_____

_____

_____

FIGURE 1 (continued)

SUBJECT HEADING DATA

ENGLISH HEADINGS   TRANSLATION

1. _____   1. _____

2. _____   2. _____

3. _____   3. _____

CROSS REFERENCE DATA

ENGLISH   TRANSLATION

_____   _____

_____   _____

_____   _____

C. OTHER INFORMATION

Is this item (check one)   ☐ Fiction   ☐ Non Fiction

Briefly describe the subject or content of the item:

_____

_____

_____

_____

_____

_____

_____

Age group most likely to use the item or for whom you think the item is intended:

☐ Adults
☐ Young adults
☐ Children
☐ Adults and children
☐ Other _____

If you can determine this item should be a reference item, check here ☐

Looking through the item can you determine when this item was printed or published?

Printed or published _____
Copyrighted _____
Other _____
☐ Cannot tell

Is there any other information about this item that you think is important?

_____

_____

_____

_____

FIGURE 1 (continued)

B. AUTHOR INFORMATION

Indicate the principal author of the text: Check one: ☐Male   ☐Female
Surname (last name)   Forename (first name)   Middle Name

① _____   _____   _____

Family name _____   How would this person be addressed in his or her native land:
Patronymic _____   _____
Given name _____   _____

Does this name include terms of address, titles of   Term of address _____
honor, or titles of nobility?   Term of nobility _____
       ☐ yes   ☐ no   Title of honor _____
                                                          Other _____

If there are additional authors on the title page, or if you can determine there are other persons responsible for the item,
enter the name(s) below and check the appropriate box(es):

② _____   _____   _____

☐Co-author   Additional information about the person or his/her name:
☐Editor
☐Compiler   _____
☐Translator   _____
☐Illustrator   _____
☐Photographer

③ _____   _____   _____

☐Co-author   Additional information about the person or his/her name:
☐Editor
☐Compiler   _____
☐Translator   _____
☐Illustrator   _____
☐Photographer

④ _____   _____   _____

☐Co-author   Additional information about the person or his/her name:
☐Editor
☐Compiler   _____
☐Translator   _____
☐Illustrator   _____
☐Photographer

If an institution, publisher or similar entity is responsible for the item, enter that name(s) here:

_____

_____

Any additional information:

_____

_____

_____

ADDITIONAL AUTHOR INFORMATION

_____

_____

_____

_____

Throughout the 1,356 hours of translation work, each of them was keenly aware that the success of our joint labors depended on the level of meaningful mutual understanding that was attained.

And it must be added that the JCPL Technical Services staff was equally creative and industrious in its collective resolve to meet the unusual demands of the Asian project.

From the experiences of all involved, it was apparent that public libraries remain pivotal centers for social responsiveness, and always and only in direct proportion to the dedication of those working in them.

MULTILINGUAL AUTHORITY CONTROL

Successful application of multilingual access techniques is inextricably tied to rigorous authority control practices. Authority control in Asian languages involves considerably more than accepted notions of author, series and subject heading integrity. It bears directly on the form, quality and meaning of transliterated data. The exigencies of polycultural semantics in translation demand extraordinary attentiveness to consistency in word order, word division, and word meaning.

Thus it was necessary to build thirty-four online authority files. These files contain subject and subject reference records, personal and corporate name records with references, and commonly used bibliographic note data. The latter were created to ensure consistent transliteration of frequently assigned bibliographic notes. In total, the files are a significant accomplishment, since they form the basis for the successful completion of future Asian cataloging in JCPL.[12]

MULTILINGUAL SUBJECT AUTHORITY FILES

A simple format was adopted for online retrieval of subject authority records—one that forgives the inability to read, write or speak any and all Asian languages. Figure 2 illustrates the basic format and specific data content of each file. Figure 3 shows representative "live" data.

Collocating individual records by language tags provided efficient retrieval of a needed heading. In the files containing strictly bilingual data, accessing the desired heading was simplified by placing

FIGURE 2. Asian Language Authority File Language Tags and Data Content

LANGUAGE TAG	FILE CONTENTS
CHINESE PIN-YIN	English heading; Pin-yin translation
CHINESE PIN-YIN BIB	English bibliographic note; Pin-yin translation
CHINESE SEE ALSO PIN-YIN	Pin-yin heading "SEE ALSO" Pin-yin heading
CHINESE SEE ALSO WADE	Wade-Giles heading "SEE ALSO" Wade-Giles heading
CHINESE SEE REF PIN	Pin-yin heading "SEE" Pin-yin heading
CHINESE SEE REF WADE	Wade-Giles heading "SEE" Wade-Giles heading
CHINESE WADE	English heading; Wade-Giles translation
CHINESE WADE BIB	English bibliographic note; Wade-Giles trans
HMONG	English heading; Hmong translation
HMONG BIB	English bibliographic note; Hmong translation
HMONG SEE ALSO REFS	Hmong heading "SEE ALSO" Hmong heading
JAPANESE	English heading; Japanese translation
JAPANESE BIB	English bibliographic note; Japanese translation
JAPANESE SEE ALSO REFS	Japanese heading "SEE ALSO" Japanese heading
KOREAN	English heading; Korean translation
KOREAN BIB	English bibliographic note; Korean translation
KOREAN SEE ALSO REFS	Korean heading "SEE ALSO" Korean heading
LAO	English heading; Lao translation
LAO BIB	English bibliographic note; Lao translation
LAO SEE ALSO REFS	Lao heading "SEE ALSO" Lao heading
THAI	English heading; Thai translation
THAI BIB	English bibliographic note; Thai translation
THAI SEE ALSO REFS	Thai heading "SEE ALSO" Thai heading
VIET	English heading; Vietnamese translation
VIET BIB	English bib note; Vietnamese translation
VIET SEE ALSO REFS	Vietnamese heading "SEE ALSO" Viet heading

the English heading ahead of the translated equivalent. The files containing monolingual cross-reference data were used in the construction of romanized vernacular cross-references. These vernacular to vernacular cross-references were created late in the project, after the basic English-vernacular vocabularies were completed.

The use of dual romanizations as shown in the Chinese files deserves special comment. In the absence of international agreement to embrace either Pin-Yin or Wade-Giles but not both (though endorsement and acceptance of both schemes is what has occurred), it seemed reasonable to offer catalog users a similar parallel choice. This was further justified by the capabilities of JCPL automated sys-

FIGURE 3. Representative Authority File Records

CHINESE PINYIN ; JOKES JAPANESE TRANSLATIONS INTO CHINESE: XIAOHUA RIBEN ZHONGWEN BEN

CHINESE PINYIN ; LITERATURE CHINESE HISTORY AND CRITICISM: WENXUE ZHONGGUO LISHI YU PIPING

CHINESE SEE ALSO PINYIN ; QIKAN ZHONGGUO; SA: ZHONGGUO RENMIN GONGHEGUO 1949- QIKAN ZHONGGUO

CHINESE SEE ALSO PINYIN ; QIKAN ZHONGGUO; SA: DAXUESHENG QIKAN

CHINESE SEE ALSO WADE ; QIKAN ZHONGGUO; SA: CHUNG HUA JEN MIN KUNG HE KUO 1949- CHI KAN CHUNG KUO

CHINESE WADE ; LITERATURE CHINESE 20TH CENTURY: WEN HSUEH CHUNG KUO ERH SHIH SHIH CHI

CHINESE WADE ; LITERATURE CHINESE 220-265 THREE KINGDOMS: WEN HSUEH CHUNG KUO 220-265 SAN KUO

JAPANESE ; PHILOSOPHY COMPARATIVE: HIKAKU TETSUGAKU

JAPANESE ; PHILOSOPHY JAPANESE 18TH CENTURY: TETSUGAKU NIHON 18 SEIKI

JAPANESE SEE ALSO REFS ; NIHON YUMOA; SA: WARAIBANASHI NIHON BUNGAKU

KOREAN ; KOREA 1592-1598 JAPANESE INVASIONS HISTORY: HANKOOK YUKSA 1592-1598 IM JIN WOI RAN

KOREAN SEE ALSO REFS ; BUCHU WA BULGYO; SA: BULGYO CHAK

LAO ; MEDICINE TERMINOLOGY FOR LAO SPEAKERS: KHAM SUB DAN KAN PED HAI KHOOM LAO

LAO BIB ; 'TEXT IN ENGLISH AND LAO': PEUM ANGKID LET LAO

LAO SEE ALSO REFS ; KAN KHOOM KAM NURD; SA: I U D

THAI ; THAILAND DESCRIPTION AND TRAVEL: KAN BUNYAI LAE TONGTEW THAI

THAI ; THAILAND HISTORY 1782-1945: PRAWATSAT THAI 2325-2588
THAI SEE ALSO REFS ; WONNAKADE THAI SA MAI PAJUBUN; SA: NIYAI THAI SA MAI PAJUBUN

VIET ; BILINGUAL MATERIALS ENGLISH VIETNAMESE VIDEO TAPES 1/2 INCH: BANG THINH THI 1/2 INCH SONG NGU ANH VIET

VIET ; BILINGUAL MATERIALS ENGLISH VIETNAMESE: SACH HAI THU TIENG ANH VIET

VIET SEE ALSO REFS ; TRUYEN TUONG TUONG TIENG VIET; SA: TRUYEN TINH CAM TIENG VIET

VIET SEE ALSO REFS ; TRUYEN TUONG TUONG TIENG VIET; SA: TRUYEN TUONG TUONG TIENG VIET THE KY 20

tems and, on a slightly more human level, by the fact that Pin-Yin romanizations are still relatively new and consequently a bit unfamiliar in this country. Although this decision added yet another tier of complexity to the handling of Chinese records, it was not an insurmountable problem since it became, in the case of subject descriptors, largely a matter of linking English headings to bi-romanized pairs of Chinese equivalents. Title entries, series entries, and author entries however, were referenced to the Wade-Giles romanization from their Pin-Yin counterparts.

Biromanizations are perfectly in harmony with the cataloging philosophy of providing users with what they reasonably might need, rather than merely what cataloging tradition dictates or, worse, automated systems mandate.

MULTILINGUAL CROSS-REFERENCES

Headings in the authority files were also used to generate a variety of cross-references. Two fundamental types are illustrated in Figure 4. Since "Type A" reflects actual usage as applied in the Asian Model Library Catalogs, it will be analyzed in detail.

Type A—English "See Also" Romanized Vernacular

This usage permits maximum staff flexibility in entering a file on behalf of a patron. Depending on a library's requirements, this may or may not be a useful technique. In either case, it has proven useful and cost-effective in the Asian Model Library Catalogs and the JEFFCAT data base. Two initial observations should be made. Since vernacular heading "A_v" represents an actual access point in the subject file, ethnic patrons may search primarily by the natural language form of any subject heading. The second point involves the creation of the subject portion of the bibliographic record. Vernacular heading "A_v" is a viable access point only when both English heading "A_e" *and* vernacular heading "A_v" are assigned to the bibliographic record at the point of subject cataloging. The result may be seen in Figure 5.

The basic syndetic infrastructure supporting subject headings, as illustrated in Figure 5, is stylized in Figure 6.

In the Asian Subject Catalog, the central subject and reference

FIGURE 4. Multilingual Cross-Reference Types

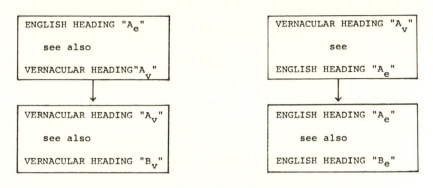

TYPE A
TYPE B

FIGURE 5. Bibliographic Records

*SIAMESE THEATRE A COLLECTION OF REPRINTS FROM THE JOURNALS OF THE SIAM SOCIETY
ASIAN MODEL LIBRARY
AUTHOR: PUBLISHER: SIAM SOCIETY
  MATTANI RUTNIN
  JOURNALS OF THE SIAM SOCIETY

              1975S   CLASSIFICATION: SP   792.09593
SUBJECTS:
  THEATRE THAILAND
LOCATIONS: VILLA

*SIANG KONG PRACHACHON   ASIAN MODEL LIBRARY
  AUTHOR: $.75 PUBLISHER: SANGRUNG
  RUANGYOD JUNTARAKERE

              1980S   CLASSIFICATION: SP   808.831 THAI
SUBJECTS:
  FICTION THAI 20TH CENTURY TRANSLATIONS FROM INDONESIAN
  FICTION INDONESIAN 20TH CENTURY TRANSLATIONS INTO THAI
  THAI LANGUAGE MATERIALS FICTION
  SHORT STORIES INDONESIAN 20TH CENTURY TRANSLATIONS INTO THAI
  SHORT STORIES THAI 20TH CENTURY TRANSLATIONS FROM INDONESIAN
  NIYAI THAI SA MAI PAJUBUN PLAE JAK INDONISIA
  NIYAI INDONISIA SA MAI PAJUBUN PLAE PHEN THAI
  NIYAI PA SA THAI
  RAUM RUANG SUNT INDONISIA SA MAI PAJUBUN PLAE PHEN THAI
  RUAM RUANG SUNT THAI SA MAI PAJUBUN PLAE JAK INDONISIA
LOCATIONS: VILLA
NOTES:
  THAI TRANSLATIONS OF SHORT STORIES ORIGINALLY WRITTEN IN UN-
  IDENTIFIED BAHASA INDONESIAN DIALECTS.
  RUANG SUNT PLAE PHEN THAI, TON CHABAB KIEN DOY.
  BUKON MIDI KLOW CHU, BOT KONG INDONESIA.

FIGURE 5 (continued)

```
*SIED ISAN      ASIAN MODEL LIBRARY
   AUTHOR:                              $.50
      VASUM AKARADEJ                    PUBLISHER: JARERNVIT

               1979S   CLASSIFICATION: SP   FICTION THAI
   SUBJECTS:
      FICTION THAI 20TH CENTURY
      THAI LANGUAGE MATERIALS FICTION
      NIYAI THAI SA MAI PAJUBUN
      NIYAI PA SA THAI
   LOCATIONS: VILLA

*SIKERIYA SONG LEMJOB   ASIAN MODEL LIBRARY
   AUTHOR:                              $7.50
      SOPARK SUWOM                      PUBLISHER: AMORNKAANPIM

               1977S   CLASSIFICATION:   FICTION THAI
   SUBJECTS:
      FICTION THAI 20TH CENTURY
      THAI LANGUAGE MATERIALS
      NIYAI THAI SA MAI PAJUBUN
      HNANG SU PA SA THAI
   LOCATIONS:  VILLA
   HOLDINGS:
      V 1          VILLA
      V 2          VILLA
```

structure in Figure 6 never actually occurs to the extent illustrated. Three translations of heading "A_e" was the maximum incidence of intermixed translations referenced from a mutually common English equivalent (counting both Chinese romanizations as one translation). The bibliographic coincidence leading to this phenomenon involved such headings as BIRTH CONTROL, WORLD WAR II 1939-1945 and BILINGUAL MATERIALS. Thus, the English-vernacular format in Figure 6 represents the maximum potential typification.

Bilingual or multilingual subject access points paired with English language headings using "see also" techniques facilitate staff entry into a non-English subject file without disruption of the English to English syndetic chain necessary for the support of a monolingual English language search. Therefore, if staff members at the Mesa County Public Library (Grand Junction, Colo.) want to search the file to determine if the Asian Model Library holds a Korean title dealing with traditional Korean folk art, the "correct" language search may be easily achieved in a framework of bilingual parity.

FIGURE 6. REFERENCE SPECIES 1: ENGLISH–MULTILINGUAL–MULTIROMANIZED HEADINGS AND INFRASTRUCTURE

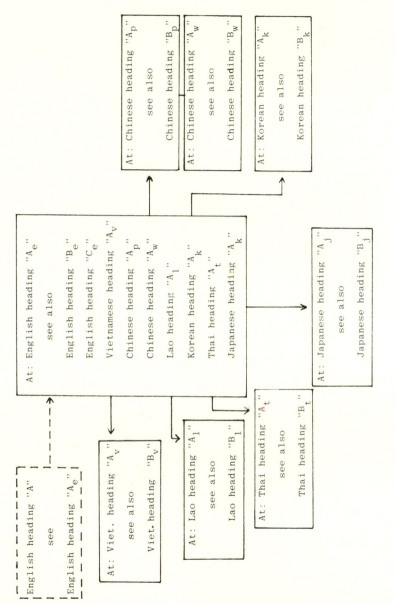

Note: All vernacular headings may have "see froms"

Vernacular romanized headings, scattered in alpha sequence throughout the subject file, facilitate direct ethnic patron entry into a non-English file at any one of the vernacular subject access points.

This produces a linguistically multilayered file where all entries are in alpha sequence and language-specific entry is fostered irrespective of the user's primary language orientation. Note that this in no way implies that heading "A_e" must be translated into every language in the catalog. Rather, it is necessary only to translate the heading into the language(s) of the text in hand, create the English to vernacular link, assign both or all headings to the bibliographic record and thereby achieve multilingual subject access. Obviously, when it is necessary to translate heading "A_e" into several languages, it is unnecessary to create "see also" links between each of the translated headings themselves.

Figure 7 shows two typical bilingual cataloging records for Chinese-language monographs and serials. The reference structure undergirding the biromanized subject headings posed a slightly different form of referencing problem. It was undesirable to intermix the two species of romanizations in the manner indicated below:

CHINESE HEADING "A_p"   CHINESE HEADING "A_w"

   see also   or,   see also

CHINESE HEADING "A_w"   CHINESE HEADING "A_p"

And since both Pin-Yin and Wade-Giles form subject headings were assigned to cataloging records, the format illustrated below was not considered to be a viable option:

CHINESE HEADING "A_p"   CHINESE HEADING "A_w"

   see   or,   see

CHINESE HEADING "A_w"   CHINESE HEADING "A_p"

The better solution seemed to be creation of unique but parallel syndetic chains for both species of romanizations. Thus, the only situation where dual level Chinese romanizations commingled was at the reference from their mutually common English language counterpart.

This format is illustrated in Figure 8. An actual string of dual

FIGURE 7. English-Chinese Bibliographic Records

*KU TIEN HSIAO SHO SAN LUN CHUN WEN HSUEH TSUNG SHU 73
ASIAN MODEL LIBRARY
AUTHOR: $2.30
LO, HENG CHUN   PUBLISHER: PRESS PURE LIT

    1976S   CLASSIFICATION: SP   895.131   CHINESE
SUBJECTS:
HAN YU TZU LIAO HSIAO SHO
HANYU ZILIAO XIAOSHUO
HAN YU TZU LIAO
HANYU ZILIAO
CHINESE LANGUAGE MATERIALS FICTION
CHINESE LANGUAGE MATERIALS
MYTHOLOGY CHINESE
HSIAO HSIAO SHENG THE GOLDEN LOTUS
FICTION CHINESE HISTORY AND CRITICISM
TSAO HSUEH CHIN CA 1717-1763 DREAM OF THE RED CHAMBER
LITERATURE CHINESE HISTORY AND CRITICISM
WENXUE ZHONGGUO LISHI YU PIPING
HSIAO HSIAO SHENG CHIN PING MEI TZU HUA
XIAO XIAOSHENG JIN BING MEI ZUHUA
HSIAO SHO CHUNG KUO LI SHIH YU PI PING
XIAOSHUO ZHONGGUO LISHI YU PIBING
TSAO HSUEH CHIN YUEH 1717-1763 HUNG LOU MENG
CAO XUEQIN YUE 1717-1763 HONG LOU MENG
WEN HSEUH CHUNG KUO LI SHIH YU PI PING
SHEN HUA CHUNG KUO
SHENHUA ZHONGGUO
LOCATIONS: VILLA
NOTES:
SUMMARY: A GENERAL DISCUSSION ON CHINESE MYTHOLOGY; IMAGES
          AS TRAGIC HEROES IN ANCIENT CHINA; AND CRITICISM OF
          SEVERAL CLASSICAL CHINESE NOVELS INCLUDING 'A
          STORY OF THE WATERSIDE', 'THE GOLDEN LOTUS', AND
          'THE DREAM OF THE RED CHAMBER'.
TIYAO PINYIN: ZHONGGUO SHENHUA TAOLUN. BAOKUO GUDAI ZHONG-
          GUO BEIJU YINXIONG, 'SHUIFU ZHUAN', 'JINGPINGMEI',
          'HONGLOUMENG' DENG ZUOPIN PINGLUN.
TI YAO WADE: CHUNG-KUO SHEN HUO TAO LUN. PAO KUO KU TAI
          CHUNG-KUO PEI CHU YING HSIUNG, 'SHUI FU CHUAN',
          'CHING PING MEI', 'HUNG LOU MENG', TENG TSO PIN
          PING LUN.

*KUANG HUA SINORAMA   ASIAN MODEL LIBRARY
                        $1.00
                        PUBLISHER: SINORAMA

    1978-   CLASSIFICATION: SP P   059 CHINESE
SUBJECTS:
CHI KAN CHUNG KUO
QIKAN ZHONGGUO
PERIODICALS CHINESE
HAN YU TZU LIAO
HANYU ZILIAO
CHINESE LANGUAGE MATERIALS

FIGURE 7 (continued)

LOCATIONS: VILLA
NOTES:
A MONTHLY MAGAZINE INTRODUCING LIFE AND POLITICS IN TAIWAN.
MOST ARTICLES HAVE BRIEF ENGLISH TRANSLATIONS FOLLOWING THE
CHINESE TEXT. LIBRARY HAS AVAILABLE VARIOUS ISSUES OF 'SINO-
RAMA'. PLEASE ASK FOR ASSISTANCE SHOULD YOU REQUIRE IT.
PINYIN: YUEKAN NEIRONG BAOKUO TAIWAN DE ZHENGZHI YU SHENG-
HUO, ZHONGGUO DE WENHUA YU CHUANTONG DENG. FU YINGWEN
GAIYAO. BEN TUSHUGUAN JUYOU GE QI ZAZHI GUANGHUA, XUYAO ZHE
QING WEN GUANLIYUAN.
WADE-GILES: YUEH CAN NEI JUNG PAO KUO TAI-WAN TE CHENG CHIH YU
SHENG HUO, CHUNG-KUO TE WEN HUA YU CHUAN TUNG TENG. FU YING
WEN KAI YAO. PEN TU SHU KUAN CHU YU KE CHI TSA CHIH 'KUANG
HUA', HSU YAO CHE CHING WEN KUAN LI YUEN.
MIN CHUEH FA YU MO KAN. CHE HSIEH HSIAO HUA SHO MING JIHPEN JEN
MIN CHU YU YU MO KAN. TUNG KUO HSIAO HUA TSUI YI LIAO CHIEH MOU
KUO JEN MIN TE HSIN LI.

level romanizations for the heading CHINESE LANGUAGE
MATERIALS is illustrated in Figure 9.

Type B—Romanized Vernacular "See" English Heading

This usage, while allowing direct access to a non-English heading
by a non-English patron (a "first hit"), also automatically forces a
double search in the subject file. This is usually undesirable and may
be quite discouraging if not realistically impossible for a patron
searching in a very large hardcopy subject catalog. A patron "hits"
vernacular heading "A_v" and no doubt is delighted. Until she/he
sees the reference. Knowing they are searching for a title with non-
English text, they understandably might interpret the reference as
what might be termed a "rude reference." It positively shouts at
them: "You should have realized that a martial arts title bearing a
Saigon imprint with text completely in quôc-ngữ would be assigned
an English language subject heading. This is sensible because that's
what our systems dictate." And therein lies another problem—accessing non-English items through English subject headings, an undesirable (but usually necessary) form of bibliographic jingoism
(see Figure 10).

If in fact we are serious about multilingual subject access, we had
better lobby mightily for an *ascriptive* cataloging rule that mandates

FIGURE 8. REFERENCE SPECIES 2: ENGLISH–BILINGUAL–BIROMANIZED CHINESE HEADING AND INFRASTRUCTURE

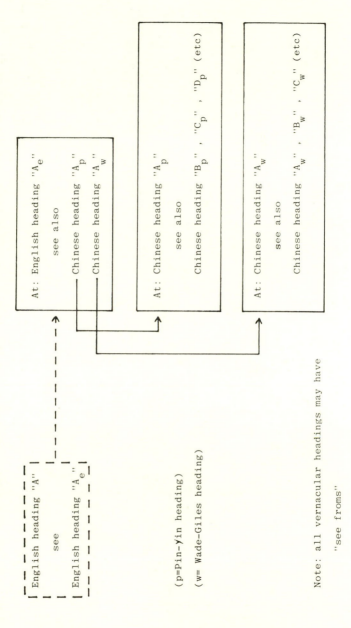

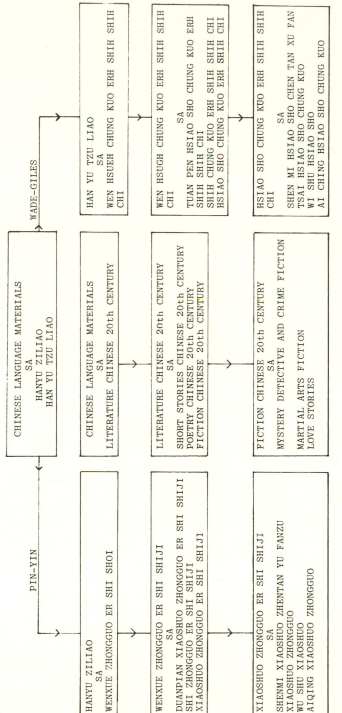

FIGURE 9. A partial syndetic branch of a bilingual biromanized subject heading infrastructure. Other subject headings in Fig. 7 have similar infrastructures.

FIGURE 10. English subject headings

```
*TRANG QUYNH      ASIAN MODEL LIBRARY
   AUTHOR:                              $4.00
   HOANG TRUC LY, 1933-                 PUBLISHER: SONG MOI
      1978?    CLASSIFICATION: SP        895.9227    VIETNAMESE
   SUBJECTS:
   HUMOROUS TALES VIETNAMESE
   HUMOROUS STORIES VIETNAMESE
   WIT AND HUMOR VIETNAMESE
   VIETNAMESE LANGUAGE MATERIALS
   LOCATIONS: VILLA
   NOTES: TEXT IN VIETNAMESE.
```

the assignment and linkage of subjects and references in the language(s) of the dominant user group. In Rush's words:

> If there are no rules concerned mainly with access, there ought to be. I believe it is just such a lack of focus on access that has caused the discipline of cataloging to become less and less well regarded, and to be increasingly derided by those who have studied in depth the concepts of communication and information transfer.[13]

Bilingual or multilingual subject analysis of this type is difficult on the local level (see Figures 11-13). But when it can be done, it should be. The realities of social pluralism demand an equally pluralistic response from librarians. Berman encapsulated the essence of the idea nicely when he wrote:

> . . .Libraries may go to much trouble and expense in picking, buying, processing, and publicizing ethnic materials, but if they don't also go to a little expense in cataloging them, the whole investment is wasted. Put in positive terms: If the stuff is worth getting, it's surely worth being handled with respect— and in such a way that people can find it.[14]

CONCLUSION

As more and more library bibliographic data become accessible online, every viable opportunity should be taken to overcome the negative aspects of romanization. Even if a library cannot currently justify online original script access because of related costs. . . that library should prepare for the time when those costs are reduced. This preparation can be accomplished by inputting romanized data into existing online systems. . . Input of romanized data now will also have immediate benefits because of the improved access offered by online systems.[15]

FIGURE 11. English-Japanese Bibliographic Records

*SEISHO NIHONGO 1955 NEN KAIYAKU   ASIAN MODEL LIBRARY
                                    PUBLISHER: JAPAN BIBLE SOC
            1955S CLASSIFICATION: SP 220.5956 JAPANESE

SUBJECTS:
  BIBLE JAPANESE AUTHORIZED 1955
  SEISHO NIHONGO 1955 NEN KAIYAKU
  NIHONGO SHOSEKI
  JAPANESE LANGUAGE MATERIALS
LOCATIONS: VILLA

*SEISHO NIHONGO 1979 NEN BAN   ASIAN MODEL LIBRARY
                                PUBLISHER: JAPAN BIBLE SOC
            1979S CLASSIFICATION: SP 220.5956 JAPANESE
SUBJECTS:
  BIBLE JAPANESE AUTHORIZED 1979
  SEISHO NIHONGO 1979 NEN BAN
  NIHONGO SHOSEKI
  JAPANESE LANGUAGE MATERIALS
LOCATIONS: VILLA

*SEIZON HOSOKURON NIHON MINZOKU NO SEKAI KAN ZEN 2 KAN ASIAN
MODEL LIBRARY
AUTHOR: PUBLISHER: SOGO BUNKA KYOT
  TOMATSU, KEIGI
            1960S CLASSIFICATION: SP 895.61 JAPANESE

SUBJECTS:
  SEIJIGAKU TETSUGAKU
  POLITICAL SCIENCE PHILOSOPHY
  SEKAI KAN
  WELTANNSCHAUNNG
  HIKAKU TETSUGAKU
  PHILOSOPHY COMPARATIVE
  TETSUGAKU NIHON
  PHILOSOPHY JAPANESE
  BUNGAKU NIHON 794 NEN IZEN
  LITERATURE JAPANESE 794 AND EARLIER
  MYTHOLOGY JAPANESE
  SHINWA NIHON
  NIHONGO SHOSEKI
  JAPANESE LANGUAGE MATERIALS
LOCATIONS: VILLA
HOLDINGS:
  V 1   VILLA
  V 2   VILLA

FIGURE 11 (continued)

NOTES:
VOLUME 1: KOJIKI HEN
VOLUME 2: SHISO HEN
SUMMARY: THIS 2 VOLUME WORK DEALS WITH COMPARATIVE PHIL-
OSOPHY OF 'RAISON D'ETRE'. VOLUME 1 ASSOCIATES 'WEL-
TANSCHAUUNG' OF JAPANESE WITH 'KOJIKI'. VOLUME 2
DISCUSSES PHILOSOPHY AS RELATED TO NATURAL AND PO-
LITICAL SCIENCES. VOLUME 2 ALSO CONTAINS COMPAR-
ATIVE STUDIES OF ORIENTAL AND EUROPEAN THOUGHT.
'KOJIKI', WHICH APPEARED IN THE 7TH CENTURY, IS THE
EARLIEST KNOWN LITERARY WORK WRITTEN IN THE JAPAN-
ESE LANGUAGE. IT CONSISTS OF 3 PARTS: MYTHOLOGY,
LEGENDS, AND HISTORY. TOMATSU FREELY DISCUSSES
THIS MYTHOLOGICAL SECTION. OTHER SECTIONS OF 'KO-
JIKI' ARE NOT INCLUDED IN THE PRESENT WORK. THE
AUTHOR SUPPORTS ARNOLD TOYNBEE'S DOGMA THAT THE
RACE WHO IS IGNORANT OF ITS OWN CLASSICS DIES OUT.
HENCE HE DEPLORES JAPANESE STUDENTS NOT EDUCATED
IN JAPANESE CLASSICS.
DAI 1 KAN: KOJIKI HEN
DAI 2 KAN: SHISO HEN
GAIYO: KONO 2 SATSU WA 'SONZAI RIYU' NO HIKAKU TETSUGAKU
NI KANSURU SHOMOTSU DE ARI, DAI 1 KAN WA 'KOJIKI' NI
YORU NIHONJIN NO SEKAIKAN O, DAI 2 KAN WA TETSUGAKU
O SHIZEN KAGAKU, SEIJIGAKU NI KANREN SASETE NO TOZAI
HIKATSU TETSUGAKU O NOBERU. 7 SEIKI NI SHIRUSARETA
'KOJIKI' WA NIHONGO DE KAKARETA BUNGAKU TO SHITE
WA MOTTOMO FURUKU, 3 BU (SHINWA, ITSUWA, REKISHI)
YORI NARU. HISSHA WA KONO SHINWA NO BUBUN O TORIA-
GETE CHUYAKU YA KOSATSU O JIYU NI KUWAETE IRU GA,
'KOJIKI' NO HOKA NO BUBUN WA KONO HON NIWA FUKUM-
ARETE INAI. HISSHA WA ANORUDO TOINBI NO 'KOTEN O SHI-
RANU MINZOKU WA SHINITAERU' TO IU SETSU O TSUYOKU
SHIJI SURU.

FIGURE 12. English-Lao Bibliographic Record

*GUIDE TO TEACHING THE LAO AND ENGLISH LAO STUDENT RESOURCE
BOOK   ASIAN MODEL LIBRARY
AUTHOR: PUBLISHER: APPLE INC
MURPHY, RICHARD P
HEARTLAND EDUCATION AGENCY
            1976S CLASSIFICATION: SP 371.1 LAO

SUBJECTS:
PEUM KHOU MEU LAO AMERICAN
PEUM KHOU MEU HAI NAI KHOU SONE ANGKID HAI KHOON LAO
PEUM KHOU MEU HAI KHOON LAO
PHASA ANGKID THEE PEEN PHASA THEE SONG HAI KHOON LAO
ENGLISH AS A SECOND LANGUAGE INSTRUCTION FOR LAO SPEAKERS
LAOTIAN AMERICANS HANDBOOKS MANUALS ETC
REFUGEES LAOTIAN HANDBOOKS MANUALS ETC
TEACHERS OF LAOTIAN REFUGEES HANDBOOKS MANUALS ETC

FIGURE 12 (continued)

LOCATIONS: VILLA
NOTES:
  KIT CONTAINS: 1 GUIDE TO TEACHING THE LAO, 1 ENGLISH LAO STU-
               DENT RESOURCE BOOK, 5 TAPE CASSETTES
  TAPE CASSETTES: SIDE 1: COUNTING AND MATH FORMULAS
              SIDE 2: MATH VOCABULARY AND MULTIPLICATION
              SIDE 3: SCHOOL
              SIDE 4: PRONOUNS
              SIDE 5: THE BODY
              SIDE 6: HEALTH
              SIDE 7: TIME, DAYS, MONTHS
              SIDE 8: SEASONS, HOLIDAYS
              SIDE 9: FORMS, USEFUL EXPRESSIONS
              SIDE 10: COLORS, FAMILY
  KHEUANG BANCHOU: 1 PEUM KAN NAMPHA KAN SONE NUK HIEN LAO,
                    1 PEUM SUBPHAYAKONE ANGKID HAI NUK HIEN
                    LAO, PHANE XIENG 5 PHANE.
  TAPE CASSETTES: SIDE 1: KAN NUB LAKE LEI BANGSOUP
              SIDE 2: KHAMSUB LAKE LEI KAN KHOON LAKE
              SIDE 3: HONGHIEN
              SIDE 4: KHAM SUBPHANAM
              SIDE 5: HANGKAI
              SIDE 6: SUKHAPHAB
              SIDE 7: VEILA, MEU, DEUAN
              SIDE 8: RADOU, MEUPHUK
              SIDE 9: HOUPHANG, KHOUAM WAO THEE ME KHOON-
                    KHA
              SIDE 10: SEE, KHOBKHOUA

FIGURE 13. English-Vietnamese Bibliographic Records

*NGUOI VO MAT TICH   ASIAN MODEL LIBRARY
  AUTHOR: $5.95
  HOANG HAI THUY   PUBLISHER: CHIEU DUONG
      1970S CLASSIFICATION: SP M FICTION VIETNAMESE

SUBJECTS:
  MYSTERY DETECTIVE AND CRIME FICTION VIETNAMESE
  FICTION VIETNAMESE 20TH CENTURY
  VIETNAMESE LANGUAGE MATERIALS FICTION
  TIEU THUYET AN MANG TIENG VIET
  TRUYEN TUONG TUONG TIENG VIET THE KY 20
  TRUYEN TUONG TUONG TIENG VIET
LOCATIONS: VILLA

*NHA THAM TU CO DON TIEU THUYET DEN   ASIAN MODEL LIBRARY
  AUTHOR: $7.50
  NGUOI THU TAM   PUBLISHER: XUAN THU
      1980? CLASSIFICATION: SP   FICTION VIETNAMESE

SUBJECTS:
  Z28 NHAN VAT TUONG TUONG
  Z28 FICTIONAL CHARACTER

FIGURE 13 (continued)

TRUYEN GIAN DIEP TUONG TUONG TIENG VIET
ESPIONAGE AND INTRIGUE FICTION VIETNAMESE
TRUYEN TUONG TUONG TIENG VIET THE KY 20
FICTION VIETNAMESE 20TH CENTURY
TRUYEN TUONG TUONG TIENG VIET
VIETNAMESE LANGUAGE MATERIALS FICTION
LOCATIONS: VILLA

*NHU BONG MAY TROI NGUYEN TAC THE VAN PHI   ASIAN MODEL LIBRARY
AUTHOR: $6.50
    QUYNH DAO   PUBLISHER: TINH HOA MIEN
    TRONG NGUYEN
        1980?   CLASSIFICATION: SP   FICTION   VIETNAMESE
SUBJECTS:
    TRUYEN TINH CAM TIENG VIET THE KY 20 DICH TU TIENG TRUNG HOA
    LOVE STORIES VIETNAMESE 20TH CENTURY TRANSLATIONS FROM CHI-
    NESE
    LOVE STORIES CHINESE 20TH CENTURY TRANSLATIONS INTO VIETNAM-
    ESE
    FICTION CHINESE 20TH CENTURY TRANSLATIONS INTO VIETNAMESE
    FICTION VIETNAMESE 20TH CENTURY TRANSLATIONS FROM CHINESE
    LOVE STORIES VIETNAMESE
    VIETNAMESE LANGUAGE MATERIALS FICTION
    TRUYEN TINH CAM TIENG TRUNG HOA THE KY 20 DICH RA TIENG VIET
    TRUYEN TUONG TUONG TIENG TRUNG HOA THE KY 20 DICH RA TIENG VIET
    TRUYEN TUONG TUONG TIENG VIET THE KY 20 DICH TU TIENG TRUNG
    HOA

Improvements on the modest methodologies previously described are already being contemplated at JCPL. Currently in the planning phase is creation of a machine-internal, user-transparent, mixed-language synonym table. We anticipate that this technique will lead ultimately to a form of "mega-access" to the items in the Asian Model Library.

It is clear that the methodologies described are not suitable to every library endeavoring to meet the informational needs of converging ethnocultural groups. Our experience with them, however, has been a positive one, as amply evidenced by the incredible demand for materials in the Asian Model Library.

The Asian Cataloging Project was conceived because of our belief that mere acquisition of Asian materials is not in any way synonymous with making them accessible.

The success of the project lies in having begun the work of meeting critical informational needs by making what is in the library accessible.

That is a significant first step for Asian librarianship in Colorado.

NOTES

1. Jefferson County Public Library provides library service to a county population of approximately 370,000 residents. The system includes 10 branch libraries, 1 bookmobile, and special services to the home-bound and county jail inmates. Annual circulation is ca. 1,500,000. The Villa Branch Library contains 56,000 volumes with annual circulation of ca. 350,000.

2. Estimates from the Office of the Coordinator of Indo-Chinese Refugees projected a total of 9,000 Indo-Chinese in Colorado in 1980. In her "Which Came First—The Chicken Or The Egg?," *Colorado Libraries* 8:22-24 Sept. 1982., Ms. Greer indicates that by 1982 the figure had risen to nearly 20,000.

3. The Colorado Resolution stated: "Be it resolved, that libraries with the assistance of appropriate groups or individuals should develop collections that reflect the cultural heritage of their communities. Be it further resolved, that libraries should place a high priority on determining special needs, and on using every resource to ensure. . . awareness of services developed." Quoted in: "Which Came First—The Chicken Or The Egg?", *Colorado Libraries* 8:22 Sept. 1982.

4. Construction of the JEFFCAT data base began in 1968. Currently, it contains 180,000 bibliographic records.

5. Wellisch, Hans H. "Bibliographic Access to Multilingual Collections," *Library Trends* 29:225 Fall 1980.

6. Ibid., pp. 229-233.

7. Ibid., pp. 234-236.

8. For several excellent discussions on the topic, see Wellisch's "Multiscript and Multilingual Bibliographic Control: Alternatives to Romanization," *Library Resources & Technical Services* 22:179-190, Spring 1978, and his: "The Exchange of Bibliographic Data in Non-Roman Scripts," *Unesco Journal of Information Science, Librarianship and Archives Administration*, 2:13-21 Jan.-March 1980. Also, C. Sumner Spalding's "Romanization Re-examined," *Library Resources & Technical Services* 21:3-12 Winter 1977.

9. Kaneko, Hideo, "Cataloging and Classifying Japanese Language Materials," *Cataloging and Classification of Non-Western Materials: Concerns, Issues and Practices*, ed. Mohammed M. Aman (Phoenix: Oryx Press, 1980), pp.145-147.

10. "Terminals Are Installed to Process Chinese, Japanese, Korean Records," *Library of Congress Information Bulletin* 24:215-216 27 June 1983.

11. Miller, R. Bruce. "Nonroman Scripts and Computer Terminal Developments," *Information Technology and Libraries* 1:146-147 June 1982.

12. Copies of these files are available for $9.95 from: Jefferson County Public Library, 10200 W. 20th Ave., Lakewood, CO 80215. (*Asian Languages Subject and Author Authority File: A Multilingual List of Headings*, ed. Paul R. Murdock (Lakewood: JCPL, 1983.)

13. Rush, James E. "AACR2 from an Information Scientist's Point of View," *Cataloging & Classification Quarterly* 3:55, Winter 1982/Spring 1983.

14. Berman, Sanford, "Ethnic Access," *The Joy of Cataloging: Essays, Letters, Reviews, and Other Explosions* (Phoenix: Oryx Press, 1981), p.109.

15. Miller, R. Bruce. "Nonroman Scripts and Computer Terminal Developments," *Information Technology and Libraries* 1:148 June 1982.

Report of the SAC
Ad-Hoc Subcommittee on Concepts
Denoted by the Term "Primitive"

ABSTRACT. The Subcommittee recommends that the use of the term "primitive" in subject analysis be substantially reduced, that its use be limited to those subject areas in which it is still widely used in our society, and that in those cases its use be more narrowly defined. Specific recommendations are made for each of the headings in LIBRARY OF CONGRESS SUBJECT HEADINGS which contains the qualifier "primitive." The nature of these recommendations varies depending on the heading and includes all of the following: Maintain the heading for the present time; Maintain the heading, but restrict its use with a scope note; Cancel the heading and use already established headings in its place; Cancel the heading and establish new headings; Expand the usefulness of non-"primitive" headings by providing for use of ethnic qualifiers, geographic subdivision, and/or "doubling"; Recatalog items with little used headings, replacing them with other appropriate headings. Recommendations are made for replacing the term "primitive" with other terms in the few remaining occurrences in the captions in the DEWEY DECIMAL CLASSIFICATION SCHEDULE. Similar specific recommendations are made for the more frequent occurrences of the term in captions in the Library of Congress Classification Schedules. The Library of Congress Subject Cataloging Division is urged to emphasize geographical area rather than evaluative characteristics when classifying materials about people.

REPORT

The SAC Ad-hoc Subcommittee on Concepts Denoted by the Term "Primitive" was created by the Subject Analysis Committee during the A.L.A. mid-winter meeting of 1981 and it first met during the annual A.L.A. convention last year. It was charged as follows:

This is the full report presented in June 1983 to the American Library Association's Subject Analysis Committee.

—To study and to recommend to the appropriate agencies changes in subject access to concepts currently labeled by "primitive," with emphasis on the LIBRARY OF CONGRESS SUBJECT HEADINGS.

—To determine which, if any, current uses of the term "primitive" are appropriate.

—To recommend an alternative method of analysis in those cases where current use of "primitive" is deemed inappropriate.

Subject Analysis Committee awareness of the need for examination of the use of the term "primitive" had been heightened by the work of two previous subcommittees: The Ad-hoc Subcommittee on Subject Analysis of African and Asian Materials and The Racism and Sexism in Subject Analysis Subcommittee. One of the recommendations of the final report (1980) of the Racism and Sexism Subcommittee was that the Subject Analysis Committee "continue the effort to find appropriate terminology to describe traditional concerns and customs. The Subcommittee. . .[did] not find the term PRIMITIVE acceptable, at least with regard to Indian customs and activities."

Discussion of this topic in both the African Studies Association Subcommittee on Cataloging and Classification and the RLG Task Force on Subject Headings for Art and Architecture provided additional impetus for the creation of a SAC subcommittee. The Cataloging Committee of the Music Library Association had made recommendations to the Library of Congress about the use of the term in music subject headings, and MUSIC CATALOGING BULLETIN, May, 1981, announced changes to be made in LIBRARY OF CONGRESS SUBJECT HEADINGS and in LC's policy for subject analysis of ethnic and national music. These changes included cancellation of the heading "Music, Primitive."

Members of the SAC Subcommittee were chosen to represent groups or disciplines, other than those with music interests, which could be expected to be concerned about the issue, including librarians with expertise in African studies, anthropology, religion, and art. At the first meetings of the Subcommittee, in June, 1981, members were given various assignments, and the remainder of this report is excerpted from or based on those individual reports.

Professional concern about the use of the term "primitive" in subject analysis pre-dates the work of the SAC Subcommittee and the various special interest groups by many years. In PREJUDICES

AND ANTIPATHIES, published in 1971, Sanford Berman discussed the problem:

> Primitive. . . inaccurately and—according to popular conceptions of the word—slurringly describes various forms and aspects of human life. No self-respecting social scientist is likely to use it. Why, then, should librarians? It is heavily overlaid with notions of inferiority, childishness, barbarity, and "state of nature" simplicity, whereas the societies, arts, economic modes, music, and religions it purportedly covers may be extremely complex, ingenious, creative, humane, and—depending on taste and WELTANSCHAUUNG—admirable. The term additionally implies, erroneously, a BYGONE period, although a "primitive" artist, for example, may be a contemporary.

Berman stated that "no self-respecting social scientist" was likely to use the term "primitive." A Subcommittee member, Greg Finnegan, analyzed the treatment of the term in three dictionaries of anthropology (Winick, C., DICTIONARY OF ANTHROPOLOGY, 1964; Panoff, M. and Perrin, M., DICTIONNAIRE DE L'ETHNOLOGIE, 1973; Hunter, D. and Whitten, P., ENCYCLOPEDIA OF ANTHROPOLOGY, 1976). His analysis did reveal use of the term, but discomfort with it, as well as with alternative terms.

> Winick, p. 437: "It ['primitive'] is not used today because it implies that nonliterate people are retarded and resist social change along the lines of western civilization, that they have not undergone any cultural evolution of their own, and that their way of life is like that of our prehistoric ancestors."

> Hunter and Whitten, p. 321: ". . .many anthropologists prefer not to use the term. . .at all, since in its popular usage it has derogatory connotations. And since the term implies earliest and original (coming as it does from the Latin PRIMITIVUS, meaning earliest or oldest), the use of PRIMITIVE to denote contemporary peoples carries the unfortunate connotation that these peoples represent the earliest stages of cultural development—which anthropologists know is not the case. Anthropologists have not agreed on a substitute term for PRIMI-

TIVE PEOPLES, although NONLITERATE PEOPLES is often encountered today.

In spite of these comments in the entry on PRIMITIVE PEOPLES, however, Hunter and Whitten did use "primitive" as a qualifier for several terms, such as, Art, Primitive and Medicine, Primitive.

Finnegan also analyzed data from AMERICAN ANTHRO-POLOGIST, from 1967 through 1982, to ascertain the level of current usage of the term. Of 630 titled articles and brief communications published during that period, only two titles used the term. One of these uses was an attack on the concept; the other was in reference to T.S. Eliot. Titles of thirty-one of the 7,146 books reviewed during that period included the word.

In the discipline of religion, another Subcommittee member, Diane Lauderdale, found "there are still prominent scholars who, while they may regret some connotations of the term, believe that the term represents a productive cross-cultural category."

In the discipline of art, the term is still in frequent use as the recent opening of the Rockefeller Wing of Primitive Art at the Metropolitan Museum in New York dramatically illustrates. THE OXFORD COMPANION TO ART defines three different ways in which the term is used, noting that two of these uses were based originally on false assumptions. Thirty-two respondents to a questionnaire distributed to the membership of the Art Library Society of North America (ARLIS/NA) and to the RLG art libraries indicated that they saw no problem with the continued use of the term "primitive," but twenty-four thought it should be eliminated. In summarizing the results of the survey and a discussion of the topic at an ARLIS meeting, Don Anderle, a Subcommittee member, made the following points: One, the results were far closer than anyone had anticipated. Two, feelings are running as high on this topic in the art community as elsewhere. Three, many libraries are resorting to various ad hoc solutions to eliminate these terms from their catalogs, but these local solutions do not appear to offer patterns which could be adopted for national level cataloging. Anderle emphasized, in addition, that "the majority, of course, favors keeping to present practices."

The Subcommittee has found it extremely difficult to reconcile various ideals while formulating recommendations for subject access to concepts denoted by "primitive." Among these frequently conflicting goals are the following:

1. To serve all elements of a multi-cultural society well by avoiding "words which connote inferiority or peculiarity" and "American/Western European ethnocentrism" (cf. J. Marshall, ON EQUAL TERMS),
2. To use access terms which are specific enough to bring together like items and exclude unlike items,
3. To provide patterns of access which are logical enough to facilitate access,
4. To choose access terms which are in common use for the concepts represented.

We have struggled not only with the formidable task of trying to achieve these various goals, but also with the nature of language itself, the shifting denotations and connotations of words and the difficulty of establishing meaning out of context.

Based on the complexity of the pattern of needs discussed above, the Subcommittee recommends that the use of the term "primitive" in subject analysis be substantially reduced, but not completely eliminated at this time; that its use be limited to those subject areas in which it is still widely used in our society; and that in those cases its use be more narrowly defined. We make specific recommendations below for maintaining or deleting each subject heading containing the term in the LIBRARY OF CONGRESS SUBJECT HEADINGS, a few recommendations about the use of the term in the DEWEY DECIMAL SCHEDULE, and recommendations regarding the use of the term in the Library of Congress classification schedules, as well as general patterns of classification in those schedules. By far the most important of these are the recommendations for changes in the LIBRARY OF CONGRESS SUBJECT HEADINGS because it is in subject headings that the pejorative connotation is most obvious to the library user.

I. LIBRARY OF CONGRESS SUBJECT HEADINGS

We make recommendations below concerning each of the headings containing the qualifier "primitive" in LIBRARY OF CONGRESS SUBJECT HEADINGS. In some cases, we recommend that the terms be maintained for the present; in most cases, however, we recommend substitution of other terms. In many of the latter cases, access to materials can be sufficiently achieved by other terms already present in the list. In some cases, we recommend establishment of new terms, whenever possible using current LC patterns for the new subjects suggested. It should be noted that we only recommend use of the qualifier "traditional" in place of "primitive" when we could find justification for that term in citation indexes or other sources. Our recommendations are based on a survey of records to which LC has assigned these headings, which was carried out by the African Studies Association's Subcommittee on Cataloging. The number of occurrences of the headings on pre-and post-1940 records was compiled by Library of Congress staff in July, 1981. In some cases the numbers are approximations rather than actual counts. The number of occurrences of the headings on MARC records was compiled by Andrea Stamm at Northwestern University in April, 1983. In some cases the post-1940 records and the MARC records duplicate each other.

  1. Agriculture, Primitive (established ca. 1906)

        Pre-1940 records: 6
        Post-1940 records: 45
        MARC records: 38

The Subcommittee recommends that the heading be cancelled. Agriculture (Indirect) although it is already established, is not an acceptable substitute, especially because the file is very large. We recommend establishing two new subjects: Agriculture, Prehistoric, because 9 out of 29 books surveyed were in fact about prehistoric agriculture; and Agriculture, Traditional, because this term is widely used in the literature. (See SOCIAL SCIENCES CITATION INDEX, 1978-81).

  2. Architecture, Primitive (established 1937)

        Pre-1940 records: 0
        Post-1940 records: 7
        MARC records: 12

The heading should be cancelled and the following already established headings should be used in its place: Architecture (Indirect); Cave dwellings (Indirect); Dwellings, Prehistoric; Architecture, ethnic qualifier; Vernacular architecture. This selection is sufficient to describe works which are now accessed by the "primitive" heading.

3. Arms and armor, Primitive (established 1910)

> Pre-1940 records: 4
> Post-1940 records: 9
> MARC records: 13

The heading should be cancelled. Arms and armor (Indirect) is already established and can be used appropriately on many records. We suggest in addition that Arms and armor, Prehistoric be reinstituted and that "doubling" be implemented using the pattern Arms and armor—place and Arms and armor, ethnic qualifier.

4. Art, Primitive (established ca. 1900)

> Pre-1940 records: 175
> Post-1940 records: 500-600
> MARC records: 221

Based on widespread current use of this term, the Subcommittee recommends that it be continued as an LC subject heading at this time. However, we are troubled not only by its pejorative connotation, but also by its lack of specificity and by the size of the file. We suggest that consideration be given to removing the provision for subdividing this heading by geographic area as a means of limiting the use of the term and the size of the file. We see a shift in attitude on the part of art librarians and urge the Subject Analysis Committee and the ARLIS/NA Cataloging Advisory Committee to continue to seek suitable alternatives.

5. Art metal-work, Primitive (established 1971)

> Pre-1940 records: 0
> Post-1940 records: 1
> MARC records: 2

The Subcommittee recommends that the two records with this subject heading (74-866565, 82-72765) be assigned Art metalwork, African—Exhibitions and Art metal-work, African—Africa, West in place of Art metal-work, Primitive, which should be cancelled.

6. Boats, Primitive (established 1979)

> Pre-1940 records: 0
> Post-1940 records: 0
> MARC records: 4

The heading should be cancelled. The Subcommittee recommends that the subject be deleted from 77-452397 since Boats and boating—Brazil is used, and that Boats and boating—Origin be substituted for the primitive subject on records 80-499706 and 80-499707, and perhaps on 82-462968.

7. Cartography, Primitive (established 1910)

Pre-1940 records: 1
Post-1940 records: 0
MARC records: 1

The Subcommittee recommends that the heading be cancelled, that Cartography—Origin be assigned as the subject heading for one record (6-5952) and that maps as a subdivision under Eskimos be established for the other (79-122328).

8. Classification, Primitive (established 1973)

Pre-1940 records: 0
Post-1940 records: 10
MARC records: 28

Two concepts are currently covered by this subject heading: (1) the classification of the universe by non-industrialized people, and (2) the zoological and botanical classifications used by non-industrialized peoples. For books on zoological or botanical classification, the already established subject headings Zoology—Classification and Botany—Classification or Ethnozoology and Ethnobotany can be used. For books on the general classification of the universe, LC already has established the subject headings Cosmology; Categories (Philosophy); and Philosophy of nature, etc. We recommend adding to these the new subject heading Cosmology, ethnic qualifier, and cancelling Classification, Primitive.

9. Clothing and dress, Primitive (established 1951)

Pre-1940 records: 0
Post-1940 records: 0
MARC records: 0

The heading should be cancelled. If a heading for the topic is needed in the future, the Subcommittee recommends the use of specific subjects whenever possible (e.g., Breechcloths, Trousers). If the item is about the clothing and dress of specific peoples, we recommend Clothing and dress with an ethnic qualifier. If a general subject is needed, we recommend Clothing and dress without a qualifier.

10. Commerce, Primitive (established 1975)

Pre-1940 records: 0

Post-1940 records: 3
MARC records: 7

The Subcommittee recommends cancellation of the heading. The current headings Economic anthropology and Commerce and the subdivision Commerce used after place names could replace the use of Commerce, Primitive on all records cited. In addition, we suggest the establishment of a new heading, Ceremonial exchange (Ethnology) for some of the records.

11. Communication, Primitive (established 1968)

Pre-1940 records: 0
Post-1940 records: 1
MARC records: 0

The Subcommittee recommends that the heading be cancelled and that the record to which it is assigned (69-99097) be reassigned Communication—Papua New Guinea and Ethnology—Papua New Guinea.

12. Decoration and ornament, Primitive (established 1926)

Pre-1940 records: 7
Post-1940 records: 7
MARC records: 2

This term should be maintained for the present time. See the comments under Art, Primitive.

13. Drama, Primitive (established 1965)

Pre-1940 records: 0
Post-1940 records: 3
MARC records: 5

The heading should be cancelled. The current subject headings Drama—Origin and Drama—History and criticism could replace Drama, Primitive. In addition, we recommend establishing Drama, Traditional. (See ARTS AND HUMANITIES CITATION INDEX, 1978-81 and SOCIAL SCIENCES CITATION INDEX, 1978.)

14. Education, Primitive (established 1957)

Pre-1940 headings: 0
Post-1940 records: 2
MARC records: 3

The Subcommittee recommends that the heading be cancelled and that Educational anthropology be used in its place on records

74-79272 and 72-13962; Education—Origin on 79-545368; and, Education—Uganda on 72-980052.

15. Erotic art, Primitive (established 1973)

> Pre-1940 records: 0
> Post-1940 records: 1
> MARC records: 1

The heading should be cancelled and the record (74-157170) be reassigned Erotic art.

16. Ethics, Primitive (established 1950)

> Pre-1940 records: 0
> Post-1940 records: 5
> MARC records: 3

Ethics (Indirect), Ethics—Origin, and Ethics, ethnic qualifier are already established LC subject headings and provide adequate access. The "primitive" heading should be cancelled.

17. Fishing, Primitive (established 1905)

> Pre-1940 records: 6
> Post-1940 records: 19
> MARC records: 8

The Subcommittee recommends cancellation of the heading. Fishing (Indirect) and Fishhooks (Indirect) are already established. Most of the books surveyed dealt with archaeological finds of fishhooks. We suggest that Fishing, Prehistoric be re-established for archaeological works and that Fishing, ethnic qualifier also be used where appropriate.

18. Fortification, Primitive (established 1910)

> Pre-1940 records: 4
> Post-1940 records: 42
> MARC records: 32

Earthworks (Archaeology) (Indirect) has already been established and could be used for the majority of the books surveyed as an acceptable substitute for the "primitive" heading. We also suggest Fortification, Prehistoric (Indirect) because the majority of books with this subject heading are actually about prehistoric sites, and Fortification, ethnic qualifier, to be used as appropriate. The "primitive" heading should be cancelled.

19. Games, Primitive (established 1948)

> Pre-1940 records: 0
> Post-1940 records: 5
> MARC records: 4

Both Games and Games, Primitive have the same recommended call number span, GN 454-456. Four of the records with Games, Primitive fall in these numbers (80-492497, 78-12577, 75-35080, 62-35538). We recommend that these records be changed to read Games. We also recommend that 76-475792 be changed to read Games—Africa, Southern. The primitive heading should be cancelled.

20. Government, Primitive (established 1959)

> Pre-1940 records: 0
> Post-1940 records: 19
> MARC records: 47

Political anthropology, Government—Origin, and the subdivision Politics and government under specific peoples have already been established. The Subcommittee recommends that Government, Primitive be cancelled and that these headings be used in its place.

21. Hunting, Primitive (established 1905)

> Pre-1940 records: 4
> Post-1940 records: 29
> MARC records: 18

The heading should be cancelled. The subject heading Hunting and gathering societies (Indirect), recently established by LC, is an excellent alternate. Approximately forty-five percent of the surveyed titles with the "primitive" heading would be more properly analyzed using this new term. LC has also established the subdivision Hunting under individual Indian tribes and the general subject heading Hunting (Indirect). We recommend that as the need arises, Hunting also be established as a subdivision under cultural-linguistic groups other than Indian tribes.

22. Industries, Primitive (established 1910)

> Pre-1940 records: 21
> Post-1940 records: 100
> MARC records: 64

LC recently clarified and narrowed the use of this heading with a scope note at the same time it established the new heading Material culture. The Subcommittee applauds this move toward narrower use of headings containing "primitive" and recommends no change.

23. Ivories, Primitive (established 1978)

> Pre-1940 records: 0
> Post-1940 records: 0
> MARC records: 1

The heading should be cancelled. The Subcommittee recommends that the subject be deleted from the one record (78-372487) as Ivories—Africa, West is already present as a subject heading.

24. Jewelry, Primitive (established 1976)

> Pre-1940 records: 0
> Post-1940 records: 0
> MARC records: 1

The heading should be cancelled. Jewelry, Prehistoric is an acceptable alternative on the one record (76-487078).

25. Kings and rulers, Primitive (established 1947)

> Pre-1940 records: 0
> Post-1940 records: 20
> MARC records: 7

The heading should be cancelled. Kings and rulers, standing alone or subdivided by Origins, and the subdivision Kings and rulers under the names of geographic areas and ethnic groups are acceptable substitutes.

26. Law, Primitive (established 1910)

> Pre-1940 records: 41
> Post-1940 records: 120
> MARC records: 42

This heading seems to be needed as a descriptor and should be maintained, although the established headings Comparative law and State, The, fit some of the titles to which it has been assigned. The Subcommittee recommends that LC supply scope notes to clearly define the use of the headings Law, Primitive and Customary law. It should be noted that Primitive law is also used as a parenthetical qualifier with a variety of headings such as Inheritance and succession (Primitive law) and Land tenure (Primitive law). The Subcommittee was unable to compile a complete list of such headings.

We urge the Subject Cataloging Subcommittee of the American Association of Law Libraries to study the use of "primitive" in these headings and in the general heading Law, Primitive and to make recommendations regarding them to the Subject Cataloging Division of the Library of Congress.

27. Man, Primitive (established 1950)

Pre-1940 records: 0
Post-1940 records: 60
MARC records: 37

The Subcommittee recommends that this heading be cancelled. An analysis of the titles to which it has been assigned revealed no distinction between the use of this heading and the heading Society, Primitive. The various headings referred to under Society, Primitive below can be used in place of Man, Primitive. In addition, the established heading Man, Prehistoric provides appropriate access to some of the records.

28. Mathematics, Primitive (established 1973)

Pre-1940 records: 0
Post-1940 records: 1
MARC records: 2

The two records with this heading are about African finger counting. We suggest that LC establish Counting (Indirect) so that Counting—Africa, Sub-Saharan can be assigned to the two records (72-91248 and 77-26586). Better still, we suggest that LC establish Finger counting (Indirect) or Finger calculation (Indirect). Mathematics, Primitive should be cancelled.

29. Medicine, Primitive (established 1905)

Pre-1940 records: 6
Post-1940 records: 45
MARC records: 60

The Subcommittee recommends that this heading be cancelled. Medical anthropology (Indirect), Medicine as a subdivision under the pattern heading for individual Indian tribes, and a number of excellent specific subjects are already established. For many of the general works surveyed, the subject Medical anthropology will suffice. However, since the term actually refers to a discipline, we suggest also the heading Medicine, Traditional, with a reference from Ethnomedicine. Medicine, Traditional is found in the SOCIAL SCI-

ENCES CITATION INDEX, 1978-1981, ARTS AND HUMAN-
ITIES CITATION INDEX, 1980 and 1982, and in subject indexes,
including Medical Subject Headings (MESH). We also recommend
that as the need arises, Medicine be established as a subdivision
under cultural-linguistic groups other than Indian tribes.

30. Money, Primitive (established 1949)

Pre-1940 records: 2
Post-1940 records: 8
MARC records: 5

Money (Indirect), Money—Origin, and many forms of money (e.g.,
Shell money, Coal money) are already established, as is Barter.
Although these headings will suffice in most cases, we suggest also
the new heading Trade goods for a specialized aspect of the subject.
The "primitive" heading should be cancelled.

31. Navigation, Primitive (established 1910)

Pre-1940 records: 1
Post-1940 records: 18
MARC records: 22

The Subcommittee recommends that the heading be cancelled. Most
of the books carrying this subject heading are about the navigation
of Polynesian and Micronesian peoples. Navigation methods of
these peoples are highly sophisticated and should not be considered
"primitive." LC has already established Maritime anthropology,
Nautical astronomy, Navigation (Indirect). The first of these is frequently assigned to Polynesian material. We recommend that in addition Navigation, ethnic qualifier be used when appropriate.

32. Oratory, Primitive (established 1975)

Pre-1940 records: 0
Post-1940 records: 2
MARC records: 3

The Subcommittee recommends cancellation and the substitution of
Sociolinguistics on the records 74-10736 and 77-21590; Oratory—
Somalia on record 81-18072; and deletion with no substitution on
75-10736.

33. Painting, Primitive (established 1971)

Pre-1940 records: 0
Post-1940 records: 2
MARC records: 1

On records 74-171018 and 74-160160 the primitive heading could be eliminated without significant loss of subject access. The primitive heading should be cancelled.

34. Philosophy, Primitive (established 1953)

> Pre-1940 records: 1
> Post-1940 records: 15
> MARC records: 20

Historically the heading seems to have been used as a catch-all for works about symbolism, psychology, and the religious thought of non-industrialized peoples. Ethnopsychology; Religion; Philosophy of nature, etc., have already been established. We recommend that Ethnophilosophy be established, patterned after the LC subject heading Ethnopsychology, and that Philosophy, Primitive be cancelled.

35. Pottery, Primitive (established 1965)

> Pre-1940 headings: 1
> Post-1940 headings: 12
> MARC records: 11

The heading should be cancelled. Many of the books with the "primitive" heading are analyses of pot sherds. We recommend the use of the established heading Pottery, Prehistoric for these books. For books about the pottery of non-industrialized peoples we suggest the headings Folk pottery and Pottery, Traditional. The juxtaposition of "pottery" with "traditional" was found several times in a search of the Scorpio data-base. Another useful heading would be Pottery—Classification.

36. Primitive property (established 1957)

> Pre-1940 records: 0
> Post-1940 records: 6
> MARC records: 2

The headings Property and Land tenure both cover the content of the books surveyed. We therefore recommend that the subject be cancelled. We recommend that the subject be deleted from 77-980617 as the other subject headings cover the content of the book well. We also recommend that the subject Property be used on 04-22285 so that it will match the record for the later edition of the same work (17-439) which has the subject without the qualifier.

37. Religion, Primitive (established 1910)

Pre-1940 records: 500
Post-1940 records: 1,000
MARC records: 150

The Subcommittee recommends that Religion, Primitive be maintained but that its use be limited with a scope note specifying that the heading be used for works about the concept or category of primitive religion and works about the religion of nonliterate, preindustrial ethnically homogeneous peoples in general, but that individual ethnographic studies should be entered under the heading for the specific people with the subheading Religion.

38. Sculpture, Primitive (established 1910)

Pre-1940 records: 15
Post-1940 records: 250
MARC records: 108

This heading should be maintained for the present time. See comments under Art, Primitive.

39. Society, Primitive (established 1910)

Pre-1940 records: 150
Post-1940 records: 850
MARC records: 171

Although the Subcommittee does not recommend cancellation of this heading, we urge the use of more specific headings such as Village communities, Tribes and clans, Blood brotherhood, whenever possible. We also recommend that Social anthropology be established following the patterns of Political anthropology and Economic anthropology and that scope notes be written for Society, Primitive; Social anthropology; and Ethnology.

40. Surgery, Primitive (established 1905)

Pre-1940 records: 3
Post-1940 records: 3
MARC records: 0

The Subcommittee recommends that the heading be cancelled. Deformities, Artificial; Self-mutilation; Circumcision; Clitoridectomy; and Trephining are established headings which cover specific forms of surgery very well. We recommend that Surgery, Ritual (Indirect) and Scarification, Ornamental (Indirect), both of which are used in the literature, be established for general works.

41. Theater, Primitive (established ?)

> Pre-1940 records: 0
> Post-1940 records: 1
> MARC records: 1

The Subcommittee recommends cancellation of the heading and that the heading on record 74-32656 be changed to Theater—Origin.

42. Transportation, Primitive (established 1905)

> Pre-1940 records: 6
> Post-1940 records: 9
> MARC records: 3

The heading should be cancelled. Specific forms of transportation are well covered by the LC subject headings. Some of these are Sleighs and sledges, Litters, Handcarts. An acceptable established alternative for general works is Transportation (Indirect)—History.

43. Warfare, Primitive (established 1974)

> Pre-1940 records: 2
> Post-1940 records: 6
> MARC records: 13

The Subcommittee recommends that the heading be cancelled. The subdivision Warfare is established for use under names of specific peoples. We recommend that LC establish Warfare, Traditional as it corresponds to Warfare, Conventional.

44. Wit and humor, Primitive (established 1968)

> Pre-1940 records: 0
> Post-1940 records: 1
> MARC records: 0

We recommend that the one record (63-37780) be reassigned either Wit and humor—Origin or Wit and humor, and that the "primitive" heading be cancelled.

45. Wood-carving, Primitive (established 1971)

> Pre-1940 records: 0
> Post-1940 records: 9
> MARC records: 22

There is a duplication of subject headings on many of the records surveyed. The first subject contains the "primitive" qualifier and the second subject is the same heading without any qualifier. We recommend that LC examine the records with this heading and eliminate this duplication by removing the "primitive" qualified subject, which should be cancelled. Wood-carving (Indirect) and Wood-carving, ethnic qualifier are acceptable alternate headings. In addition, our analysis of the titles under the Wood-carving headings indicated the need for a scope note to distinguish between the use of the headings Wood-carving and Sculpture.

II. DEWEY DECIMAL SCHEDULE

A Subcommittee member, Janie Morris, compared the Dewey 18 and 19 editions to see which areas of the schedules covered "primitive" topics and whether there had been any change in the use of terms relating to "primitive" subjects from one edition to another. She found that essentially the same topics were covered in both editions, but that the terminology varied. Typically in Dewey 18 the category of people referred to is called "primitive" or "preliterate" whereas in Dewey 19 they are referred to as "nonliterate." Furthermore, the phrase "including primitive traditions" was omitted from explanatory notes in Dewey 19. Morris was also able to ascertain that the numbers relating to nonliterate people are used sparingly by the Library of Congress Decimal Classification Division. If the PROPOSED REVISION OF 780 MUSIC is adopted, a separate number for music of nonliterate people (781.71 in Dewey 18 and 19) will be eliminated.

The Subcommittee discussed the use of the term "nonliterate" and was somewhat uncomfortable with it since literacy is not always the distinguishing factor. "Traditional societies" was suggested as an alternative, but was felt to be vague and ambiguous. For lack of a better term, the Subcommittee recommends retention of "nonliterate."

The Subcommittee also discussed the retention of the term "primitive law" in Dewey 19. The alternatives "customary law" and "law of traditional societies" were suggested. "Law of traditional societies" was dismissed as also being vague and ambiguous. Morris surveyed people with expertise regarding the term "customary law" and found that it is a broader term than the concept referred to at 340.52. Therefore, to maintain consistency with terms used throughout the schedule, the Subcommittee recommends that the wording at 340.52 be changed to "Law of nonliterate peoples."

The Subcommittee recommends the following revisions between

classification numbers 615.88 and 615.889 to eliminate the use the term "primitive" in that area:

—Change the note at 615.88 to read for For folk, traditional, ancient, medieval remedies, see 615.89,
—Delete 615.882 Folk medicine,
—Revise 615.899 to read Folk, traditional, ancient, medieval remedies.

The word "Primitive" is also used in Dewey 19 in the area of suspension bridges. The Subcommittee recommends that bridges be categorized according to type, rather than according to whether they are early or modern. This would parallel the change in treatment of weapons in Dewey 19. (See 623.441.) The following terms are suggested for bridges:

624.5   Suspension bridges
.52   Non-metal

Rope bridges of hammock and basket types

.55   Metal
Wire-cable, self-anchored, eye-barchain, rope-strand cable suspension bridges.
Including plate-girder suspension bridges (formerly 624.7).

The Subcommittee applauds the efforts of the Decimal Classification Editorial Policy Committee and the Dewey Division to remove offensive terms from the schedule and the Division's practice of using separate classification of "primitive" subjects sparingly.

III. LIBRARY OF CONGRESS CLASSIFICATION SCHEDULES

A. Current Treatment of Peoples of the Non-Western World in LCC

In 1976, the G Schedule and particularly the GN section underwent major revision and restructuring. LC attempted to objectively define the ethnological and ethnographic subfields of anthropology. The word "primitive" as a qualifier for customs and institutions was removed and the terms "preliterate and/or folk societies" were introduced. Specific instruction is now given to place materials on specific topics relating to a particular group in D-F, thus arranging by geographical location rather than by subjective description of the level of the culture. Recently the section of the D schedule for African countries has been revised and expanded to include "ethnography" for each country's itemization.

Because of the generally perceived role of anthropology as the examiner of the primitive peoples of the world, there exists in LCC an inherent bias which will be difficult to eliminate. Works studying a western culture using anthropological techniques are classed geographically in D-F or in HM (Social History). In many areas of the LCC, this subtle distinction between "primitive" and "civilized" is made through notes referring to GN and particularly in chronological arrangement where "primitive" is equated with prehistoric and before the division of "ancient, medieval, and modern." (See the R schedule examples below.) Depending on the date of revision, varying degrees of insensitivity are displayed in the structure of individual schedules.

B. Caption Language in LCC

Since few of the captions in LCC actually employ the word "primitive," LC could adopt uniform and neutral language to describe preliterate and folk societies with minimum disruption, and we recommend that this be done. While the phrase "preliterate and/or folk societies" is not accepted by all social scientists, the use of this term in place of "primitive" would conform to existing LC language in GN 301-699. Also, the simple addition of the qualifier (Ethnology) to a term removes a major portion of the judgmental overtones of "primitive." Other options include elimination of portions of the caption, adding "ethno-" to a base word, or introduction of the concept of "origins" to the caption. The special problems of the N Schedule can only be itemized at this time. We suggest that the ARLIS/NA Committee on Cataloging Problems review the schedule and make recommendations for appropriate changes.

C. Summary Recommendations

1. We request that LC alter the language of the current captions to eliminate the term "primitive" and other words carrying judgmental overtones from captions.

2. We encourage LC to class by geographical area rather than evaluative characteristics.
3. We encourage LC, SAC, and other professional groups to remain aware of the improvements in language used to define preliterate people and/or folk societies and to initiate or recommend future changes as appropriate.

D. Itemization of the Use of the Word "Primitive" in the Captions, Notes, and Index Terms of the Library of Congress Classification Schedules, with Recommendations for Changes

BL-BX (2nd Edition, 1962)

BL (370)	Classification of religions. Primitive peoples, see GN 470-474 RECOMMENDATION: Substitute "Preliterate and/or folk societies," or "Religion (Ethnology)" for "Primitive peoples." (These terms conform to captions and notes used in GN 301-699.)
BL 900-975	Other primitive European religions RECOMMENDATION: Use "early" for "primitive."
BL 2670	Religions of primitive peoples (General), see GN 470+ Comment: Added in list 197. RECOMMENDATION: Use "preliterate and/or folk societies" for "primitive peoples."
BV 6	Worship (Public & Private). History. By period. Primitive and early church Comment: Retain "primitive." The term is not pejorative in this context as it refers to the church in its pure form.
BV 416 .M5	Hymnology. Hymns. Hymnbooks. Other Methodist churches. Primitive Methodist Church. Comment: Retain "primitive"; proper name.
BV 716	Ecclesiastical theology. Church law. Sources.

.A3 &   Primitive and early church. Ancient church
.A15   orders (Collective)
             Comment: Retain "primitive." The term is
             not pejorative in this context as it refers to the
             church in its pure form.

BX 6380-   Old School, Old Order or Primitive Baptists,
   6389   "Hardshell Baptists"
             Comment: Retain "primitive"; proper name.

BX 6460-   National Primitive Baptist Convention of the
   6460.9   U.S.A. Formerly Colored Primitive Bap-
             tists
             Comment: Changed in List 185. Retain
             "primitive"; proper name.

BX 7771-   Primitive Friends
   7772   Comment: Retain "primitive"; proper name.

BX 8370-   Primitive Methodist Church
   8379   Comment: Retain "primitive"; proper name.

BL-BX   Deities
             Primitive European
   Index   RECOMMENDATION: Use "Early."

C (3rd Edition, 1975)

CE 15   Comparative chronology
                Primitive, see GN 476.3
             RECOMMENDATION: Substitute "Chron-
             ology (Ethnology)."

G (4th Edition, 1976)

G 81   History of geography. General special
                Cf. GN 476.4, Primitive geography
             RECOMMENDATION: Substitute one of the
             following: "Geography (Ethnology")) or
             "Ethnological geography."

GN 296   Medical anthropology
                Cf. GN 477, Primitive medicine
             Comment: Note realigned in List 190.
             RECOMMENDATION: Use "Medicine
             (Ethnology)."

Note
before
GN 301

Ethnology. Social and cultural anthropology
Many topics provided for here represent concepts also encompassed by the discipline of sociology in HM. In cases of overlap, the following principle should normally apply, unless specific instructions are made to the contrary. Class here those works which deal with the nature of human societies in general, as well as those works which deal specifically with preliterate and/or folk societies. For those works which deal principally with modern civilization, see HM.
Comment: This note illustrates the difficulty LC has had finding appropriate terms to describe the discipline of anthropology and its subfields of ethnology and ethnography. Although many object to the terms "preliterate" and "folk societies," they are more acceptable than "primitive."

GN 492

Cultural traits, customs, and institutions.
Political organization. Political anthropology.
Cf. JC 20+, The primitive state (Political theory)
Comment: Probably retained in G (4th Edition) to conform with language used at JC 20+.
RECOMMENDATION: Alter JC 20+.

GN 493-494

Social control
Cf. K 190, Primitive law
Comment: Probably retained in G (4th Edition) to conform to usage at K 190.
RECOMMENDATION: Alter K 190.

Note
before
GT

Manner and customs (General)
Class here comprehensive works on social life and customs, as well as works on certain specific customs. For general works on the broader topic of civilization, i.e., the aggregate of characteristics displayed in the collec-

tive life of literate peoples, including intellectual life, the arts, etc., as well as social life and customs, see CB. For general works on the social life and customs of preliterate and folk societies, see GN 301+.
Comment: Good example of the division in LC thinking on the concepts of civilization and the relationship of literacy.

GV 571 Sports. History. General works. By period
    Preliterate, see GN 454+
Comment: Awkward compromise as GV 573 is defined as the ancient period of sports history. The implication is that preliterate is chronological and older than "ancient."

H-HG (4th Edition, 1981)

Note Economic history and conditions. History.
before By period. Prehistoric, primitive, see GN
HC 31 448+
    RECOMMENDATION: Substitute "Preliterate and/or folk societies" for "Prehistoric, primitive."

Line Land use. History. Primitive
before RECOMMENDATION: Change line to Pre-
HD 115 literate and/or folk societies, see GN449+.
    Enclose numbers 115, 117, 118, 119, 121 in parentheses.

HD 4843 Labor. History. Primitive
    RECOMMENDATION: Change line to Early, see GN 448.5+. Enclose 4843 in parentheses.

HE (155) Transportation and communications. History.
    Primitive, see GN 438+
    RECOMMENDATION: Substitute "Preliterate and/or folk societies" for "Primitive."

HF (361) Commerce. History. Ancient. Primitive, see
    GN 450+
    RECOMMENDATION: Substitute "Preliterate and/or folk societies" for "Primitive."

HG 231   Money. General works.
                     Primitive, see GN 450.5
                     RECOMMENDATION: Use "Preliterate and/or folk societies" instead of "Primitive."

HM-HX (4th Edition, 1980)

HQ 504   Family. Marriage. Home. History. Primitive. Origins.
                     Cf. GN 480+, The family among savages
                     RECOMMENDATION: Eliminate "primitive" as "origins" covers the concept sufficiently; change "The family among savages to "The family (Ethnology)."

HS 407   Freemasonry among primitive races
                     Cf. GN 490.8, Anthropology
                     Comment: The Subcommittee could find no evidence of use of this number.
                     RECOMMENDATION: Delete line.

HV 6118   Causes of crime. Criminal etiology. Primitive conceptions. Fall of man. Dualism. Freedom of will, etc.
                     RECOMMENDATION: Omit "Primitive conceptions."

HV 8505   Penology. Prisons. Penitentiaries. Punishment and reform. History and antiquities. Primitive.
                     RECOMMENDATION: Eliminate "primitive" and allow "antiquities" to cover the concept.

J (2nd Edition, 1966)

JA 81   History of political science. General
                     Primitive, see JC 20
                     RECOMMENDATION: Change caption at JC 20.

JC 20-24   The primitive state
                     Cf. GN 490-495
                     RECOMMENDATION: Substitute "Formative state. Early state."

JC 26-29   Tribal institutions
           Cf. GN 488-495
               The family in relation to primitive political organization and institutions, see GN, HM, HQ
           RECOMMENDATION: Use "preliterate and/or folk" rather than "primitive."
           Forms of state. Primitive

JC (369)   Family. Patriarchy. Matriarchy, see JC 20-29

JC (370)   Tribe. Clan, see JC 20-29

JC (371)   Mark. Village. Commune, see JC 31-45

JC (373)   Theocracy
           Cf. JC 20-89
           RECOMMENDATION: Use "Formative state" rather than "Primitive."

J Index   Primitive state   JC 20-45
           RECOMMENDATION: Use "Formative state" rather than "Primitive state."

K (1st Edition, 1977)

Note   Ethnological jurisprudence. Primitive law.
before   Class here works on the laws of preliterate
K 190   people in general, not limited to a particular region or country. For works on the primitive law of special areas or tribes, see customary law in the subclass for the appropriate region or country.
           RECOMMENDATION: Eliminate Primitive law after Ethnological jurisprudence in the heading and the word primitive in the fourth line of the text.

K 325   Historical jurisprudence. General works
           Primitive law, ethnological jurisprudence see K190+
           RECOMMENDATION: Use only the term "Ethnological jurisprudence."

K 520+   Comparative law. International Uniform Law
                Cf. K 190+, Primitive law
                RECOMMENDATION: Use "Ethnological
                jurisprudence" in place of "Primitive law."

K 589   Modern and ancient law
                Primitive law, see K 190+
                RECOMMENDATION: Use "Ethnological
                jurisprudence" for "Primitive law."

K Index   Primitive law K 190+
                RECOMMENDATION: Eliminate entry

L Index   Primitive education GN 488.5
                RECOMMENDATION: Cancel. GN was
                completely restructured in 4th edition.

M (3rd Edition, 1978)

ML 156.4   Bibliography. Catalogs. Sound recordings.
                Discography. Lists. By topic, A-Z
                .P7 Primitive music
                RECOMMENDATION: Cancel ".P7 Prim-
                itive music;" substitute appropriate cutter
                number for acceptable music term covering
                the concept of ethnic music.

M Index   Primitive music
                Discography: ML 156.4.P7
                RECOMMENDATION: Delete entire entry
                and cover concept with some form of "eth-
                nomusicology."

N (4th Edition, 1970)

Note   Primitive art.
before   Used here to denote art produced outside the
N 5311   traditions of the art of Europe, the Medi-
                terranean area, and Asia. That is, the art of
                the Negro peoples of sub-Saharan Africa; of
                the inhabitants of the islands of the Pacific

Ocean, Australia and some areas off the coast of Southeast Asia.

Does not include "primitive" or "naive" artists who, while seemingly untutored, work in the traditions of European folk art or easel painting.

Cf. E-F, American Indian art
GN 429-434, Primitive arts and crafts
N 7432.5.P7, Naive art
NB 62-64, Primitive sculpture
NC 54, Primitive drawing
ND 1482.P7, Naive painting
NK 1177, Primitive ornament

Comment: The term "primitive" in the art world appears to be a necessary evil; to the layperson, primitive carries a connotation of crude, rudimentary and unlearned, which should cover artists irrespective of their national origins. The singling out of those living in certain areas as "primitive" is unnecessary as there is ample provision for division of all art subjects by geographical location or chronological subdivision.

RECOMMENDATION: Change "Negro" in fourth line of text to "black."

In this N section, the captions with a form of primitive are reproduced without further comment in most cases.

N 6494

History. Modern art. By century. 20th century. Special aspects or movements, A-Z
.P7 Primitivism. Groupe Henri Rousseau
Comment: "Groupe Henri Rousseau" added in List 179.

History. Special countries. America.

N (6501.5)

Primitive American art, see E 59.A7; E 98.A7; F1219.3.A7; etc.

N 7428.5

General special. Influences and relationships between cultures
e.g., Comparisons of ancient and modern

art; comparisons of primitive and modern art

List 178

N 7428.5 Comparative art
Including influences and relationships be-tween cultures, e.g., comparisons of an-cient and modern art; comparisons of prim-itive and modern art

List 193

N 7428.5 Comparative art

N 7429 Influences and relationships between cultures, e.g., comparisons of ancient and modern art; comparisons of primitive and modern art

N 7432.5 Technique, composition, etc. Styles. Special styles, A-Z
.P7 Primitivism. Naive art
Especially the "naive" art produced in coun-tries whose culture is basically modern Eu-ropean, or derived from it
Prefer N 5311 where applicable

Architecture. History. Primitive
Cf. Gn 413-415. Ethnology

NA 205 General works

NA (207) Primitive American, see E-F

Sculpture. History

NB 61.5 Prehistoric sculpture

Primitive sculpture. (Includes note found be-fore N 5311)

NB 62 General works

NB 64 General special
Special countries, see NB 201-1113

NC 54 History of drawing. Primitive
Cf. NK 1177, Primitive ornament

NC 55 — Ancient

ND 1482 — Painting. Technique. Styles. General styles, A-Z
    .P7 Primitive painting. Naive painting (Includes note below N 7432.5.P7)

NK 605 — Decorative arts. Primitive

NK 1177 — Decoration and ornament. History. Primitive ornament. Evolution of decorative art
    Cf. GN 419, Anthropology
    NC 54, Primitive drawing

NK 3795 — Other arts and art industries. Ceramics. History. Primitive
    For aspects other than aesthetic, see GN 433

N Index — Primitive art: N 5310.7-5313
    Architecture: NA 205
    Ceramics: GN 433, NK 3795
    Decoration and ornament: NK 1177
    Decorative arts: NK 605
    Drawing, design: NC 54
    Illustration: NC 54
    Sculpture: NB 62-64
    See also Naive art; Primitivism (Art); Primitivism as a style in art
    Primitive art, American E 59.A7, F 1219.3. A7, etc.
    Primitivism
      Visual arts
        General
          Canadian primitivism: N 6540.5.P7
          United States primitivism: N 6505.5 .P74
        By period
          Colonial period
          American primitivism. N 6505.5.P7
          17th-18th centuries
          English primitivism: N 6766.5.P74
          19th century
          American primitivism: N 6510.5.P7

20th century
American primitivism: N 6512.5.P7
Belgian primitivism: N 6968.5.P74
Canadian primitivism: N 6546.5.P7
Dutch primitivism: N 6948.5.P74
French primitivism: N 6848.5.P7
German primitivism: N 6868.5.P7
Hungarian primitivism: N 6820.5.P7
Italian primitivism: N 6818.5.P7
Romanian primitivism: N 7228.5.P7
Swedish primitivism: N 7088.5.P7
Yugoslavian primitivism: N7242.5.P7

Comment: The index terms under "Primitivism" were altered by List 178; these areas in the N schedule were not included as they are repetitious and the formal name of a style of European art.

Q (6th Edition, 1973)

Q 141.2   Elementary mathematics. Numeration, number concept, numeration systems. History
Cf. GN 476.1, Primitive numeration
RECOMMENDATION: Use "Numeration (Ethnology)" rather than "Primitive numeration."

Q Index   Primitive numeration (Anthropology): GN 476.1
RECOMMENDATION: Eliminate "Primitive" and use "Numeration (Ethnology)."

R (4th Edition, 1980)

R 131+   Medicine. History
Cf. GN 477+, Primitive medicine
GR 880, Folk medicine
RECOMMENDATION: Substitute "Medicine (Ethnology)" for "Primitive medicine."

RD 22   Surgery. History. Primitive
Cf. GN 477.5+, Ethnology

RECOMMENDATION: Use "Origins" rather than "Primitive."

RG 53   Gynecology and obstetrics. History. Primitive
RECOMMENDATION: Use "Origins" rather than "Primitive."

RG 512   Obstetrics. History. Primitive
RECOMMENDATION: Use "Origins" rather than "Primitive."

T (5th Edition, 1971)

T (32)   Technology. History. Primitive peoples, see
GN 429-434
RECOMMENDATION: Replace caption with "Technology. History. Material culture, see GH 429-434. For material culture of individual peoples, see the D, E, and F schedules."

TH 16   Building construction. History and description. Ancient
Including primitive construction
RECOMMENDATION: Omit phrase "Including primitive construction."

TJ 901   Hydraulic machinery. Pumps and pumping engines.
General special.
Including ancient and primitive pumps.
RECOMMENDATION: Alter last line to read "Including history."

T Index   Primitive industries: GN 429-434
RECOMMENDATION: Use "Industries (Ethnology) and Material culture."

Z (5th Edition, 1980)

Religions (non-Christian)

Z 7833   General bibliography. General special bibliography.

Including primitive religions, sex worship, phallicism, etc.
RECOMMENDATION: Substitute "religion (ethnology)" or "religions of preliterate and/or folk societies" for "primitive religions."

Z Index

Primitive religions: Z 7833
RECOMMENDATION: Use "Religion (Ethnology)."

Two Changed Headings: Documentation

Sanford Berman

I.

On October 15, 1981, I sent this letter to *The Star* (National Hansen's Disease Center, Carville, LA 70721):

Dear Friends,

As the enclosed pages from both our own catalog and the National Library of Medicine's MEDICAL SUBJECT HEADINGS 1980 indicate, "Leprosy" is now the subject heading prevalent, or favored, in most library catalogs and indexes. The October 1981 *Consumer Health Info*, however, on p. 6 cites an article in your May/June issue titled "Why not Hansen's disease instead of Leprosy?" Because we are concerned at Hennepin County Library to employ terminology that is relatively objective and unbiased, I'd very much appreciate a copy of that article, together with any other information and arguments you can supply regarding the merit of substituting "Hansen's Disease" for "Leprosy." If convinced by the documentation, we will immediately make such a change here, and duly report it to the library community by means of our bi-monthly HCL CATALOGING BULLETIN.

With thanks in advance for whatever material
    you can send,
Sanford Berman
Head Cataloger

cc: *Consumer Health Info* (Eleanor Otterness, Editor, c/o Group Health Plan, Inc., 2500 Como Avenue, St. Paul, MN 55108)

P.S. Just for the record: ''Hansen's Disease'' *does* appear in the HCL catalog, as well as in ''MeSH,'' as a cross-reference to ''Leprosy'':

Hansen's Disease. *See* Leprosy.

Louis Boudreaux, Chair of the *Star* Editorial Board, replied on October 30th:

Dear Sir:

It is most encouraging to learn that the Hennepin County Library is desirous of promoting objective and unbiased nomenclature and terminology wherever possible. In compliance with your request for facts and authoritative opinions put forth by THE STAR and others who strongly oppose the pejorative term ''leprosy'' for a specific disease considered to be feebly communicable and totally unrelated to the ingnominious Biblical scourge, we are sending you a collection of articles and documents in support of universal recognition of ''Hansen's disease.'' After reviewing the material, I am sure you will agree that the continued association of ''leprosy'' with Hansen's disease would only serve to perpetuate the stigma.

If Hansen's disease does become the accepted nomenclature, and it certainly should since it is more humane, dignified and scientifically accurate, it may be necessary to also say that it is sometimes erroneously associated with Biblical leprosy. However, we cannot hope to achieve ultimate success until the definition of Hansen's disease is accompanied by a new glossary of related terms such as *M. hansenii* (Hansen's bacillus) in place of *M. leprae*, *Virchowian* in place of *lepromatous*, *Mitsuda* in place of *lepromin*, E.N.H., etc. These terms are already in rather wide use.

Thank you very much for your interest in this extremely important matter. If Hansen's disease does become the primary entry for this disease in your cataloging we would certainly like to know.

That prompted another missive, dated November 3, 1981:

Louis Boudreaux, Chair
STAR Editorial Board
Box 325
Carville, LA 70721

Dear Mr. Boudreaux,

Many thanks for your October 30th letter and generous documentation concerning the term, "Leprosy." Since we are committed to employing humane, non-pejorative nomenclature, particularly names favored by the affected persons or groups themselves, we find your arguments for replacing LEPROSY with HANSEN'S DISEASE persuasive. Accordingly, we are now abandoning LEPROSY as a subject heading. In the next edition of our catalog (on microfiche), HANSEN'S DISEASE will appear in place of the currently-used form LEPROSY. This new heading will be cross-referenced from both "H.D." and "'Leprosy'"; e.g.,

> H.D. *See* HANSEN'S DISEASE.
> "Leprosy." *See* HANSEN'S DISEASE.

Further, we will fully report this reform in the next (Jan./Feb. 1982) issue of our bimonthly *HCL cataloging bulletin*, scheduled for publication in early or mid-December. That report will include extensive citations, culled from *The Star*, as shown on the enclosed sheet. Once they appear, I will immediately forward copies of the revamped catalog-entries and *Cataloging bulletin* report.

With best wishes to you and your colleagues,

Sanford Berman
Head Cataloger

cc: John Likins, Editor, *PLAFSEP* (c/o Wellesley Free Library, P.O. Box 308, Wellesley, MA 02181)

Eleanor Otterness, Editor, *Consumer Health Info* (c/o Group Health Plan, Inc., 2500 Como Avenue, St. Paul, MN 55108)

Mary Kay Pietris, Chief, Subject Cataloging Division, The Library of Congress (Washington, D.C. 20540)

The Editor, *Medical Subject Headings* (National Library of Medicine, 8600 Rockville Pike, Bethesda, MD 20209)

Marvin Scilken, Editor, *Unabashed Librarian* (G.P.O. Box 2631, NYC 10001)

Karl Nyren, Editor, *LJ/SLJ Hotline* (1800 Avenue of the Americas, NYC 10036)

This is what appeared on the enclosed sheet:
Hansen's Disease.**

cn LC form: LEPROSY. Authority: Abraham Rotberg, "Mexico City: 'Hansen's Disease' vs. 'Leprosy,'" *The star: radiating the light of truth on Hansen's Disease*, v. 38, no. 1 (1978), p. 1 ("The terminology has officially been banned by the governments of Brazil, Portugal and Surinam and officially abandoned by the U.S. Public Health Service's regulations...It is time to expel from modern medicine the pejorative which extensive inquiries throughout the English-speaking world have proven beyond any doubt to be the disintegrator of the patient's personality, the label that blocks education, the continued psychic pain and trauma and the most negative of all medical terms''); *Star* Editorial Board, "There is no middle of the road," *The Star*, v. 38, no. 1 (1978), p. 1 ("Financial pleas for sufferers of HD may not fill the mission coffers as readily, but the constant use of these archaic terms are not improving the psycho-social welfare of the patient either''); "Editorial policy on terminology," *The star*, v. 40, no. 1 (Sept./Oct. 1980), p. 1 ("The *Star* stands firmly in its opposition to the use of the term 'leprosy'''); "The name's the thing," *The star*, v. 40, no. 1 (Sept./Oct. 1980), p. 2, 16 ("The point of the story is that the facts about HD did not frighten him very much. It was the word 'leprosy' that did. He wasn't petrified of the disease itself, only its name. The word 'leprosy' causes one of the biggest problems that people with HD have''); Bhagwant Singh Dalawari, "Why not 'Hansen's Disease' instead of 'Leprosy'?" *The star*, v. 40, no. 5 (May/June 1981), p. 5, 16 ("Now the point is this: should a particular name for this disease be used because it evokes pity, provides more funds for helping the patients, *even if it hurts their pride; preserves their dehumanised form?...I see no reason why the opinion of pa-*

tients who have survived the shock, who have come into them-
selves and are human beings in their own right should not be-
come the decisive factor in determining the terminology. And
the educated, developed patient has repeatedly pleaded for
'H.D.' because, in the words of 19th century etymologist William Matthews, the word 'leprosy' was 'sharper than drawn
swords, which give more pain than a score of blows...'
...My humble impression is that it is just not correct, even re-
ligiously, to parade the derogatory vocabulary which humili-
ates the patient, even if the purpose is to help him economically. Moral, spiritual bruises will not be healed by material
help''); Louis Boudreaux, "Four decades of progress," *The*
star, v. 41, no. 1 (Sept./Oct. 1981), p. 8 ("1951-1961: *The*
star...was applying more and more pressure to bring about
long-overdue recognition of patients' rights, especially the
very basic right of replacing the debasing terms 'leper' and
'leprosy' with the humane, dignified, and accurate term
Hansen's disease''); Fay Diers Lindsay, "Father Damien was
not a leper!," *The star*, v. 41, no. 1 (Sept./Oct. 1981), p. 12
("The word 'leper' is as bad as the word 'nigger.' It was out-
lawed by those who work with this disease, at their International Congress of 1948, and is very, very offensive when used
in any way...").

sf H. D.
"Leprosy"
xx Skin—Diseases

A few months later, Fay Diers Lindsay, who operates AIGA Publications (744 Frances Harriet Drive, Baton Rouge, LA 70815), un-
expectedly wrote:

Dear Mr. Berman,

Enclosed is a flyer announcing our first effort for sale, and
copies of our for free efforts, too, but this letter is really in the
nature of a fan letter to you. I was a volunteer at THE STAR,
Carville, for the last 21 months, and I have never felt happier
than I did about the change in terminology in the Hennepin County Library cataloging! I'm not even sure that many realize what a
splendid thing that was, and what a milestone that it really is to

have a library change its cataloging, and moreover, to announce it to all other libraries as you did. I am very pleased to have a part in the documentation, and I have written Mr. Dalawari of India, too. I know he will be tremendously pleased as well.

And the entire exchange prompted this never-published "Letter to the Editor" of the *Minneapolis Tribune*, dated January 15, 1982:

Friends,

This morning's TRIBUNE on page 15B ran a news item bannered "Report: Drug resistance may increase leprosy cases." The text, like the banner, repeatedly mentioned "leprosy" and "leprosy patients."

Until a month or two ago, the "leprosy" reference wouldn't have troubled me. But it does now. Because I've learned that the people described as "leprosy patients" in the New York Times Service article emphatically do *not* wish to be called either "leprosy patients" or—even more commonly—"lepers." And they insist that the disease itself should be known as Hansen's Disease.

Following correspondence with an organized group of patients at the Public Health Service's National Hansen's Disease Center in Carville, Louisiana, we changed the relevant subject heading used in our library catalog from the previous "LEPROSY" to "HANSEN'S DISEASE," and similarly substituted "HANSEN'S DISEASE PATIENTS" for "LEPERS."

The enclosed documentation explains the objections to "leprosy" and "lepers" in much detail. The arguments, I trust you'll agree, are at once serious and compelling.

I invite the TRIBUNE to join Hennepin County Library in using more sensitive and accurate terminology with respect to the disease produced by "Hansen's bacillus" and the people it afflicts.

II.

This "Commentary" appeared on p. 151 of the May/June 1982 *Rehabilitation Literature* (v. 43, nos. 5/6):

"Work Centers"—New Term, New Pride

Among the more insidious labeling processes occurring in our society today is that applied to persons with disabilities. "Handicap" (vaguely reminiscent of horse races or golf courses) and "invalid" (not valid?) are just a few of the negatively connoted terms still in use. Happily—as with many of the labels applied to minority groups—these pejorative terms have fallen into some disrepute, phrases such as "persons who have disabilities" replacing them. These new expressions are intended to correctly separate the disabling condition from the person.

At a time when individual strengths are being hailed and the more objectionable anomalies of our language are being routed, it is appropriate that the seemingly acceptable term "sheltered workshop" is being held in question as well. If it does bite the dust, then it is to be hoped that along with it will go both the frequent misconception that persons at the "workshops" are not really workers but are instead engaged in a hobby of some sort, and the patronizing consensus that such settings function as giveaways or freebies (i.e., "shelter": safety in a storm), an attitude which significantly decreases their integrity.

The new and preferred term is "work center." It's been lauded in Congress by Senator Weicker, endorsed by the National Easter Seal Society, and recently adopted by National Industries for the Severely Handicapped (NISH). Other major organizations are considering endorsing it as well. The "work center" term is designed to at last give credit as workers to those persons having such severe disabilities that they cannot presently work in a normal societal work setting, but who nevertheless do work in the facilities.

Workshop, if not associated with crafts, has by some persons even been associated with "sweat shop," hordes of indistinguishable persons toiling out their existence at sewing machines. In a work center, people work together toward common goals; that is, the earning of an honorable wage by producing goods that other people truly need.

As a program, the "work center" philosophy is designed to facilitate a more self-supporting posture in this area of rehabilitation—good for center survival in hard economic times and good for the morale of people working in the center. Why not, it's finally being asked, run "work centers" (workshops) more like businesses, with businesslike names and businesslike philosophies? Why not consider attaining more favorable economic returns? Why not choose to survive the eighties, and survive them with dignity?

In speaking of work centers recently, John Garrison, Executive Director of the National Easter Seal Society, said, "We're proud that the Easter Seal Society has been able to forge a new path in this important area. But we're eager for others to join with us. It's a concept that should have been considered long ago."

The impact of the words we so easily write or speak is always worth thinking about. Just two words may mean so much to the dignity of so many. And the possibility that after all these years what we thought wasn't for profit could be—not in a greedy way, but in a way that assures the dignity of persons involved—that's exciting as well.

Work center. A positive new concept in rehabilitation bolstered by a positive new term...we encourage you to make it a part of your vocabulary.

That triggered this letter, dated July 2, 1982:

The Editor
Rehabilitation Literature
National Easter Seal Society
2023 W. Ogden Avenue
Chicago, IL 60612

Dear Colleague,

A co-worker here recently shared your May/June 1982 "Commentary" dealing with the term, "Work Centers." Since our official policy concerning subject headings used in the library catalog is "to eliminate sexist, racist, ageist, and other biased or inaccurate terms," we are now replacing SHELTERED WORKSHOPS with WORK CENTERS. We will report this change to the library community in the next issue of our bi-monthly *HCL Cataloging Bulletin* (sample issue being sent "Library rate" for your information). This is the draft entry:

Work centers.

cn LC [Library of Congress] form: SHELTERED WORKSHOPS. Authority: "Commentary: 'work centers'—new term, new pride,'' *Rehabilitation literature*, v. 43, nos. 5/6 (May/June 1982), p. 151 ("At a time when individual strengths are being hailed and the more objectionable anomalies of our language are being routed, it is appropriate that the seemingly acceptable term, 'sheltered workshop' is being held in question as well. If it does bite the dust, then it is to be hoped that along with it will go both the frequent misconception that persons at the 'workshops' are not really workers but are instead engaged in a hobby of some sort, and the patronizing consensus that such settings function as giveaways or freebies...an attitude which significantly decreases their integrity. The new and preferred term is 'work center.' It's been lauded in Congress by Senator Weicker, endorsed by the National Easter Seal Society, and recently adopted by National Industries for the Severely Handicapped...The 'work center' term is designed to at last give credit as *workers* to those persons having such severe disabilities that they cannot presently work in a normal societal work setting, but who nevertheless do *work* in the facilities'').

pn Here are entered materials on facilities where severely disabled persons work, "earning an honorable wage by producing goods that other people truly need."

sf Centers for disabled workers
    Disabled workers' centers
    Severely disabled workers' centers
    "Sheltered workshops"
    "Workshops, Sheltered"

xx Disabled persons—Employment
    Disabled workers
    Physically disabled persons—Employment
    Vocational rehabilitation centers

The "pn" is a "public note" that will appear immediately following the subject heading in the catalog. The "sf's" are "see" references, and the "xx's" represent "see also from" connections: e.g.,

DISABLED WORKERS. *See also* WORK CENTERS.
Severely disabled workers' centers. *See* WORK CENTERS.

Trusting you'll find it of some interest, I'm enclosing correspondence and background data relating to another recent term-substitution: HANSEN'S DISEASE replacing LEPROSY. And also enclosed are a few sample pages concerning handicapist terminology from a work co-authored by one of our staff, Emmett Davis (*Mainstreaming library service for disabled people*).

With best wishes,

Sanford Berman
Head Cataloger

cc: Emmett Davis (HCL Cataloging Section)

Jan Price (HCL Government Center Information Center Library)

John Likins, Editor, *PLAFSEP* (Wellesley Free Library, Massachusetts)

Norman Grunewald, Program Specialist, National Easter Seal Society

Mary Kay Pietris, Chief, Subject Cataloging Division, The Library of Congress (Washington, DC 20540)

Eleanor Otterness, Editor *Consumer Health Info* (Room 336, Group Health Plan, Inc., 2829 University Ave., S.E. Minneapolis, MN 55414)

Mrs. Tom Cook, Jr. and John Garrison, President and Executive Director of the National Easter Society, jointly wrote on July 12th:

Dear Mr. Berman:

We at the National Easter Seal Society are heartened to hear of the leadership role taken by the Hennepin County Library in formally adopting the term "work center" to designate vocational rehabilitation facilities. Hennepin County Library, through this action, emerges as a model for the entire library community. We welcome you as a partner and look forward to working with you as efforts to effect this positive change are implemented.

And Norman D. Grunewald, Society Program Specialist, added on October 14th:

Dear Sanford:

Please excuse the undue delay in responding to your recent mailings indicating the new designation of work centers in the Hennepin County Library system. We applaud your actions and thank you not only for converting to the work center term but also promoting it so effectively.

I will soon be forwarding a copy of those national organizations which have also endorsed or supported the work center term. We are making good progress....largely due to people such as yourself. Thanks.

Out of the Kitchen—
But Not Into the Catalog

Sanford Berman

Despite laudable efforts at the Library of Congress to achieve sex equity in subject cataloging—e.g., the contraction of forms like WOMEN AS LIBRARIANS to WOMEN LIBRARIANS and either the "neutralization" of various occupational terms (e.g., LONGSHOREMEN becoming STEVEDORES) or creation of counterpart female headings (e.g., COWBOYS/COWGIRLS)—significant nomenclature remains sexist, in effect declaring women to be a kind of subspecies. And women's materials still suffer routine undercataloging, most relevant literature, especially fiction, enjoying no subject access and many vital topics continuing to be ignored. A few specifics:

Sexist terminology

CITY COUNCILMEN
COLOR OF MAN
FALL OF MAN
FISHERMEN
FOSSIL MAN
LUMBERMEN
MAN
MAN (CHRISTIAN THEOLOGY)
MAN (HINDUISM [JUDAISM, etc.])
MAN, PREHISTORIC
MAN, PRIMITIVE [sic!]
MAN (THEOLOGY)
MANPOWER
MANPOWER PLANNING
MANPOWER POLICY

167

MANPOWER POLICY, RURAL
WHALEMEN
WILD MEN

Missing terminology

AFRO-AMERICAN FEMINISM
AFRO-AMERICAN LESBIANS
ANARCHA-FEMINISM
ANTI-PORNOGRAPHY MOVEMENT
BATTERED WOMEN
BATTERED WOMEN'S SERVICES
CHILD CARE (EMPLOYEE BENEFIT)
CHILD SUPPORT ENFORCEMENT
CHRISTIAN FEMINISM
DISABLED MOTHERS
DISPLACED HOMEMAKER SERVICES
ECO-FEMINISM
FAMILY PLANNING
FAMILY PLANNING SERVICES
FEMINIST ART
FEMINIST COLLECTIVES
FEMINIST CRITICISM
FEMINIST DRAMA
FEMINIST ESSAYS
FEMINIST FICTION
FEMINIST FILM CRITICISM
FEMINIST HUMOR
FEMINIST PERIODICALS
FEMINIST SPIRITUALITY
FEMINIST THEOLOGY
GAY MEN'S WIVES
INTERNSHIP PROGRAMS FOR WOMEN
JEWISH LESBIANS
LESBIAN AUTHORS
LESBIAN FEMINISM
LESBIAN MOTHERS
LESBIAN TEENAGERS
NONSEXIST CHILDREARING
NONSEXIST WRITING GUIDELINES

PARENTAL NOTIFICATION LAWS
PAY EQUITY
PREGNANCY COUNSELING
PREGNANT WORKERS
RADICAL FEMINISM
SEXISM IN CATALOGING
  [CHILDREN'S LITERATURE, CHRISTIANITY, FILMS,
  PSYCHOTHERAPY, SPORTS, etc.]
SOCIALIST FEMINISM
SUBURBAN WOMEN
SUPERHEROINE COMICS
VIOLENCE AGAINST WOMEN
WOMEN'S BOOKSTORES
WOMEN'S FINANCIAL INSTITUTIONS
WOMEN'S MOVEMENT
WOMEN'S MUSIC
WOMEN'S POWER
WOMEN'S PUBLISHERS
WOMEN'S RESISTANCE AND REVOLTS
WOMEN'S SHELTERS
WORKING CLASS WOMEN

CASES

These, as examples, are subject tracings that recent women-related works didn't get because of an overly parsimonious assignment policy at LC and/or the failure to innovate needed headings:

Albert, Gail.
  Matters of chance. 1982.
  1. Women neurobiologists—Fiction.
2. Jewish-American women—Fiction.

Barth, Richard.
  One dollar death. 1982.
  1. Binton, Margaret—Fiction.
2. Women detectives—Fiction.

Beck, Evelyn Torton, editor.
  Nice Jewish girls: a Lesbian anthology. 1982.
  1. Jewish Lesbians.

Cho, Emily.
  Looking, working, living terrific 24
  hours a day. 1982.
  1. Women's clothing.

Climo, Shirley.
  Cobweb Christmas. 1982.
  1. Senior women—Fiction.

Cróss, Amanda.
  The James Joyce murder. 1982.
  1. Fansler, Kate—Fiction.
2. Women detectives—Fiction.

Danky, James P., editor.
Women's periodicals and newspapers from the 18th Century to 1981: a union list of the holdings of Madison, Wisconsin libraries. 1982.
1. Women's periodicals—Bibliography—Union lists. 2. Feminist periodicals—Bibliography—Union lists.

De Pauw, Linda Grant.
Seafaring women. 1982.
1. Women sailors. 2. Women pirates.

Horn, Patrice D.
Sex in the office. 1982.
1. Sex in offices, 2. Sexual harassment.

Irwin, Hadley.
What about grandma? 1982.
1. Grandmothers—Fiction.
2. Mother and daughter—Fiction.
3. Sixteen-year-old girls—Fiction.

Day, Dorothy,
By little and by little: the selected writings of Dorothy Day. 1983.
1. Women radicals—Correspondence, reminiscences, etc.
2. Women, Catholic—Personal narratives.

Griffin, Susan.
Made from this earth: an anthology of writings. 1982.
1. Feminist essays. 2. Feminist poetry. 3. Feminist drama.

Hull, Gloria T., editor.
All the women are White, all the Blacks are men, but some of us are brave; Black women's studies. 1982.
1. Afro-American feminism. 2. Women's writings, Afro-American—Bibliography. 3. Black Women's Studies.

Ruether, Rosemary Radford.
Sexism and God-talk: toward a feminist theology. 1983.
1. Sexism in Christianity. 2. Christian feminism. 3. Feminist theology.

Dorfman, Ariel.
Widows. 1983.
1. Women's resistance and revolts—Fiction.

Plotz, Helen, compiler.
Saturday's children: poems of work. 1982.
1. Women workers—Poetry.

Lee, Barbara.
The woman's guide to the stock market. 1982.
1. Women—Personal finance.

Lewis, Shannon.
Personal habits. 1982.
1. Nuns—Fiction

Mays, Lucinda.
The candle and the mirror, 1982.
1. Women labor organizers—Fiction.

Morris, Michelle.
If I should die before I wake. 1982.
1. Father and daughter—Fiction.
2. Seventeen-year-old girls—Fiction. 3. Incest—Fiction.

Sachs, Marilyn.
Call me Ruth. 1982.
1. Women labor unionists—Fiction. 2. Women garment workers—Fiction.

Basic sources on subject cataloging women's materials

"At Random: Notes, Comments, Etc.," *HCL Cataloging Bulletin*, #6/7 (April 5, 1974), p. 39-42.
Berman, Sanford, "Man/Woman/Sex," in *Prejudices and Antipathies* (Scarecrow Press, 1971), p. 174-205.
Berman, Sanford, "Webster's Fourth," *Humanist*, v. 42, no. 6 (Nov./Dec. 1982), p. 66.
Biermaier, Carla Knutson, "Mistresses, Consorts & Cataloging," *WLW Journal*, v. 5, no. 6 (Nov./Dec. 1980), p. 5-7.

"Conference Kaleidoscope: Sexism," *SRRT Newsletter*, #32 (Aug. 1974), p. 4-5.

Dickinson, Elizabeth, "Word Game," *Canadian Library Journal*, v. 31, no. 4 (Aug. 1974), p. 338-43.

Marshall, Joan K., *On Equal Terms: a Thesaurus for Nonsexist Indexing and Cataloging* (Neal-Schuman, 1977), 152p.

Marshall, Joan K., "Sexist Subject Headings: an Update," *HCL Cataloging Bulletin*, #17 (Oct. 1, 1975), p. 38-42.

"Why All the Fuss Over 'Humanizing' and 'Desexifying' Subject Forms?," *HCL Cataloging Bulletin*, #5 (Jan. 21, 1974), p. 21-5.

Beyond the Pale:
Subject Access to Judaica

Sanford Berman

It's reasonable to expect that the subject treatment of Jewish materials in library catalogs should do two things:

- Provide full and swift access to those materials by both Jews themselves and interested Gentiles.
- Use headings that:
    - Specifically and accurately represent or denote Jewish subjects.
    - Don't bias the library patron against either the materials or the topics.
    - Reflect the language, experience, and viewpoint of *Jews*, not Gentiles, of *victims*, not victimizers.

The two fundamental goals or functions, then, are: access and equity. But, unfortunately, they are not the reality of Judaica subject cataloging, at least not as performed by the Library of Congress (LC) and its lockstep followers.

While it can safely—and sadly—be argued that no ethnic or religious groups, apart from WASPs, enjoy truly adequate and equitable subject treatment, Jews undoubtedly fare worse than all others. It's anybody's guess *why* that's the case, but there's no mystery whatever about how it happens. There are two modes: First, through the content and form of the vocabulary. And, second, by the way that vocabulary is actually applied.

This is a revised and expanded version of a paper first presented at the Association of Jewish Libraries Convention, Cincinnati, June 18, 1979, later published in the author's *Joy of Cataloging* (Phoenix, AZ: Oryx Press, 1981), and then reprinted in *Shmate*, v. 1, no. 3 (Sept./Oct. 1982).

1. THE VOCABULARY PROBLEM ITSELF DIVIDES INTO SEVERAL ASPECTS

• Clearly defamatory, palpably Goyish terminology like JEW-ISH QUESTION and—until very recently—that whole sequence of assinine and demeaning headings: JEWS *AS* FARMERS, JEWS *AS* SOLDIERS, JEWS *AS* SCIENTISTS, etc. (which incidentally co-existed for decades with JEWISH CRIMINALS, no "as" considered necessary to express doubt about a Jew's fitness for being a crook).

• A special or peculiar approach to Jews and Judaica, exemplified by the almost exclusive use of—JEWS as an ethnic subdivision under topics like CAPITALISTS AND FINANCIERS and RADICALISM, and the concurrent appearance of JEWS, AMERICAN and JEWS—UNITED STATES in *LCSH*, with no clear differentiation between the two forms.

• A failure to create and assign headings for Jewish-related subjects amply represented in both print and audiovisual media; e.g.,

ALIYAH BETH

ANTISEMITISM IN CHRISTIANITY

ANTISEMITISM IN THE ARMED FORCES [applied at HCL to Harold W. Felton's 1978 biography of Uriah Phillips Levy]

ANTISEMITISM IN THE NEW TESTAMENT [assigned at HCL, with a—FICTION subhead, to Ben Friedman's 1977 novel, *The Anguish of Father Rafti*.]

BEIRUT MASSACRE, SEPTEMBER 16-18, 1982—ISRAELI PARTICIPATION

BILINGUAL MATERIALS—ENGLISH/HEBREW and the corollary BILINGUAL MATERIALS—ENGLISH/YIDDISH

CANADA AND THE JEWISH HOLOCAUST (1933-1945)

CHRISTIAN CHURCH AND THE JEWISH HOLOCAUST (1933-1945)

CHRISTIAN ZIONISM

CONCENTRATION CAMP SURVIVORS

GAY SYNAGOGUES

GEFILTE FISH

GHETTOES [in the LC scheme still only a *see* reference to JEWS—SEGREGATION]

HOMOPHOBIA IN JUDAISM

HUMANISTIC JUDAISM

ISRAELI-OCCUPIED TERRITORIES

JEWISH-AMERICAN DETECTIVES

JEWISH-AMERICAN LABOR LEADERS

JEWISH-AMERICAN POLITICIANS

JEWISH-AMERICAN RADICALS

JEWISH CONSERVATISM

JEWISH GAYS

JEWISH LESBIANS [applicable, e.g., to Evelyn Torton Beck's 1982 *Nice Jewish Girls: a Lesbian anthology*]

JEWISH RADICALISM

JEWISH SOCIALISM

JEWISH RESISTANCE AND REVOLTS [which at HCL parallels rubrics for AFRICAN RESISTANCE AND REVOLTS, NATIVE AMERICAN RESISTANCE AND REVOLTS, WOMEN'S RESISTANCE AND REVOLTS, etc.]

KLEZMER MUSIC [assigned at HCL to Klezmorim's 1977 LP, *East Side Wedding*]

LEBANON—HISTORY—ISRAELI INVASION, 1982 [applicable, e.g., to Jacobo Timerman's *Longest War: Israel in Lebanon* (1982)]

NAZI FUGITIVES [applicable, e.g., to M. Bar-Zohar's *Avengers* (1967), S. Wiesenthal's *Murderers among Us* (1967), and H. Blum's *Wanted! The Search for Nazis in America* (1977).]

NAZI HUNTERS [assigned at HCL to material by and about Simon Wiesenthal]

PALESTINIAN ARABS—RIGHTS

PALESTINIAN STATE (PROPOSED)

SEXISM IN JUDAISM

SHTETL [Hennepin, emphatically not a "Jewish" library, has already assigned SHTETL to more than two dozen works, and the *Index to Jewish Periodicals* acknowledges the topic with a heading for JEWS IN EUROPE—SHTETL.]

SKOKIE CASE

UNITED STATES AND THE JEWISH HOLOCAUST (1933-1945)

YIDDISH THEATER

WEST BANK (JORDAN RIVER)—ISRAELI SETTLE-MENTS

folkloric persons and places like CHELM and SCHLEMIEHL.

fictional characters like DAVID SMALL, the protagonist of Harry Kemelman's "Rabbi" stories, SADIE SHAPIRO, who stars in a series of novels by Robert Kimmel Smith, and "SILKY" PINCUS, Leo Rosten's imaginary shamus.

and literary prizes—like the SCHWARTZ JUVENILE BOOK AWARDS, BERNARD H. MARKS AWARD BOOKS, and EDWARD LEWIS WALLANT BOOK AWARDS— that could be applied as labels or tags to the laureate works themselves, making it easy to identify those award winners actually in the collection.

• A failure to introduce helpful cross-references to existing terms, links that would benefit Jewish and non-Jewish catalog users alike; e.g.,

HOLOCAUST, JEWISH (1933-1945)

   x Shoah

SYNAGOGUES

   x Jewish synagogues
      Shuls
      Temples, Jewish

BIBLE. O.T.

x Bible, Jewish
Jewish Bible

BIBLE. O.T. PENTA-
TEUCH.

x Five Books of Moses

JEWS—PERSECUTIONS

x Pogroms
Programs

MYSTICISM—JUDAISM

x Jewish mysticism

JEWS—DIASPORA

x Jewish Diaspora
Jews—Galut

YOM KIPPUR

x Day of Repentance
(Judaism)

ENTEBBE AIRPORT RAID,
1976

x Israeli Raid, Entebbe
Airport, 1976
Uganda Airport Raid,
1976

• Awkwardly or oddly formulated terms that impair quick access
or, in catalogs with few cross-references, totally prevent finding the
sought-after topic; e.g.,

AMERICAN LITERA- TURE—JEWISH AUTHORS	instead of	JEWISH-AMERICAN LITERATURE
WARSAW—HISTORY —UPRISING OF 1943	instead of	WARSAW GHETTO UPRISING, 1943
AMAUROTIC FAMILY IDIOCY	instead of	TAY-SACHS' DIS- EASE (used by the *In- dex to Jewish Period- icals*)
NATIONAL SOCIAL- ISM	instead of	NAZISM
SLAUGHTERING AND SLAUGHTER- HOUSES—JEWS	instead of	the more accurate and far less insensitive SCHECTING (or SHECHTING)

• A failure to recognize the Jewish dimension of certain notable
events through *see also* connections; e.g.,

AUSCHWITZ TRIAL, FRANKFURT AM MAIN, 1963-1965

xx Holocaust, Jewish (1933-1945)
Jews—Persecutions [or Jews, European—Persecutions]

BABIY YAR MASSACRE, 1941

xx Antisemitism—Ukraine
Holocaust, Jewish (1933-1945)
Jews—Persecutions [or Jews, Ukrainian—Persecutions]

• A pervasive and overwhelming "Christian primacy" among the multitude of headings that deal with religion. In nearly every string of descriptors concerning a special facet of spirituality, worship, or faith, Christianity comes first. There are forms for GOD (AFRICAN RELIGION), GOD (HINDUISM), GOD (ISLAM), and GOD (JUDAISM), but not for GOD (CHRISTIANITY). Why? Because the unglossed, the unmodified GOD, the primary divinity, the God-Before-All-Other-Gods, is unabashedly and undeniably *Christian*. And the same pattern obtains for countless other topics, including ANGELS, SERMONS, CHILDREN'S SERMONS, HERESIES AND HERETICS, PRAYER, ESCHATOLOGY, CONFIRMATION, PROVIDENCE AND GOVERNMENT OF GOD, DEVOTIONAL LITERATURE, and THEOLOGY (indeed, the lately added "see" references to the unmodified term THEOLOGY, are from "Christian theology" and "Theology, Christian"!). Aside from considerations of ethics and fairness, this Christocentrism unquestionably violates the "Establishment Clause" of the First Amendment.

2. THE ASSIGNMENT PROBLEM IS BEST ILLUSTRATED WITH REAL CASES

• In 1978, Pantheon Books reissued Izzy Stone's *Underground to Palestine*, including a new introduction and epilogue. LC assigned three subject tracings: WORLD WAR, 1939-1945—REFUGEES; WORLD WAR, 1939-1945—JEWS; and STONE, ISIDOR F. The last head, for the author, would be redundant in a dictionary catalog; the first two are appropriate, but not nearly specific nor accurate enough. HCL added: ISRAEL—IMMIGRATION AND EMIGRA-

TION—HISTORY; ZIONISM; PALESTINIAN ARABS; PAL-
ESTINE—IMMIGRATION AND EMIGRATION—HISTORY;
ALIYAH BETH—PERSONAL NARRATIVES; and ISRAELI-
ARAB RELATIONS (Just for the record, the current LC "equiv-
alent" to ISRAELI-ARAB RELATIONS is JEWISH-ARAB RE-
LATIONS, which crazily implies that *all* Jews—everywhere—have
had, or are now having, "relations" with Arabs. Both the *Sears List
of Subject Headings* and *Subject Headings for Church or Synagogue
Libraries* wisely employ the unambiguous "Israeli" form).

• To Marilyn Hirsh's 1978 "easy book," *Potato Pancakes All
Around: A Hanukkah Tale*, LC's juvenalia catalogers applied one
heading: HANUKKAH—FICTION. And composed this summary:

> A wandering peddler teaches the villagers how to make potato
> pancakes from a crust of bread.

Okay, as far as it goes. But, again, it doesn't go far enough. HCL
inserted this extra note:

> Includes "Grandma Yetta's and Grandma Sophie's recipe for
> potato pancakes," as well as "a brief explanation of Hanukkah
> and its history."

And assigned four more headings, all subdivided by—FICTION:
PEDDLERS AND PEDDLING; LATKES; COOKING, JEWISH;
and SHTETL.

• Crowell, in 1977, published Lulla Rosenfeld's *Bright Star of
Exile*, subtitled *Jacob Adler and the Yiddish Theater*. LC's trio of
subject headings: ADLER, JACOB, 1855-1926; THEATER—
JEWS; and ACTORS, JEWISH—BIOGRAPHY. The first tracing,
for Adler himself, is unexceptional. However, the next two nicely
manage to both bury the "Yiddish" element and mask the biog-
raphee's true identity. HCL replaced them with YIDDISH
THEATER and ACTORS AND ACTRESSES, JEWISH-AMER-
ICAN. Also, to further enhance access by readers who might recall
only a portion of the title, Hennepin made title added-entries for
"Star of exile" and "Exile star."

• Maggie Rennert's *Shelanu, an Israel Journal*, appeared in
1979. It got three LC subject tracings: ISRAEL—DESCRIPTION
AND TRAVEL; AUTHORS, AMERICAN—20TH CENTURY—
BIOGRAPHY; and the wonderfully Byzantine RENNERT, MAG-

GIE—HOMES AND HAUNTS—ISRAEL—BEERSHEBA. HCL
left the first heading alone, changed the second to AUTHORS,
JEWISH-AMERICAN—DIARIES, and replaced the convoluted
Beersheba Monster with ISRAEL AND JEWISH-AMERICANS, a
homemade descriptor. Also, Hennepin made an entry for the permuted title, "An Israel journal," on the premise that some title
searchers might forget the first word, "Shelanu."
   • Stein and Day, in 1979, issued M. Hirsh Goldberg's *Just
Because They're Jewish*. LC assigned a total of four added entries:
one for the title plus three for subjects (JEWS—HISTORY,
JEWS—ANECDOTES, FACETIAE, SATIRE, ETC., and
JEWS—PUBLIC OPINION). That cataloging conveys the unmis-
takable impression that Goldberg's tome is basically a lighthearted
review of the Jewish experience and of popular ideas about Jews.
Well, Goldberg's style is surely informal, but the substance of his
book is definitely not "funny," nor does it qualify as a "balanced,"
good-and-bad rundown of "popular opinion" through the ages.
HCL made two notes to clarify the author's intent and what's really
inside the work:

> On title page: If anything can be misconstrued about the Jews,
> it will be. . .and has been.

> PARTIAL CONTENTS: The Jews in stereotype. -About that
> religion that brought you the Ten Commandments. -Praise the
> Lord and pass the ammunition. -Sticks and stones may break
> your bones, but names can kill you. -To Hell with Hitler: a
> journey inside the Holocaust.

   Of the three original subject headings, Hennepin kept only the
first, JEWS—HISTORY, and expanded the treatment with: ANTI-
SEMITISM; JEWISH SOLDIERS; MISCONCEPTIONS (an HCL
innovation); JUDAISM; HOLOCAUST, JEWISH (1933-1945);
JEWISH RESISTANCE AND REVOLTS; and JEWS—MISCEL-
LANEA.
   • Yael Dayan's 1979 novel, *Three Weeks in October*, published
by Delacorte & Friede, got one LC subject tracing, for ISRAEL-
ARAB WAR, 1973—FICTION. Which is perfectly valid. It might
also, however, have been assigned SOLDIERS—ISRAEL—FIC-
TION and the genre heading, ISRAELI FICTION, which can be
valuable—particularly in smaller collections—for collocating or list-

ing together all such works. (LC applies genre tracings solely to anthologies by *various* authors, not to novels, plays, or poetry by a *single* writer.)

• *Quitting Time*, a 1982 novel by Leonard Kriegel, unsurprisingly emerged from the LC cataloging process without *any* topical access points. But it merited these: JEWISH-AMERICAN LABOR LEADERS—FICTION, C.I.O.—FICTION, JEWISH-AMERICAN RADICALS—FICTION, and COMMUNISM AND LABOR UNIONS—FICTION.

• A collective of radical Jews in Chicago has been producing the tabloid, *Chutzpah*, for about nine years. In 1977, New Glide Publications, a small alternative press in San Francisco, issued *Chutzpah: a Jewish Liberation Anthology*. The table of contents includes captions like "Singing in a strange land: Jewish life in America," "Anti-Semitism," "The joy of socialism, the heartbreak of capitalism," and "Two peoples, two states: self-determination in the Middle East." Among the individual essays are "Role models for Jewish women," "The Jewish sorority: sisterhood perverted," "Why we write about Gay Liberation," "Dilemma of a Jewish Lesbian," "Anti-Semites are surfacing like roaches from the woodwork," "That's funny, you don't look Anti-Semitic: perspective on the American left," "Feminist frustration with the forefathers," "Magnus Hirschfeld: Gay Liberation's Zeyde," and "In forests and ghettos: Jewish resistance to the Nazis." All of this any cataloger could have determined purely from the "front matter," without reading a word of text or knowing anything in advance about the collective and its scruffy-looking newspaper. How was it subject-cataloged? With *one* heading: JEWS—HISTORY—20TH CENTURY—ADDRESSES, ESSAYS, LECTURES. Instead of that feeble, imprecise, and misleading treatment, which also happens to mask or submerge several key, controversial topics that are otherwise hard to find much about, it should have been assigned at least these nine tracings: JEWISH RESISTANCE AND REVOLTS; ANTISEMITISM; JEWISH WOMEN; JEWISH RADICALISM; PALESTINIAN STATE (PROPOSED); ISRAELI-ARAB RELATIONS; JEWISH GAYS; SEXISM IN JUDAISM; and JEWISH-AMERICANS. Further, there could have been—but wasn't—a title added-entry for "Jewish liberation anthology."

• LC applied three subject descriptors to Hans Askenasy's 1978 study, *Are We All Nazis?*: VIOLENCE; SOCIAL PSYCHIATRY; and HOMICIDE—PSYCHOLOGICAL ASPECTS. It deserved

more: AUSCHWITZ (CONCENTRATION CAMP); NAZIS—
PSYCHOLOGY; HOLOCAUST, JEWISH (1933-1945)—PSY-
CHOLOGICAL ASPECTS; OBEDIENCE; and ATROCITIES—
PSYCHOLOGICAL ASPECTS.

• LC's handling of *The Maimie Papers*, issued in 1977 by the
Feminist Press, and Lee Seldes' *Legacy of Mark Rothko*, a 1978
Holt title, neglects in both cases to recognize the Jewishness of the
principal figures, one a prostitute, the other a painter.

• Beverly Brodsky McDermott's 1976 *Golem: A Jewish Legend*,
got two subject tracings from LC, one for JUDAH LOW BEN
BEZALEEL and the other for GOLEM, both subdivided by—JU-
VENILE LITERATURE. Except for the ageist subhead, those are
fine—but insufficient. Even though explicitly subtitled "a Jewish
legend," and of obvious relevance to Jews, where's the explicitly
"Jewish" entry point? Missing. Nor did LC's cataloging express
other major aspects of this powerful rendering, elements that might
prove of special interest and worth to Jewish readers, adults as well
as children. These are the additional tracings applied at Hennepin:
GHETTOES, JEWISH—PRAGUE—FOLKLORE; JEWS,
CZECHOSLOVAK—PERSECUTIONS—FOLKLORE; LEG-
ENDS, JEWISH; and RABBIS—FOLKLORE.

• On October 14, 1982, this letter went to Mary Kay Pietris,
chief of LC's Subject Cataloging Division:

Dear Mary Kay,

According to the CIP for Marilyn Sach's *Call me Ruth*
(Doubleday, 1982), LC's juvenalia catalogers composed this
annotation:

SUMMARY: The daughter of a Russian immigrant family,
newly arrived in Manhattan in 1908, has conflicting feelings
about her mother's increasingly radical union involvement.

and assigned 4 subject headings:

1. Russian Americans—Fiction. 2. New York (N.Y.)—
Fiction. 3. Emigration and immigration—Fiction. 4. Labor
unions—Fiction.

Both the annotation and first subject tracing seriously distort
the book's thematic content, for while the subject family im-
migrated *from* Russia, they were not ethnic "Russians," but
rather Jews. This is apparent on the very first page of the text:

In the old country, my name was Rifka and my mother's name was Faigel...

Mama was standing barelegged in the water, her skirts hiked up around her waist, rinsing off the large, white Passover tablecloth, for the holiday had just ended.

And is further confirmed by the jacket subtitle: "A warm and moving story about the struggles of a young Jewish immigrant in New York City at the turn of the century."

By contrast, this is how we cataloged the work at Hennepin:

SUMMARY: The daughter of a Jewish immigrant family from Russia, newly arrived in Manhattan in 1908, has conflicting feelings about her mother's increasingly radical union involvement.

1. Women labor unionists—Fiction. 2. Girls, Jewish-American—New York (City)—Fiction. 3. Women garment workers—Fiction. 4. Americanization—Fiction. 5. Mother and daughter—Fiction. 6. Immigrants—New York (City)—Fiction. 7. New York (City)—Fiction.

With a hearty SHALOM!

Sanford Berman
Head Cataloger
Hennepin County Library

• Robert Greenfield's 1982 novel, *Temple*, assigned no subject tracings by LC, should be accessible via ORTHODOX JUDA-ISM—UNITED STATES—FICTION and JEWISH-AMERICAN FAMILIES—FICTION, while Icchokas Meras' 1980 work, *Stalemate*, likewise rendered unfindable by subject, warranted at least a tracing for GHETTOES, JEWISH—VILNA—FICTION.

• LC children's book catalogers applied only one subject descriptor to Barbara Cohen's 1982 *Gooseberries To Oranges:* UNITED STATES—EMIGRATION AND IMMIGRATION—FICTION. Further, the annotation made no reference to the Jewish theme. HCL's note and tracings:

SUMMARY: A young Jewish girl reminisces about the journey from her cholera-ravaged village in Russia to the United States where she is reunited with her father.

1. United States—Immigration and emigration—Fiction. 2. Father-separated children—Fiction. 3. Girls, Jewish-American—New York (City)—Fiction. 4. Immigrants—New York (City)—Fiction.

• HCL assigned HOLOCAUST SURVIVORS—FICTION and AUTHORS, JEWISH—20TH CENTURY—FICTION to Raymond Federman's *Twofold Vibration* (1982). LC had assigned no headings.
• W. D. Rubinstein's 1982 title, *The Left, The Right, and the Jews*, deserved tracings for JEWISH RADICALISM, JEWISH CONSERVATISM, CONSERVATIVES—RELATIONS WITH JEWS, and RADICALS—RELATIONS WITH JEWS. It didn't get them from LC.

If this, then, is the sorry and even shameful state of Judaica subject cataloging, what can be done about it? Well, there are two things: one is to lobby the Library of Congress, the source of most of our "outside copy," whether in the form of cards, MARC (Machine Readable Cataloging) records, or CIP (Cataloging in Publication), and also the agency responsible for the world's principal English-language subject heading scheme, the "authority" for subject cataloging in most libraries. But don't expect instant results. And don't expect that LC, even if it were miraculously sensitized and reformed overnight, would be able to do certain things for your particular library. Which raises the second point: That the best way to improve subject access and equity in your own library is to locally undertake as many reforms as your resources allow. For instance, in no event can LC—no matter how enlightened—make necessary cross-references in your catalog. Or assign retrospective award or prize headings. You have to do it. Regardless of when LC abandons or alters JEWISH QUESTION, if you find the heading inaccurate and indefensible, you should eliminate it from your active subject thesaurus and recatalog the titles it has already been assigned to. If you get a new filmstrip on latke making and there's no "latke" heading in the LC subject list, it's up to you to devise and apply a suitable descriptor. If you want your catalog to show all of the Israeli drama, fiction, or poetry you've got—not just anthologies—you'll have to assign the relevant headings yourself to incoming or existing material because LC will probably never do so for novels, plays, and verse by single authors. This "do-it-yourself" approach may strike some as tedious and even sinful, since it indisputably violates the holy canons of standardization and "follow-the-leader." However, the foregoing litany of neglect, if not abuse, should have demonstrated that the "leader" can't be wholly trusted. And what applies to local *librarians* can also apply to local library *users*. As consumers they should insist not only that their libraries *stock* Judaica, but also that it be fully and fairly cataloged so that a) the material can be easily found and used, and b) the catalog itself doesn't convey antisemitic messages.

To reinforce that conclusion about LC-unresponsiveness, here is the history of what is probably the only serious lobbying effort in the past decade: On August 26, 1975, the newly formed ALA Jewish Caucus sent the following letter to the chief of LC's Subject Cataloging Division:

ALA's Jewish Caucus applauds LC's increasing sensitivity to the needs and views of American ethnic groups—manifest, for instance, in Mr. Mumford's reply to the October 1974 Nashville Seminar resolution (cf. *HCL Cataloging Bulletin*, nos. 11-13, pp. 80-2) and such recent subject-heading innovations as ITALIAN-AMERICANS, JAPANESE-AMERICANS, and SCANDINAVIAN-AMERICANS (1974 LCSH supplement). Given this new and welcome responsiveness, we herewith request immediate attention to three areas of special concern to us:

1. Offensive/archaic nomenclature

JEWISH QUESTION, for reasons already well stated in the literature, must be dismantled. Since, in fact, this form has been applied to works dealing with the relationship between Jews and non-Jews, we suggest its replacement with the completely accurate and altogether neutral JEWS—RELATIONS WITH GENTILES, which would allow permutations like JEWS IN EUROPE—RELATIONS WITH GENTILES, etc. On no account should "Jewish Question" again defile library catalogs, even as a cross-reference.

We trust that all extant JEWS AS . . . constructions will be speedily supplanted by nondefamatory, contracted forms; e.g., JEWISH FARMERS and JEWISH SOLDIERS instead of the present JEWS AS FARMERS and JEWS AS SOLDIERS.

2. Omissions/inadequacies

JEWS IN THE UNITED STATES should be promptly complemented by JEWISH-AMERICANS, applicable to material on Jewish citizens and permanent residents in America. This form would totally harmonize with ITALIAN-AMERICANS, JAPANESE-AMERICANS, etc. Also required are such spin-off forms as JEWISH-AMERICAN FICTION; JEWISH-AMERICAN LITERATURE; JEWISH-AMERICAN WOMEN; etc.

We further recommend the deliberate creation and conscientious assignment of Jewish-related rubrics for which literary warrant has long existed and whose employment should measurably enhance access to the relevant materials for Jews and Gentiles alike. Examples: KIBBUTZ; SHTETL; JEWISH RESISTANCE AND REVOLTS; BOYS, JEWISH; and BAS-MITZVAH. Additionally, several cross-references can be usefully introduced to existing primary heads; e.g.,

COOKERY, JEWISH

   x Cookery, Kosher
     Kosher cookery

Unless subdivided by place, JEWISH-ARAB RELATIONS is seriously inaccurate and misleading. We believe ISRAELI-ARAB RELATIONS would prove an appropriate substitute.

3. Christian primacy

The manifold religious headings—like GOD and ANGELS—which automatically endow Christianity with preeminence are altogether unacceptable and must be transformed so that *all* religions enjoy absolute equity. In the two above-cited cases, this can be painlessly accomplished by appending the gloss (CHRISTIANITY), and reserving application of the unglossed form to genuinely comparative or multifaith materials.

We look forward to quick action on these matters. And wish to express our thanks in advance for your cooperation.

The SCD chief replied on December 4, 1975:

I had hoped to be able to answer your letter. . . with an answer that all the questions raised had been considered and solved as requested but I cannot. The fact is that I have been away so much in the past months and we have come to a grinding halt in major changes until we have decided on implementation in our own catalogs.

As a pledge of good faith, however, I did want to let you know that the points are valid ones. I see nothing insurmountable in a resolution along the lines you ask. But I don't think I can give you a final answer until after the first of the year.

Thank you for your considered and specific recommendations. That gives us a point of departure so we can make the best use of our time which we have to subtract from that meant for current cataloging.

Now, the answer was a bit tardy, but certainly sympathetic, inspiring hope for fairly fast reforms. Yet, to this day few of the Caucus requests—only the truncation of "as" forms, establishment of BAT MITZVAH and KIBBUTZIM, and addition of "Kosher" cross-references—have actually been implemented. There are still no "Jewish-American" forms; "God" remains unreservedly Christian; and as recently as June 6, 1979, the present chief of LC's Subject Cataloging Division wrote Herb Zafren of Hebrew Union College that "elimination of [JEWISH QUESTION] has been considered in the past but has not been achieved because of the difficulty of determining what heading(s) would replace it"—that "explanation" notwithstanding at least three known and weighty precedents: the use of JEWS AND GENTILES by *Sears*, of JEWS AND NON-JEWS by the *Index to Jewish Periodicals*, and Hennepin's nine-year-old JEWS—RELATIONS WITH GENTILES. Beyond these precedents, there are two more in LC practice: the recent replacement of RACE QUESTION by RACE RELATIONS and the use of—GOVERNMENT RELATIONS as a subhead under various INDIAN headings, which, in the form of JEWS—GOVERNMENT RELATIONS, might easily be applied to some of the works presently saddled with JEWISH QUESTION. And if, for research purposes, it's desirable to trace the history of the concept itself, however odious, a little imagination could produce an acceptable form like "JEWISH QUESTION" (ANTISEMITIC DOCTRINE).

To continue the saga. This very paper went to Daniel Boorstin, Librarian of Congress, shortly after the June 1979 AJL convention. Nothing happened. So on January 29, 1981, a *Joy of Cataloging* photocopy traveled to Washington with this note:

Dear Mr. Boorstin,

About 1½ years ago I sent you a typescript version of this article. By first-class mail. To date, I have received no reply, not even an acknowledgement. But I think it's worth trying again.

That finally prompted a "response":

Dear Mr. Berman,

Many thanks for sending us a copy of your article from *The Joy of Cataloging*. We appreciate your thinking of the Library of Congress.

Sincerely,

Daniel J. Boorstin
The Librarian of Congress

In sum, there's no realistic basis for expecting much from LC—not soon, anyway—although it would surely be worthwhile for prestigious organizations like the Association of Jewish Libraries and the Church and Synagogue Library Association to firmly demand improvements. It may not seem very professional or high-minded, but the fact is that LC tends to be most "responsive" when it's most threatened, when it's publicly ridiculed or chastised. That's how Black and women's groups not long ago secured a number of overdue subject-cataloging changes.

If there is any one message with respect to the "Jewish Question" in subject cataloging," it is probably that—just as with other varieties or manifestations of either Goyish unconcern or outright anti-Semitism—Jewish librarians and library-users must take care of themselves. LC won't do a thing unless forced. And even then, what they produce may not be 100 percent kosher. So it needs to be checked. And corrected. And otherwise made to work. By the people it most affects. By people who are resolved never again to be humiliated nor oppressed. By people who understand that the weapons of oppression include not only whips and guns, but also words.

Postscript: Finally, in June 1983, nearly 13 years after the heading had been publicly and thoroughly denounced, LC agreed to scrap JEWISH QUESTION. Marjorie Greenfield, an irate Jewish-

American librarian, persuaded the Anti-Defamation League to intercede. And that did it. However, the extensive correspondence between Frances M. Sonnenschein, Director of ADL's National Education Department, Mary K. D. Pietris, Chief of LC's Subject Cataloging Division, and Dr. David Cohen, Director of the Ethnic Materials Information Exchange at Queens College, reveals no commitment by the Library of Congress to similarly correct the many other inequities in Judaica subject cataloging. Although the heading has now been dropped, the "Jewish Question" persists.

SOURCES

Baker, Zachary M. "Problems in Judaica Cataloging." *HCL Cataloging Bulletin*, nos. 23-24 (September 1, 1976): 54-6.

Berman, Sanford. "Cataloger's Corner." *Jewish Librarians Caucus Newsletter*, April 1977; Summer 1978; Winter 1978; Spring 1979.

_____ "Counter-cataloging." *Library Journal* (May 1, 1972): 1640.

_____ "Ethnic Access." In *Joy of Cataloging*. Phoenix, AZ: Oryx Press, 1981, pp. 105-9.

_____ "Golems and Goddesses." *HCL Cataloging Bulletin*, no. 22 (July 1, 1976): 29-31.

_____ *Prejudices and Antipathies*. Metuchen, NJ: Scarecrow Press, 1971, pp. 22-5, 35-8, 55-6, 61-3, 84, 86-8.

_____ "Reference, Readers and Fiction: New Approaches." *Reference Librarian*, nos. 1/2 (Fall/Winter 1981): 45-53.

_____ "Title Access: the Need, the Policy, and the Practice." *Technicalities*, v. 1, no. 1 (Dec. 1980): 6-7.

"Jewish Caucus Asks for 'Quick Action' on LCSH Bias, Omissions." *HCL Cataloging Bulletin*, no. 17 (October 1, 1975): 43-4. Discussion: *HCL Cataloging Bulletin*, no. 20 (March 1, 1976): 3-4.

Kersten, Dorothy B. *Subject Headings for Church or Synagogue Libraries*. Bryn Mawr, PA: Church and Synagogue Library Association, 1978, p. 13.

Westby, Barbara M., ed. *Sears List of Subject Headings*. 12th ed. New York: H. W. Wilson, 1982, pp. 278, 329, 331-2.

"Teen" Subject Headings: A Selection From the Hennepin County Library Authority File

Sanford Berman

What follows is a sampling of teen-related subject headings developed and used at the Hennepin County (Minnesota) Library over the past decade. Although operating within the framework of Library of Congress subject cataloging, HCL has deliberately changed some LC rubrics to make them more findable and familiar, while innovating other descriptors to represent topics not recognized in the LC scheme. Further, the HCL thesaurus is constantly expanded and enriched with cross-references and "public notes."

Abbreviations/symbols
cn = cataloger's note (does not appear in catalog)
HCL = Hennepin County Library
LC = Library of Congress
pn = public note (appears in catalog)
sa = "see also" reference (appears in catalog)
sf = "see from" or "x" reference (appears in catalog)

Abortion counseling.
    sa Parental notification laws.
    sf Counseling, Abortion.

Afro-American teenagers.
    cn HCL form.
    sa Teenage boys, Afro-American. /Teenage girls, Afro-American.
    sf Black American teenagers. /Black teenagers. /Teenagers, Black.

Afro-American teenagers—Employment.
sa Unemployed Afro-American teenagers.

Afro-American teenagers—Fiction.

Afro-American youth.
sa Afro-American children. /Afro-American teenagers. /Boys,
Afro-American. /Girls, Afro-American.
sf Black youth. /Youth, Afro-American. /Youth, Black.

Arthritic teenagers.
cn HCL form.
sf Teenagers, Arthritic.

Arthritic teenagers—Fiction.

Blind teenagers.
cn HCL form.
sf Teenagers, Blind.

Brain-damaged teenagers.
cn HCL form.
sf Teenagers, Brain-damaged.

Cheyenne teenagers.
cn HCL form.
sf Teenagers, Cheyenne.

Christian church work with teenagers.
cn LC form: CHURCH WORK WITH ADOLESCENTS.
sf Teenagers—Christian church work.

Christian teenagers.
cn HCL form.
sa Hutterite teenagers.
sf Teenagers, Christian.

Consumer education for teenagers.
cn HCL form.
sf Teenagers—Consumer education.

Cooking and teenagers.
cn HCL form.
sa Teenage cooks.
sf Teenagers and cooking.

Counseling for teenage girls.
cn HCL form.
sa Parental notification laws.
sf Teenage girls—Counseling.

Counseling for teenage girls—Twin Cities metropolitan area.
sf Twin Cities metropolitan area—Counseling for teenage girls.

Counseling for teenage girls—Twin Cities metropolitan area-Directories.

Counseling for teenagers.
cn HCL form.
sa Counseling for teenage girls.
sf Teenagers—Counseling.

Cuban-American teenagers.
cn HCL form.
sf Teenagers, Cuban-American.

Deaf teenagers.
cn HCL form.
sf Teenagers, Deaf.

Deaf teenagers—Interviews.
sf Interviews—Deaf teenagers.

Depression in teenagers.
cn HCL form.
sf Depression, Teenage. /Teenage depression. /Teenagers' depression.

Developmentally disabled teenagers.
cn HCL form.
sf Mentally disabled teenagers. /Mentally "handicapped" teenagers. /Mentally "retarded" teenagers. /"Retarded" teenagers. /Teenagers, Developmentally disabled. /Teenagers, Mentally disabled. /Teenagers, "Retarded."

Developmentally disabled teenagers—Education.

Developmentally disabled teenagers—Family relationships.

Developmentally disabled teenagers—Family relationships—Fiction.

Developmentally disabled teenagers—Fiction.

Developmentally disabled teenagers—Personal narratives.

Diabetic teenagers.
  cn HCL form.
  sf Diabetes in teenagers. /Teenagers, Diabetic.

Disabled teenagers.
  cn HCL form.
  sa Developmentally disabled teenagers. /Learning disabled teen-
    agers. /Physically disabled teenagers.
  sf "Handicapped" teenagers. /Teenagers, Disabled. /Teenagers,
    "Handicapped."

Disabled teenagers—Education.
  sa Mainstreaming (Education). /Special education.

Disabled teenagers—Employment.

Disabled teenagers—Fiction.
  sa Developmentally disabled teenagers—Fiction. /Physically dis-
    abled teenagers—Fiction.

Disabled teenagers—Lifestyles.

Disabled teenagers—Self-help materials.

Drew, Nancy.
  cn Fictional character. Creator: Carolyn Keene.
  sf Nancy Drew.

Drew, Nancy—Fiction.

Epileptic teenagers.
  cn HCL form.
  sf Epileptics, Teenage. /Teenage epileptics. /Teenagers, Epi-
    leptic.

Europe—Description and travel—Guidebooks (for teenagers).
  cn HCL form. Make dual entry under TRAVEL—GUIDE-
    BOOKS (FOR TEENAGERS).

Family planning services.
  cn HCL form.
  sa Family planning information systems. /Parental notification
    laws. /Pregnancy counseling. /Pregnancy testing.

Family violence.
  cn Class in 301.4274.
  pn Additional material on this subject may be found in the Pamphlet Collection.
  sa Child abuse. /Family and child abuse. /Husband battering. /Marital rape. /Police and family violence. /Teenage abuse. /Woman battering.
  sf Conjugal violence. /Domestic assault. /Domestic violence. /Household violence. /Violence in the family.

Fein, Doris.
  cn Fictional character. Creator: T. Ernesto Bethancourt.
  sf Doris Fein. /Fine, Doris.

Fein, Doris—Fiction.

Gay teenagers.
  cn HCL form.
  sa Lesbian teenagers.
  sf Teenage gays. /Teenagers, Gay.

Gay teenagers—Fiction.

Gay teenagers—Personal narratives.

Generation gap.
  cn LC form: CONFLICT OF GENERATIONS. Not subdivided by—UNITED STATES.
  sa Children and adults. /Intergenerational communication. /Teenagers and adults.
  sf Conflict of generations. /Gap, Generation.

German-American teenagers.
  cn HCL form.
  sf Teenagers, German-American.

Grooming for teenage girls.
  cn HCL form.
  sf Teenage girls' grooming. /Teenagers—Grooming.

High school students.
  cn Not subdivided by—UNITED STATES.
  sa High school frosh. /High school juniors. /High school seniors. /High school sophomores. /Teenagers.
  sf Students, High school.

Hutterite teenagers.
  cn HCL form.
  sf Teenagers, Hutterite.

Igbo teenagers.
  cn HCL form.
  sf Teenagers, Igbo.

Jewish-American teenagers.
  cn HCL form.
  sa Teenage boys, Jewish-American. /Teenage girls, Jewish-American.
  sf Teenagers, Jewish-American.

Job hunting for teenagers.
  cn HCL form.
  sf Teenagers—Job hunting.

Juvenile delinquency.
  pn Additional material on this subject may be found in the Pamphlet Collection.
  sa Juvenile corrections. /Juvenile delinquents. /Juvenile justice system. /Leisure and juvenile delinquency. /Middle class delinquency. /Police services for juveniles. /School vandalism. /Social work with delinquents and criminals. /Violence in schools. /Violence in teenagers.
  sf Delinquency, Juvenile.

Juvenile delinquents.
  sa Juvenile court waivers. /Juvenile delinquency. /Police services for juveniles. /Rehabilitation of juvenile delinquents. /Social work with delinquents and criminals. /Teenage murderers. /Teenage sex offenders.
  sf Criminals, Juvenile. /Delinquent teenagers. /Delinquents, Juvenile. /Delinquents, Teenage. /J Ds. /Offenders, Juvenile. /Teenage criminals. /Teenage delinquents. /Teenage offenders.

Latino teenagers.
  cn HCL form. Not subdivided by—UNITED STATES.
  sa Chicano teenage girls. /Cuban-American teenagers.
  sf Hispanic teenagers.

Latino teenagers—Drug use.

Latino teenagers—Employment.

Learning disabled teenagers.
  cn HCL form. Class in 371.926.
  sf Teenagers, Learning disabled.

Lesbian teenagers.
  cn HCL form.
  sa Gay teenagers.
  sf Teenage Lesbians. /Teenagers, Lesbian.

Lesbian teenagers—Fiction.

Lesbian teenagers—Personal narratives.

McKinley, Maggie.
  cn Fictional character. Creator: Joan Lingard.
  sf Maggie McKinley. /McKinley, Margaret.

McKinley, Maggie—Fiction.

Mentally ill teenagers.
  cn HCL form.
  sa Teenagers—Psychiatric care. /Teenagers—Psychotherapy.

Mentally ill teenagers—Case studies.

Mentally ill teenagers—Drama.

Mentally ill teenagers—Family relationships.

Mentally ill teenagers—Psychiatric care.
  cn LC form: ADOLESCENT PSYCHIATRY.
  sa Teenage sex offenders—Psychiatric care. /Teenagers—Psychotherapy.
  sf Adolescent psychiatry. /Psychiatric care—Mentally ill teenagers. /Psychiatric care—Teenagers. /Teenagers—Psychiatric care.

Minority teenagers.
  cn HCL form. Not subdivided by—UNITED STATES.
  sa Afro-American teenagers. /Jewish-American teenagers. /Latino teenagers. /"Mulatto" teenagers. /Teenagers, Native American.
  sf Teenagers, Minority.

Minority teenagers—Employment.
  sa Afro-American teenagers—Employment. /Latino teenagers—Employment.

Netsilik teenagers.
    cn HCL form.
    sf Teenagers, Netsilik.

Overweight teenagers.
    cn HCL form.
    sf Teenagers, Overweight.

Overweight teenagers—Fiction.

Overweight teenagers—Nutrition.

Parental notification laws.
    cn HCL form.
    sf Notification laws, Parental. /"Squeal" laws. /Teen notification laws.

Pennington, Patrick.
    cn Fictional character. Creator: K. M. Peyton.
    sf Pat Pennington. /Patrick Pennington. /Penn Pennington.

Pennington, Patrick—Fiction.

Poor teenagers.
    cn HCL form.
    sf Teenagers, Poor.

Popular music.
    cn LC form: MUSIC, POPULAR (SONGS, ETC.). Class in 780.42. Not subdivided by—UNITED STATES.
    sa Best sellers (Records, tapes, etc.). /Blues (Songs, etc.). /Country-rock music. /Disco music. /Jazz music. /Ragtime music. /Reggae music. /Rhythm and blues music. /Rock music. / Salsa music. /Ska music. /Soul music. /Teenagers and music.
    sf Music, Popular. /Pop music.

Sex education for teenagers.
    cn LC form: SEX INSTRUCTION FOR YOUTH.
    sa Teenage pregnancy. /Teenagers—Sexuality.
    sf Teenagers' sex education.

Sexuality.
    cn LC form: SEX.
    pn Additional materials on this subject may be found in the Pamphlet Collection.
    sa Anal sex. /Analingus. /Animals—Sexual behavior. /Aphrodisiacs. /Bestiality. /Birth control. /Bisexuality. /Children—

Sexuality. /Cohabitation. /Coitus interruptus. /Cunnilingus. /
Dating (Social customs). /Disabled persons—Sexuality. /Erot-
ica. /Extramarital relations. /Fellatio. /Fetishism (Sexuality). /Heterosexuality. /Homosexuality. /Incest. /Interracial
sex. /Lesbianism. /Masturbation. /Men—Sexuality. /Or-
gasm. /Pedophilia. /Pheromones. /Prostitution. /Puberty. /Re-
productive system. /Sadomasochism. /Seniors—Sexuality. /
Sex and health. /Sex counseling and therapy. /Sex education. /
Sex in business. /Sex in institutions (group homes, etc.). /
Sex manuals. /Sex research. /Sexual revolution. /Single people—Sexuality. /Swinging and swingers. /Teenagers—Sexuality. /Transsexuals. /Transvestism and transvestites. /Voyeur-
ism. /Women—Sexuality.
  sf Copulation. /Human sexuality. /Intercourse, Sexual. /Love-
     making. /Sexual activity. /Sexual behavior.

Teenage
  cn LC form: ADOLESCENCE.
  sa Puberty. /Puberty rites. /Teenagers.
  sf Adolescence. /Teen age.

Teenage abuse.
  cn HCL form. Class in 362.7044.
  sa Child abuse.
  sf Abuse of teenagers. /Adolescent abuse. /Teenager abuse. /
     Youth abuse.

Teenage abuse victims.
  cn HCL form.
  sf Abused teenagers. /Victims, Teenage abuse.

Teenage abuse victims—Group psychotherapy.

Teenage actors and actresses.
  cn HCL form.
  sf Actors and actresses, Teenage. /Teenage actresses. /Actresses,
     Teenage.

Teenage adventurers.
  cn HCL form.
  sf Adventurers, Teenage.

Teenage alcoholics.
  cn HCL form.
  sa Alateen groups.
  sf Alcoholic teenagers. /Alcoholics, Teenage.

Teenage artists.
  cn LC form: YOUTH AS ARTISTS.
  sf Artists, Teenage.

Teenage athletes.
  cn HCL form.
  sf Athletes, Teenage.

Teenage automobile racing drivers.
  cn HCL form.
  sf Automobile racing drivers, Teenage. /Racing drivers, Teenage. /Teenage racing drivers.

Teenage boys.
  cn LC form: ADOLESCENT BOYS.
  sa Eighteen-year-old boys. /Fifteen-year-old boys. /Fourteen-year-old boys. /Juvenile delinquents (Boys.) /Nineteen-year-old boys. /Seventeen-year-old boys. /Sixteen-year-old boys. /Teenage fathers. /Thirteen-year-old boys.
  sf Adolescent boys. /Boys, Teenage.

Teenage boys, Chinese-American.
  cn HCL form.
  sf Chinese-American teenage boys.

Teenage boys—Comedies.

Teenage boys—Humor.
  sa Teenage boys—Comedies.
  sf Humor—Teenage boys.

Teenage boys, Irish-American.
  cn HCL form.
  sf Irish-American teenage boys.

Teenage boys, Italian-American.
  cn HCL form.
  sf Italian-American teenage boys.

Teenage boys—Lifestyles
  cn HCL form.

Teenage boys, Native American.
  cn HCL form.
  sf Amerindian teenage boys. /Indian teenage boys. /Native American teenage boys. /Teenage boys, Amerindian.

Teenage boys—Sexuality.
  cn HCL form.
  sa Sex education for teenagers. /Teenage fathers. /Teenagers—
    Sexuality.

Teenage cooks.
  cn HCL form.
  sf Cooks, Teenage.

Teenage cowhands.
  cn HCL form.
  sf Cowhands, Teenage.

Teenage dancers.
  cn HCL form.
  sf Dancers, Teenage.

Teenage detectives.
  cn HCL form.
  sf Detectives, Teenage.

Teenage drug abusers.
  cn HCL form.
  sa Teenage alcoholics.
  sf Drug abusers, Teenage. /Youth drug abusers.

Teenage drug abusers—Treatment.

Teenage fathers.
  cn HCL form. Class in 301.43154.
  sa Teenage marriage. /Teenage parents.
  sf Fathers, Teenage.

Teenage filmmakers.
  cn HCL form.
  sf Filmmakers, Teenage.

Teenage girls.
  cn LC form: ADOLESCENT GIRLS.
  sa Counseling for teenage girls. /Eighteen-year-old girls. /Fif-
    teen-year-old girls. /Fourteen-year-old girls. /Grooming for
    teenage girls. /Juvenile delinquents (Girls). /Nineteen-year-
    old girls. /Seventeen-year-old girls. /Sixteen-year-old girls. /
    Teenage mothers. /Teenage pregnancy. /Thirteen-year-old
    girls. /Young women.
  sf Adolescent girls. /Girls, Teenage.

Teenage girls, Afro-American.
cn HCL form.
sf Afro-American teenage girls.

Teenage girls—Diaries.
sf Diaries—Teenage girls.

Teenage girls—Employment.
sa Teenagers—Employment.

Teenage girls—England.
sa Teenage girls—Cornwall, England. /Teenage girls—Liverpool. /Teenage girls—London.

Teenage girls—Fiction.

Teenage girls—Health.
sa Anorexia nervosa. /Teenage girls—Nutrition. /Teenagers—Health.

Teenage girls, Japanese-American.
cn HCL form.
sf Japanese-American teenage girls.

Teenage girls, Jewish-American.
cn HCL form.
sf Jewish-American teenage girls.

Teenage girls—Nutrition.
sf Nutrition for teenage girls.

Teenage girls—Periodicals.

Teenage girls
cn HCL form.
sa Counseling for teenage girls. /Teenage mothers' services. / Teenage pregnancy and services.

Teenage girls—Sexuality.
sa Sex education for teenagers. /Teenage pregnancy. /Teenagers—Sexuality.

Teenage girls—Sexuality—Fiction.

Teenage health services.
cn HCL form. Class in 362.19893.
sa EPSDT program.

sf Adolescent health services. /Health services for teenagers. / Teenagers—Health services.

Teenage health services—Directories.

Teenage heroes and heroines.
cn HCL form.
sf Heroes and heroines, Teenage. /Teenage heroines.

Teenage inventors.
cn HCL form.
sf Inventors, Teenage.

Teenage literature.
pn Here are entered materials on literature written especially for teenagers. For works on teenagers' reading interests and attitudes, as well as the encouragement of teenage reading, see TEENAGERS—BOOKS AND READING.
sa Teenagers' plays. /Teenagers' writings.
sf High school students' literature. /Literature for teenagers. / Literature, Teenage. /Literature, Y A. /Literature, Young adults. /Y A literature. /Young adult literature.

Teenage literature—Bibliography.

Teenage literature, Easy-to-read.
cn HCL form.
sf Books for reluctant readers. /Easy reading for teenagers. /Easy teenage reading. /Easy-to-read teenage literature. /Hi-low books for teenagers. /High interest/low-vocabulary books. / Low-vocabulary/high-interest books. /Reluctant readers' materials. /Teen hi-low books. /Teenage easy reading. /Teenagers' hi-low books.

Teenage literature, Easy-to-read—Bibliography.

Teenage literature, Easy-to-read—Reviews.

Teenage literature—History and criticism.

Teenage literature—Stories, plots, etc.

Teenage literature—Study and teaching.

Teenage literature writing.
cn HCL form.

sf Teenage literature—Authorship. /Teenage literature—Technique. /Writing for teenagers.

Teenage marriage.
    cn HCL form. Not subdivided by—UNITED STATES. Class in 301.43154.
    sa Counseling for teenagers. /Social work with youth. /Teenage parents. /Teenage pregnancy.
    sf Adolescent marriage. /Marriage, Teenage. /Teen marriage.

Teenage marriage—Case studies.

Teenage marriage—Fiction.

Teenage marriage—Law and legislation.

Teenage mothers.
    cn LC form: ADOLESCENT MOTHERS. Not subdivided by—UNITED STATES. Class in 301.43154.
    sa Teenage marriage. /Teenage parents. /Teenage pregnancy.
    sf Mothers, Teenage.

Teenage mothers—Case studies.

Teenage mothers—Fiction.

Teenage mothers' services.

Teenage murderers.
    cn HCL form.
    sf Murderers, Teenage.

Teenage neglect.
    cn HCL form. Class in 362.7044.
    sa Child neglect.
    sf Adolescent neglect. /Neglect of adolescents. /Neglect of teenagers. /Teenager neglect. /Youth neglect.

Teenage parents.
    cn LC form: ADOLESCENT PARENTS. Class in 301.43154.
    sa Teenage fathers. /Teenage mothers.
    sf Adolescent parents. /Parents, Teenage.

Teenage parents—Family relationships.

Teenage parents' services.
    sa Teenage mothers' services.

Teenage pregnancy.
cn LC forms: PREGNANT SCHOOLGIRLS; PREGNANCY, ADOLESCENT. Not subdivided by—UNITED STATES. Class in 301.43154.
pn Additional material on this subject may be found in the Pamphlet Collection.
sa Counseling for teenage girls. /Social work with teenage girls. / Teenage mothers. /Unmarried mothers.
sf Adolescent pregnancy. /Pregnant teenagers. /Teenagers, Pregnant.

Teenage pregnancy—Information services.

Teenage pregnancy
sa Parental notification laws. /Teenage pregnancy—Information services.

Teenage rebels.
cn HCL form.
sf Rebels, Teenage.

Teenage revolutionaries.
cn HCL form.
sf Revolutionaries, Teenage.

Teenage revolutionaries—China.
sf China—Teenage revolutionaries. /Chinese teenage revolutionaries.

Teenage romance.
cn HCL form.
sf Romance, Teenage. /Romantic love, Teenage.

Teenage romance—Fiction.
sf Romantic stories.

Teenage romance—Humor.
sf Humor—Teenage romance.

Teenage sailors.
cn HCL form.
sf Sailors, Teenage.

Teenage sex offenders.
cn HCL form.
sf Sex offenders, Teenage.

Teenage sex offenders—Psychiatric care.

Teenage soldiers.
cn HCL form.
sf Soldiers, Teenage.

Teenage spies.
cn HCL form.
sf Spies, Teenage.

Teenage unemployment.
cn HCL form. Not subdivided by—UNITED STATES.
sa Teenagers—Employment. /Unemployed Afro-American teenagers. /Youth employment policy.
sf Teenagers—Unemployment. /Unemployed teenagers. /Youth
unemployment.

Teenage unemployment—Personal narratives.

Teenage unemployment services.

Teenage unemployment—Statistics.

Teenage volunteer workers.
cn HCL form.
sa Candy stripers.
sf Volunteer workers, Teenage. /Youth volunteer workers.

Teenage workers.
cn HCL form.
sa Teenage unemployment. /Teenage volunteer workers. /Teen-
agers—Employment. /Youth employment policy.
sf Workers, Teenage.

Teenagers.
cn LC form: YOUTH. Class in 301.4315.
pn Here are entered materials on persons 13 to 19 years old. Additional information may be found in the Pamphlet Collection,
and for works specifically on the 18-25 age group, see
YOUNG ADULTS.
sa Adoption of older children. /Blind teenagers. /Consumer education for teenagers. /Disabled teenagers. /Eighteen-year-
olds. /Epileptic teenagers. /Fifteen-year-olds. /Fourteen-year-
olds. /Gay teenagers. /High school students. /Hutterite
teenagers. /Igbo teenagers. /Juvenile delinquents. /Learning

disabled teenagers. /Lesbian teenagers. /Minority teenagers. / Netsilik teenagers. /Overweight teenagers. /Poor teenagers. / Puberty. /Seventeen-year-olds. /Sixteen-year-olds. /Thirteen-year-olds. /Unemployed teenagers. /Vocational guidance for teenagers. /Working class teenagers. /Youth advocacy.
sf Adolescents. /YAs. /Juniors.

Teenagers and adults.
sa Generation gap. /Teenage abuse. /Teenage neglect. /Teenagers and seniors.
sf Adults and teenagers.

Teenagers and automobiles.
cn HCL form.
sa Teenage automobile racing drivers.
sf Automobiles and teenagers. /Cars and teenagers. /Teenagers and cars.

Teenagers and death.
cn LC form: YOUTH AND DEATH.
sf Death and teenagers. /Family changes and teenagers. /Teenagers and family changes. /Youth and death.

Teenagers and dogs.
cn HCL form.
sf Dogs and teenagers.

Teenagers and music.
cn HCL form.
sa Teenage musicians.
sf Music and teenagers.

Teenagers and seniors.
cn HCL form.
sa Generation gap. /Intergenerational communication.
sf Seniors and teenagers.

Teenagers' art.
cn HCL form.
sf Art, Teenagers'.

Teenagers—Bibliography.

Teenagers—Biography.

Teenagers—Books and reading.
   pn Here are entered materials on teenagers' reading interests and attitudes, as well as the encouragement of teenage reading. For materials on literature written especially for teenagers, see TEENAGE LITERATURE.
   sa Teenagers' library services.
   sf Books and reading for teenagers. /Books and reading for young adults. /Teenage reading interests. /Teenagers' reading. /Y A reading interests. /Young adult reading interests.

Teenagers—Drug use.
   cn HCL form.
   sa Teenage drug abusers. /Teenagers—Alcohol use. /Teenagers—Marijuana use.
   sf Drugs and teenagers. /Drugs and youth. /Teenagers and drugs. /Youth and drugs.

Teenagers—Employment.
   cn LC form: YOUTH—EMPLOYMENT.
   sa Disabled teenagers—Employment. /Job hunting for teenagers. /Minority teenagers—Employment. /Part-time employment. /Summer employment. /Teenage girls—Employment. / Teenage unemployment. /Teenage workers. /Vocational guidance for teenagers. /Youth employment policy.
   sf High school students—Employment. /Youth—Employment.

Teenagers—Family relationships.

Teenagers—Fiction.

Teenagers' films.
   cn HCL form.
   sf Films, Teenagers'.

Teenagers—Health.
   cn LC form: YOUTH—HEALTH AND HYGIENE.
   sa Acne. /Arthritic teenagers. /Braces (Dentistry). /Diabetic teenagers. /Disabled teenagers. /Epileptic teenagers. /Teenage abuse. /Teenage drug abusers. /Teenage girls—Health. /Teenage health services. /Teenage neglect. /Teenagers—Medical care. /Teenagers—Mental health. /Teenagers—Nutrition. / Terminally ill teenagers.

Teenagers—Legal status, laws, etc.
   sa Emancipation of minors. /Juvenile justice system. /Parental

notification laws. /Teenage marriage—Law and legislation. / Teenagers—Rights.

Teenagers—Marijuana use.

Teenagers—Medical care.
cn LC form: YOUTH—MEDICAL CARE. Class in 362.19893.
sa Teenage health services. /Teenagers—Psychiatric care.
sf Adolescent medical care. /Medical care for teenagers. /Teenage medical care. /Youth—Medical care.

Teenagers—Mental health.
cn LC form: YOUTH—MENTAL HEALTH.
sa Counseling for teenagers. /Depression in teenagers. /Mentally ill teenagers. /Teenage psychopathology. /Teenagers—Psychotherapy. /Teenagers—Suicidal behavior. /Violence in teenagers.
sf Disturbed teenagers. /Emotional problems of teenagers. /Emotionally disturbed teenagers. /Mental health—Teenagers. / Teenagers' emotional problems. /Youth—Mental health.

Teenagers, Native American.
cn LC form: INDIANS OF NORTH AMERICA—YOUTH.
sa Cheyenne teenagers. /Teenage boys, Native American. /Teenage girls, Native American.
sf Amerindian teenagers. /Indian teenagers. /Indians of North America—Teenagers. /Indians of North America—Youth. / Native American teenagers. /Teenagers, Amerindian. /Teenagers, Indian.

Teenagers—Nutrition.
cn LC form: YOUTH—NUTRITION.
sa Overweight teenagers—Nutrition.
sf Nutrition for teenagers. /Youth—Nutrition.

Teenagers' periodicals.
cn HCL form.
sf Periodicals, Teenagers'. /Teenage periodicals. /Teen magazines.

Teenagers' plays.
cn HCL form.
sf Drama for teenagers. /Drama, Teenage. /Plays for teenagers. /Plays, Teenagers'. /Teenage plays.

Teenagers' plays—Indexes.

Teenagers—Poetry.

Teenagers—Portraits.

Teenagers—Psychology.
  cn LC form: ADOLESCENT PSYCHOLOGY.
  sa Teenagers and death. /Teenagers—Mental health. /Teen-
    agers—Psychotherapy.
  sf Teenage psychology. /Adolescent psychology.

Teenagers—Psychotherapy.
  cn LC form: ADOLESCENT PSYCHOTHERAPY.
  sf Adolescent psychotherapy. /Psychotherapy for teenagers.

Teenagers—Rights.
  cn HCL form.
  sa Emancipation of minors. /Students—Rights. /Youth advocacy.
  sf Minors (Law)—Rights. /Juvenile rights.

Teenagers—Sexuality.
  cn LC form: YOUTH—SEXUALITY.
  sa Sex education for teenagers. /Teenage marriage. /Teenage
    pregnancy.
  sf Adolescent sexuality. /Sexuality of teenagers. /Teenage sex-
    uality. /Youth—Sexuality.

Teenagers—Sexuality—Bibliography.

Teenagers—Sexuality—Fiction.

Teenagers—Sexuality—Periodicals.

Teenagers—Suicidal behavior.
  cn LC form: YOUTH—SUICIDAL BEHAVIOR. Class in
    616.85844.
  sf Adolescent suicide. /Suicide, Teenage. /Teenage suicide. /
    Youth—Suicidal behavior.

Teenagers' writings.
  cn LC form: YOUTHS' WRITINGS.
  pn Here are entered collections of works written by teenagers.

Television and teenagers.
  cn LC form: TELEVISION AND YOUTH.

sf Teenagers and television. /Television and youth. /Youth and television.

Terminally ill teenagers.
cn HCL form.
sf Teenagers, Terminally ill.

Travel—Guidebooks (for teenagers)
cn HCL form.
sf Teenage travel guides. /Teenagers—Travel guides.

Unemployed Afro-American teenagers.
cn HCL form.
sf Afro-American teenage unemployment. /Afro-American teenagers—Unemployment. /Black teenage unemployment. /Black teenagers' unemployment. /Black youth unemployment. /Unemployed Afro-American youth. /Unemployed Black teenagers.

Violence in teenagers.
cn HCL form.
sa Juvenile delinquents. /Teenage murderers.
sf Teenage violence. /Teenagers, Violent. /Violent teenagers.

Violence in teenagers—Prevention.

Vocational guidance for teenagers.
cn HCL form.
sf Career guidance for teenagers. /Teenagers—Vocational guidance.

Working class teenagers.
cn HCL form.
sa Poor teenagers. /Teenage workers.
sf Teenagers, Working class.

Young adults.
cn Class in 301.432.
pn Here are entered materials on persons 18 to 25 years old.
sa Eighteen-year-olds. /Nineteen-year-olds. /Teenagers.
sf YAs.

Youth.
pn Additional graphic material on this subject may be found in the HCL Picture File.

sa Children. /Teenagers. /Young adults.
sf Juniors.

Youth projects and services.
cn LC form: YOUTH—SERVICES FOR.
sa Aftercare services for youth. /Christian church work with teenagers. /Counseling for teenagers. /Independent Living Subsidy Program (Oregon). /Juvenile delinquency projects and services. /Runaway youth services. /Social work with youth. / Teenage girls' services. /Teenage health services. /Youth shelters.
sf Teenage projects and services. /Teenage services. /Teenagers' services. /Youth programs. /Youth services.

Youth—Rights.
cn HCL form.
sa Children's rights. /Students—Rights. /Teenagers—Rights. / Youth advocacy. /Youth Liberation Movement.
sf Minors (Law)—Rights. /Juvenile rights.

RESOURCES/READINGS

Berman, Sanford, "Kid's Stuff: a Grabbag of HCL Subject Headings for (Mostly) Children's Literature," in his *Joy of Cataloging* (Phoenix, AZ: Oryx Press, 1981), p. 163-5.
Hennepin County Library Cataloging Section, 12601 Ridgedale Drive, Minnetonka, MN 55343; (612) 541-8570.

Tools for Tinkering

Sanford Berman

The purpose of subject cataloging is to make material accessible by topic, to pinpoint items in the collection that either deal with specific themes and subjects or represent particular genres. The instruments of access are subject headings, either independently formulated or selected from a standard thesaurus, which are assigned to given works and so become the means for identifying what they're about or what form they appear in. To facilitate searching, the subject vocabulary ought to be contemporary, accurate, and predictable; related headings should be clearly indicated and synonymous terms employed as *see*-references; and the assignment policy must be generous enough to fully and fairly reflect the content or form of each work.

The most widely used thesaurus at present is the *Library of Congress Subject Headings* (*LCSH*). The most significant source for subject-cataloging direction and "copy" is the Library of Congress itself. Anyone even modestly familiar with LCSH and LC practice knows that while the system and principles are firmly established and basically sound, they don't adequately "do the job." Too often the vocabulary is archaic, inaccurate, and unpredictable, compelling often deadly second look-ups. Too often the scheme fails to indicate genuinely related headings or to convert common synonyms into cross-references. Too often both old and new subjects go unrecognized. And too often not enough subject tracings are applied to make a work properly findable. Without sudden, large-scale reforms in Washington, this situation is likely to continue indefinitely, meaning that individual libraries, networks, and bibliographic utilities—if truly committed to enhancing subject access—must assume some responsibility for improving the currently dismal scene. That is, to whatever degree they can manage, they've got to "tinker." And these resources may help.

An earlier version of this paper, "Do-It-Yourself Cataloging: Sources and Tools," appeared in *Library Journal*, April 15, 1982, p. 785-6.

213

GUIDELINES/PRINCIPLES

Berman, Sanford, "Access/equity," in *Joy of Cataloging*. Oryx, 1981, p. 61-155. $16.50.

> Includes 20 pieces. See especially "Easy Access vs. Authenticity" (p. 83), "Ethnic Access" (p. 105-09), "Gay Access" (p. 110-12), "Access to Alternatives" (p. 124-48), and "Proposed: a Subject Cataloging Code for Public, School, and Community College Libraries" (p. 149-52), which posits ten vocabulary and four assignment rules.

_____, "Catalog Access to Consumer Health Information," *Technicalities*, v. 2, no. 1 (Jan. 1982), p. 6-7.

> Identifies "four problem areas in. . .subject cataloging practice": awkward/technical/clinical nomenclature; missing vocabulary; inadequate cross-referencing; and "miserly heading assignment." Includes many examples and suggests concrete reforms.

_____, "Reference, Readers, and Fiction: New Approaches," *Reference Librarian*, Nos. 1 & 2 (Fall/Winter 1981), p. 45-53.

> An argument for heightening access to fictional genres, characters, and places, together with practical suggestions for doing so. Includes rosters of genre and "unreal" headings devised and applied at Hennepin County Library (e.g., ECO-FICTION; OCCULT FICTION; SMILEY, GEORGE; TARZAN; MARPLE, MISS JANE; NARNIA; CATFISH BEND; DREW, NANCY; PADDINGTON-THE-BEAR). For an update, see "Fiction Access," *Technicalities*, v. 2, no. 7 (July 1982), p. 7, 16.

Library of Congress. Subject Cataloging Division. "Authority Research for Subject Heading Proposals," *Cataloging Service Bulletin*, no. 16 (Spring 1982), pp. 52-55.

> These guidelines, illustrating "how the Division selects forms for new headings. . .will assist other libraries in doing research to establish new headings themselves." Specifies "where to search for authority" and features 6 complete search-records, e.g., for a current news topic, historical event, and "contemporary public affairs issue."

Marshall, Joan K., "Principles for Establishing Subject Headings Relating to People and Peoples," in *On Equal Terms: a Thesaurus for Nonsexist Indexing and Cataloging*. Neal-Schuman, 1977, p. 6-10.

> The six-point document, with commentary, jointly endorsed in 1975 by ALA's Subject Analysis Committee and the Library of Congress.

AUTHORITY CONTROL/CATALOG MAINTENANCE

Berman, Sanford, "A Model Authority File for Names, Subjects, and Dewey Numbers," in *Joy of Cataloging*. Oryx, 1981, p. 210-21. $16.50.

> A prototype, featuring primary headings, cataloger's notes, "public" notes, and three kinds of cross-references.

Dowell, Arlene Taylor, "Subject Headings," in *Cataloging with Copy*. Libraries Unlimited, 1976, p. 111-34. $16.50.

> A sound, detailed treatment of subject-related maintenance, including data on filing, notes, and cross-references.

Likins, John, "How I Run My Authority File Good," *Unabashed Librarian*, No. 33 (1979), p. 25-26.

> Down-to-earth advice from the technical services director of a medium-sized public library on how to create and maintain an authority file.

Preston, Gregor A., "Coping with Subject Heading Changes," *Library Resources & Technical Services*, Vol. 24, No. 1 (Winter 1980), p. 64-68.

> Offers "three methods—Standard, Interfiling, and Split Files—for preserving card catalog integrity," and discusses "tools and routines for subject maintenance. . .."

Scilken, Marvin H., "Changing Subject Headings," *Unabashed Librarian*, No. 1 (November 1971), p. 26.

> Simple, graphic tips from the U*L editor and director of the Orange, New Jersey Public Library for economically managing card catalog reforms.

VOCABULARIES

Barnhart Dictionary of New English Since 1963. Barnhart/Harper, 1973. 512p. $14.95.

"Lexical index of the new words. . .which have come into the common or working vocabulary of the English-speaking world during the period from 1963 to 1972." Entries include phonetic spelling, definition, illustrative quotations, and etymological notes. Supplemented by *Second Barnhart Dictionary of New English* (1980).

Berman, Sanford, "Career-Related Subject Headings," *RQ*, Vol. 20, No. 1 (Fall 1980), p. 110.

An inventory of "non-standard," job-connected descriptors appearing in the HCL catalog.

————, "Cumulative Subject Index," *Sources: A Guide to Print and Nonprint Materials Available from Organizations, Industry, Government Agencies, and Specialized Publishers*, Vol. 3, No. 3 (1980), p. 155-85; Vol. 4, No. 3 (1981), p. 179-216; Vol. 5, No. 3 (1982), p. 165-206.

Since the indexed, multimedia material spans nearly all topical areas, the index itself—consisting of "natural order," up-to-date terms with plentiful "see" and "see also" references—constitutes a universal mini-thesaurus, particularly appropriate for handling print and AV items on both "solid" and current subjects (e.g., ADULT BASIC EDUCATION, AGRIBUSINESS, ANTI-NUCLEAR MOVEMENT, CREATIONISM, CHILDREN'S THEATER, COHABITATION, HEMORRHOIDS, HUMAN SERVICES, LABOR EDUCATION, LITERARY CRITICISM, OCCUPATIONAL HEALTH AND SAFETY, SENIOR CENTERS, WORKING MOTHERS).

————, "Kids' Stuff: a Grabbag of HCL Subject Headings for (Mostly) Children's Media," in *Joy of Cataloging*. Oryx, 1981, p. 163-65. $16.50.

More than 400 juvenalia descriptors developed and used at Hennepin County Library. Sample headings: BEDTIME,

BILINGUAL MATERIALS, BLIND CHILDREN'S MATE-
RIALS, BOBBSEY TWINS, DISOBEDIENCE, FIRST DAY
IN SCHOOL, MOVING TO A NEW NEIGHBORHOOD,
SILLINESS.

―――, "Nitty-Gritty Subject Heads: a Selection of People-Help-
ing Descriptors LC Hasn't Got around to Yet," in *Joy of Cataloging*. Oryx, 1981, p. 96, $16.50.

A core list of 69 headings, from AFFIRMATIVE ACTION
ORGANIZATIONS, CENTERS, ETC. to YOUTH SHEL-
TERS, plus sample contact-notes exemplifying "how the catalog might easily perform a local information-and-referral
function."

Chicano Thesaurus for Indexing Chicano Materials. Santa Barbara,
CA 93106: Office of the Librarian, Univ. of California. 1979. 77p.
$7.50.

"Three segments: alphabetical; permuted; and hierarchical."
All first-segment terms appear in noninverted form with ample
cross-references. The list "has been adopted as the indexing
tool for the Chicano Periodical Index Project and is likewise
being used in several Chicano Studies Libraries/Collections in
the Southwestern U.S. for indexing and/or cataloging monographs, off-prints, newsclipping files, pamphlets. . .period-
ical literature, etc." Sample headings: BARRIO,
BRACEROS, CURANDERISMO, SALSA, UNDOCU-
MENTED WORKERS.

Hennepin County Library. *Authority File*. 1977- . q. $30; $7.50 for
single cumulations.

A 42x microfiche service, combining in one alphabetical sequence all name, corporate, topical, and series headings
employed in the HCL catalog (i.e., over 250,000 terms, more
than 75,000 being "topical"). Also includes both cataloger's
and "public" notes, as well as nearly 53,000 cross-references.

―――. *Cataloging Bulletin*. 1973- . bi-m. $12, institutions; $6, individuals; $1.50 back issues. Indexes: Nos. 1-10 ($3), 11-20 ($5),
21-30 ($5), 31-40 ($5). Orders for both *Authority File* and *Bulletin*

to: Secretary, Technical Services Div., Hennepin County Library, 12601 Ridgedale Drive, Minnetonka, MN 55343.

> Reports HCL subject heading innovations and changes, citing authorities, precedents, and applications.

HUD Research Thesaurus. GPO. 1980. 68p. $5. Stock No. 023-000-00-676-7. SuDoc No. HH 1.56/2:980/1.

> "Contains approximately 2500 terms. . .representing concepts used to index the literature in the HUD USER data base." A "natural order" list, especially rich in housing and urban affairs nomenclature, it includes full cross-referencing and occasional scope-notes. Sample headings: CONDOMINIUM CONVERSION, ENERGY EFFICIENT HOUSING, HOME SAFETY, HUMAN SERVICES INFORMATION SYSTEMS, MASS TRANSIT, NEWS MEDIA, ONE-PERSON HOUSEHOLDS, URBAN PLANNING.

Legislative Indexing Vocabulary. Congressional Research Service, Library of Congress. 14th ed. 1982. 331p. "Internal document; not for sale." Request through member of Congress.

> "Scope of the LIV encompasses the broad research areas of public affairs assigned to. . .the Congressional Research Service, stressing the social sciences as well as policy aspects of the pure and applied sciences. . .Cross-references show both hierarchical and collateral relations among terms." Descriptor form is noninverted. Sample headings: IMMIGRATION POLICY, INFORMATION POLICY, INSANITY DEFENSE, LANDFILL SITING, NEW RIGHT, NO-TILLAGE, THE SEVENTIES, SUSPECTS' RIGHTS, TEENAGE PREGNANCY, THIRD WORLD, TUITION TAX CREDITS, UNDERGROUND ECONOMY.

Miller, Don Ethan. *The Book of Jargon: An Essential Guide to the Inside Languages of Today.* Macmillan, 1981. 347p. $16.95.

> "Medicalese, legalese, computerese, TV talk, basic jock and 20 other varieties of American jargon." A topically arranged list of relatively short definitions, its great value is likely to be the section of "New Age and New Therapies," which pin-

points such otherwise fugitive terms as "rebirthing," "wicca," "Bach Flower Remedies," "Bates Eye Method," "Eckanckar," "reflexology," and "transpersonal psychology." While the clothbound edition inexplicably lacks a word index, one is promised for the upcoming paperback version.

Music Index Subject Heading List. 1949- a. $8. Orders to: Information Coordinators, 1435-37 Randolph St., Detroit, MI 48226.

"Two lists of subheadings, one general, one for use under instruments, and a separate list of geographical headings (which are also used as subheadings) precede the main subject heading list." Composed of both "direct" and inverted rubrics, as well as bountiful cross-references, the main sequence features highly specific descriptors for folk, popular, and classical music alike. Sample headings: ARIA, ARPEGGIO, LABOR SONGS, REGGAE CONCERTS, RENAISSANCE MUSIC, TAPE INDUSTRY.

National Criminal Justice Thesaurus: Descriptors for Indexing Law Enforcement and Criminal Justice Information. Rockville, MD 20850: Nat'l. Criminal Justice Reference Service, Box 6000. 1980. 334p.

A "KWOC list" follows three fully cross-referenced sequences of "substantive," organizational, and geographic descriptors. The "substantive" section includes many scopenotes. Sample headings: COMMUNITY CONTROL OF POLICE, COMMUNITY CRIME PREVENTION PROGRAMS, STATUS OFFENDERS.

Political Science Thesaurus II: Rev. and expanded 2d ed. Pittsburgh, PA 15260: NASA Industrial Applications Center, Univ. of Pittsburgh, 710 LIS Building. 1979. 675p. $65.

"Organized into two parts: 1). . .terms of political science, and 2). . .geographical/political areas. . .Each descriptor. . . is displayed with its hierarchical structuring and other cross-references," plus occasional scope-notes. A thorough, extremely specialized vocabulary (e.g., PUBLIC POLICY MANAGEMENT, PUBLIC POLICY PLANNING, PUBLIC POLICY STUDIES).

Population/Family Planning Thesaurus, 2d ed. Carolina Population Center Library, 1978. 286p. $20.00. Orders to: University of North Carolina, University Square 300A, Chapel Hill, NC 27514.

"An alphabetical and hierarchical display of terms drawn from population-related literature in the Social Sciences," every entry including a succinct scope-note. Sample headings: ABORTION COUNSELING, BIRTH SPACING, COHABI-TATION, COITUS INTERRUPTUS, FAMILY PLAN-NING, FAMILY PLANNING EDUCATION, FAMILY PLANNING LIBRARIES, FAMILY PLANNING MOVE-MENT, FAMILY PLANNING POLICY, IUD'S, PILL-A-MONTH, URBAN PLANNING. Includes a 9-page, 77-term supplement (1981).

Second Barnhart Dictionary of New English. Barnhart/Harper. 1980. 520p. $19.95.

Companion to *Barnhart Dictionary of New English since 1963* (1973), containing entries derived from 1973-1979. Together, BDNE1 and BDNE2 constitute the best, most useful reservoir of "new word" information. Updated by *The Barnhart Dictionary Companion*: 1982- q. $50.00 p.a. Orders to: P.O. Box 247, Cold Spring, NY 10516.

Thesaurus of ERIC Descriptors. 9th ed. Oryx, 1982. 569p. $35.00.

"Over 8000 terms and cross-references," mainly dealing with education and related topics. Sample headings: CLASSROOM DESIGN, CLASSROOM ENVIRONMENT, COLLEGE BOUND STUDENTS, READING PROGRAMS, READING SKILLS, READING TESTS, SENSORY EXPERIENCE. 10th ed. due Jan. 1984 @ $45.00.

Words That Mean Business: 3,000 Terms for Access to Business Information. Neal-Schuman, 1981. 235pp. $49.95.

Compiled by Warner-Eddison Associates, this "natural order" thesaurus abounds in both cross-references and scope-notes. Four separate vocabularies—for "Agencies and Organizations," "Major Companies," "Currencies of the World," and "Standard Subject Heading Subdivisions"—follow the main list. Sample headings: AGRIBUSINESS, AIR POLLU-

TION CONTROL, ALTERNATIVE ENERGY SOURCES, BIOTECHNOLOGY INDUSTRIES, CORPORATE RESPONSIBILITY, EMPLOYEE BENEFITS, HIGH TECHNOLOGY INDUSTRIES, JOB SHARING, KEOGH PLANS, TRADE FAIRS, WORKING HOURS.

Contributors

SANFORD BERMAN, Head Cataloger at the Hennepin County (Minnesota) Library since 1973, has authored *Prejudices and Antipathies: a Tract on the LC Subject Heads Concerning People* (Scarecrow Press, 1971) and *The Joy of Cataloging* (Oryx Press, 1981). In 1981, he garnered the American Library Association's Margaret Mann Citation for "outstanding achievement in cataloging and classification."

DIANE CHOQUETTE, Head of Public Services and Special Collections at the Graduate Theological Union Library, Berkeley, has been in charge of the New Religious Movements Research Collection since 1971. Her *New Religious Movements in America: an Annotated Bibliography* will shortly be published by Greenwood Press.

LIONELLE ELSESSER, Chief of Library Service at the Veterans Administration Medical Center in Minneapolis since 1981, has authored the Medical Library Association syllabus for *C.E.636: Patient Education*, as well as various articles and book chapters on patient and consumer health education. A frequent instructor/lecturer in these and related subjects, she planned and now coordinates the Patient Education Center/Library (V.A.M.C., Minneapolis), which opened in 1978 as a unique library-based teaching and materials development center.

ELLEN KOGER spent 5 years as Assistant Director for Technical Services at the Nampa (Idaho) Public Library. She is currently Assistant Librarian at Treasure Valley Community College in Ontario, Oregon.

JOHN LIKINS, Technical Services Librarian at the Wellesley (Massachusetts) Free Library since 1977, has compiled two silly subject heading lists, *From ADZES to ZUTPHEN* and *From BATBANDING TO ZOONOSES*; edited the Massachusetts Library Association's *PLAFSEP* [PROCESSING (LIBRARIES)—ANEC-

DOTES, FACETIAE, SATIRE, ETC.—PERIODICALS] from 1977 to 1981; and is presently updating *EL SALVADOR—HISTORY—CIVIL WAR, 1977- —BIBLIOGRAPHY.* While his native tongue is English, Mr. Likins has thought only in subject headings since mid-1974.

PAUL R. MURDOCK, Cataloging Unit Head at the Jefferson County (Colorado) Public Library since 1979, has been involved with development of innovative cataloging networks for a number of years, including the Denver (Colorado) area consortium called IRVING, which will link dissimilar computers for the purpose of sharing information. Recently, he has helped formulate and design a cataloging system, including online authority files, for a large Sperry-Univac computer.

SAC AD-HOC SUBCOMMITTEE ON CONCEPTS DENOTED BY THE TERM "PRIMITIVE" members: JoAnne Anderson (San Diego Public Library); Don Anderle (New York Public Library); Gregory A. Finnegan (Roosevelt University Library); Carol Fleishauer (Stanford University Libraries), Chairperson; Gail Junion (Jerome Library, Bowling Green State University); Diane Lauderdale (Chicago Cluster of Theological Schools); and Janie Morris (William R. Perkins Library, Duke University).

SHIRLEY A. SMITH, Field Consultant with the West Virginia Library Commission since 1978, not only developed a statewide information and referral file (SIR), but has also written a cookbook.

AUDREY TAYLOR, Head Librarian at Aurora High School, York Region Board of Education (Ontario, Canada), since 1971, and Director of the PRECIS Project since 1976, has written numerous articles on PRECIS as well as *Precis Indexing: Development of a Working Model for a School Library Cataloguing/Information Retrieval Network* (Ministry of Education, Ontario, 1982).

Index